SpringerBriefs in Economics

For further volumes:
http://www.springer.com/series/8876

For Heidi,

Our great friend
and excellent
financial
advisor.

Fred

Frederick Betz

Why Bank Panics Matter

Cross-Disciplinary Economic Theory

Springer

Frederick Betz
Portland State University
Portland, ON, USA

ISSN 2191-5504 ISSN 2191-5512 (electronic)
ISBN 978-3-319-01756-3 ISBN 978-3-319-01757-0 (eBook)
DOI 10.1007/978-3-319-01757-0
Springer Cham Heidelberg New York Dordrecht London

Library of Congress Control Number: 2013949284

Printed on acid-free paper

Springer is part of Springer Science+Business Media (www.springer.com)

For Nancy, My Lovely Wife

Preface

Bank panics have always mattered, because they are devastating to national economies, creating recessions and sometimes depressions. Previously, bank panics were national, depressing only a nation. But now they can be global, capable of breaking the economies of not one but several nations. The reason that bank panics are now global is due to information technology (computers and the Internet), which has stitched together a global financial system. But the whole global financial system is unregulated. Can we understand how such a global financial system evolved, but with technology so far ahead of proper regulation?

And why do bank panics still occur? Despite over a hundred years of modern economic theory and many excellent historical studies about bank panics, panics are still poorly understood and certainly not yet preventable. Partly this has been a failure of modern economic theory about bank panics. Economics has been a narrow and single discipline, while bank panics are a complex societal phenomena.

For example, within the historical context of the Euro-bank crisis beginning in 2010, there occurred in 2013 the collapse of the banks of Greek Cyprus. In this Cypriot bank panic, there was again something common to the histories of all bank panics—just plain, old-fashioned, bad banking practices. Cypriot banks were serving as an "offshore" bank for tax evasion and money laundering—bad practices. But exacerbating the harm was the leverage effect upon the Euro-bank system with the computerized Internet connection of Cypriot banks to Europe and Russia, all without proper regulation.

Landon Thomas Jr. reported: "NICOSIA, Cyprus—With time running out until Cyprus's devastated banks must reopen their doors to the public, Cypriot and European officials are scrambling to put in place a set of measures that would allow jittery depositors access to their savings while preventing many billions of euros from fleeing the country. But the situation is now looking even worse than anticipated… (There is) the shock that the island's small economy has endured from the extended closure of its banks." (Thomas 2013a)

When all the banks close, a modern economy stops. Shops close. Employees are not paid. Factories shut down. Tourists do not vacation. The government cannot finance services. Modern economies run on money. Banks are the transmitters of money, the agency of financial transactions. Even the banks' automated teller machines need to be resupplied frequently with cash.

But when banks close, who fixes them? Governments. Landon Thomas further reported: "The bailout package being put together by the troika of international lenders—the International Monetary Fund, the European Central Bank and the European Commission—will consist of about 10 billion euros ($12.9 billion dollars) in loans for Cyprus itself." (Thomas 2013a)

But when banks fail, who bears the cost? Depositors, shareholders, and bank employees. Landon Thomas wrote: "The cost of bailing out the island's two largest banks, Bank of Cyprus and Laiki Bank, is to be borne by the banks' large but uninsured depositors. At a news conference on Tuesday, the governor of Cyprus's central bank, Panicos O. Demetriades, said that he expected big depositors at the Bank of Cyprus to get a 'haircut,' or loss, of about 40 percent on their 14 billion euros in long-term deposits. In exchange, depositors will receive shares in a recapitalized bank." (Thomas 2013a)

Depositors are important to opening a bank again. But there were two kinds of depositors in Cypriot banks: Cypriot citizens and wealthy Russians. Tony Barber commented: "Cyprus acquired dubious friends, such as Slobodan Milosevic, the Serbian dictator whose war-mongering regime, hit by Western sanctions, used the island for financial operations. Post-communist Russians came to Cyprus too." (Barber 2013)

Cyprus' financial business was principally for foreign depositors wanting a "lightly taxed hideaway for cash." Why in the world is there a need for such hideaways? To avoid taxes and to launder illegally acquired wealth. Peter Siegel, Karin Hope, and Quentin Peel reported: "…Nicos Anastasiades (a lawyer and career politician) had assumed the country's presidency just two weeks earlier. Like many in Cyprus, he has ties to Russian interests—his family law practice has two Russian billionaires on its books. And other members of the Cypriot governing class felt pressure to protect the country's banking sector, which counts Russians among its most important customers. Failing to grasp the depth of such ties would prove a fatal blind spot (to European officials). 'The discussion in Cyprus was not about small savers,' says a senior German official. 'It was about people who fly in Lear jets.' By the end of the week (March 18–24), there would be 13 private jets belonging to Russian owners of Cypriot companies parked at Larnaca International Airport, ready to decamp with millions held in the two main banks. Cyprus has long been a popular tax haven for Russian businessmen, legitimate and not." (Spiegel et al. 2013)

The Cypriot bank panic was not just about the euro banking system (which is studied in the discipline of economics), but it was also about the ties between Cypriot politicians and Russian billionaires (which is studied in the discipline of sociology and political science). Thus to understand the Cypriot bank panic, one needs a cross-disciplinary social science perspective.

Would the European regulatory officials let the Lear jets fly away from Cyprus, with the millions of euros deposited by wealthy Russians? Apparently not. Liz Alderman reported: "The Cypriot government on Wednesday announced severe restrictions on access to funds held in the country's banks, hoping to curb what is nonetheless likely to be a rush to withdraw money when the banks open Thursday (March 28) for the first time in nearly two weeks. The measures, which are supposed to be in effect for only a week but could be extended, will prohibit electronic transfers of funds from Cyprus to other countries. In addition, individuals will not be allowed to take more than 3,000 euros in cash outside the country, well below the current ceiling of 10,000 euros, or $13,000. The cap on withdrawals from automated teller machines will rise to 300 euros per day from 100 euros, but credit and debit card charges will be capped at 5,000 euros per person per month. Banks will not cash checks, though they will accept checks as deposits. Bank clients will also not be able to withdraw money from fixed-term deposits before their maturity date" (Alderman 2013a).

Russian political influence was important in Cyprus but not so important in Europe. Landon Thomas further reported: "Might the largest shareholder of the troubled Bank of Cyprus end up being a Russian oligarch, furious that he's just lost a lot of his money in the bank's bailout? That conceivably could happen under the terms by which big depositors in the Bank of Cyprus, the country's biggest, will be forced to help pay for the international bailout of the Cypriot banking industry… By Wednesday evening it was not known how much of a loss, or haircut, would be demanded from depositors on their amounts exceeding €100,000, or $128,000. The figure of 40 percent was commonly cited by people involved in the assessment, but that number could go higher…" (Thomas 2013b).

What was the failure here? It had been failure in bank regulation. Liz Alderman summarized: "Banking experts say that the reason Cyprus, as well as Spain and Ireland, have needed bailouts is because Brussels has left to national regulators the very large responsibility of ensuring that their banks do not engage in risky conduct that could threaten the broader euro monetary system. In the case of Spain and Ireland, it was banks lending recklessly in real estate bubbles; with Cyprus, it was having too large an exposure to Greek government bonds. 'What we really need is to have stronger central control of banks on a Europe-wide basis,' said Karel Lannoo, the chief executive of the Brussels-based Center for European Policy Studies and an expert on bank regulation in Europe. 'Capital controls result from bad bank behavior,' he said. 'We need to have unified regulations with regard to how banks conduct their business.'" (Alderman 2013a, b)

What is important in the regulation of financial systems is to balance a public good against private good in banking. This distinction between public and private good can be vividly seen in the impacts of the Cypriot bank bailout upon its two classes of depositors: Cypriot citizens and Russian oligarchs.

About the tragedy for Greek Cypriots, Landon Thomas reported: "For 20 years, Mr. Agrotis was a stockbroker at the Bank of Cyprus, the country's largest financial institution, and until the shares were recently wiped out, he and his family had much of their wealth tied up in the bank via shares, bonds, retirement funds and—now—frozen deposits. Under terms of the bailout, shareholders' equity in the bank has been eliminated… Within Cyprus, as the realization sinks in of how badly the national economy might be ravaged by the combination of capital controls on the flow of money out of the country and an indefinite freeze on the bulk of bank deposits, frustration is flaming into full rage." (Thomas 2013c)

Joe Nocera had no sympathy for the Russians using the Cypriot banks: "I realize this is a somewhat irresponsible thought, but I keep wondering why anyone should care if some Russian oligarchs and businesses—and corrupt officials—lose a bundle in Cyprus... It turns out that much of the hot money held in the Cypriot banking system is Russian. Russian companies like the low taxes that come with having entities in Cyprus. Because of the wink, wink, nod, nod relationship between Cyprus and Russia, rubles deposited in Cypriot banks are as untraceable as dollars once were in Swiss bank accounts... Corrupt officials who embezzle money have long found Cyprus to be a friendly haven." (Nocera 2013a, b)

Bank panics, stability of financial systems, societal benefits of banking, and proper regulation of global financial systems are topics for a cross-disciplinary review of bank panics and economic theory. Bank panics continue to matter. Information technology, applied to financial technology in banking systems, now makes panics matter even more. How can the global financial system be made to properly work?

Portland, ON Frederick Betz

References

Alderman, L. (2013a, March 27). Cyprus sets up tight controls as banks prepare to reopen. *New York Times*.

Alderman, L. (2013b, April 11). Future looks bleaker than anticipated in cyprus, its creditors claim. *New York Times*.

Barber, T. (2013, March 23–24). The tremors hitting Cyprus could shake the world. *Financial Times*.

Nocera, J. (2013a, March 27). The new Russian Mob. *New York Times*.

Nocera, J. (2013b, July 20). Financial scandal scorecard. *New York Times*.

Spiegel, P., & Hope, K., & Peel, Q. (2013). A poor diagnosis, a bitter pill. *Financial Times*.

Thomas, L., Jr. (2013a, March 26). In Cyprus, big losses expected on deposits. *New York Times*.

Thomas, L., Jr. (2013b, March 27). Big depositors may become big, angry shareholders in Cyprus. *New York Times*.

Thomas, L., Jr. (2013c, March 28). In Cyprus feeling the pain of a bailout. *New York Times*.

Contents

Chapter 1
Reality and Theory

Introduction

Bank panics have long been experienced, and even extensively studied, as economic history. Yet the full explanation of panics remains contentious. Why do bank panics occur? How can recovery be made from the recessions triggered by bank panics? Can proper government policy prevent bank panics? Since the nineteenth century, these have been central questions in economics.

For example, there was a famous financial crisis in 1907, triggered by an attempt by Augustus Heinze to control (corner) stock in his copper company (which we will later review). An observer, back in 1907, O. M. W. Sprague, had written: "...the significance of this Heinze-Morse episode (is) as an example of a deep-seated cause of weakness in the American financial world...danger arises when, by securing possession of a majority of its shares, an individual or group of closely associated individuals gain control of a bank for the purpose of furthering their own private undertakings." (Sprague 1908)

Financial crises continued, as the economic historians, Charles P. Kindleberger and Robert Z. Aliber, wrote: "The years since the early 1970s are unprecedented in terms of the volatility in the prices of commodities, currencies, real estate and stocks. There have been four waves of financial crises; a large number of banks in three, four, or more countries collapsed at about the same time. Each wave was followed by a recession, and the economic slowdown that began in 2008 was the most severe and most global since the great Depression of the 1930s." (Kindleberger and Aliber 2011)

Historical Case: 2009 US Congress Independent Commission

In 2009, the US Congress established an inquiry to investigate the Global Financial Crisis of 2008; and Phil Angelides was appointed Chairman of the US Congress Financial Crisis Inquiry Commission. In 2011, Angelides talked about his

F. Betz, *Why Bank Panics Matter: Cross-Disciplinary Economic Theory*, SpringerBriefs in Economics, DOI 10.1007/978-3-319-01757-0_1,

experience: "I came into my position as chairman of the commission with what I thought was a reasonable understanding of the American financial system, and I had this quaint notion that it was a system designed to allocate capital to the economy for the purposes of creating jobs in enterprise and long-term sustained wealth for our society. I must tell you that over the course of the last year and half, I, along with my fellow commissioners, undertook a journey of revelation. As we did our investigation, we were surprised, we were shocked, we were fascinated and often appalled at what we found. I often felt as if I had entered my local community bank, had opened a door that I wasn't suppose to open, and when I opened it, I saw a casino floor as big as New York, New York. And, I may add, that unlike Claude Raines in Casablanca, I was truly shocked at the level of gambling that was going on in Wall Street." (Angelides 2011)

Phil Angelides had practiced in real estate investment for two decades. Also he served as Treasurer of the State of California, and he participated on the boards of two large pension funds. From his experience with investment and development, he had assumed that the US financial system was principally funding investments in production and development in its economic system. He hadn't realized how the US banking system after the 1990s had turned from this economic function toward casino banking. From the 1980s through the 1990s, what happened in the US economic system was a vast outsourcing of manufacturing to Asia. By 1990, labor costs in US manufacturing were less than 10 % of direct costs on average, or less than 5 % of overall costs. Outsourcing of manufacturing from the USA to Asia was less about labor costs than about capital costs of investment in manufacturing.

When manufacturing left, there were few opportunities in the USA for traditional investment in economic production. Yet money kept flowing into the USA, particularly from oil-rich producers. Sovereign oil companies (owned by governments) controlled 70 % of the world's oil in Russia, Saudi Arabia, Nigeria, Kuwait, Iran, Libya, Nigeria, Venezuela, etc. In the economies of these sovereign companies, large wealth was being accumulated by individuals, needing places for investment. Ben S. Bernanke wrote: "Large and growing amounts of foreign funds flowed into the USA. This created a demand for various types of financial assets... Foreign investors had these funds to lend, either because they had a very high personal savings rate or because of high oil prices... A 'flood' of funds reached the USA financial markets." (Bernake 2007)

Thus, in the 1980s, the US financial system turned away from investment in production and toward trading, particularly trading ownership of corporations. This trading occurred as "leveraged buyouts," leveraged and financed by junk bonds. Michael Millikan helped develop this casino market through Drexel (Buck 1988). From 1981 to 1985, one-quarter of US corporations changed ownership, with "junk-bond" financing. Corporations were taken private and loaded with new debt from the leveraged buyouts. They could not invest in new products and improved manufacturing, because they had to focus on paying off the enormous debt to buy them out—transferred from the hedge funds to the corporations' books. This accelerated the outsourcing of US manufacturing to Asia. This 1980s financial movement created the new trading firms, which evolved into hedge funds by the 1990s.

Then in 1999, trading was integrated into commercial banking. Investment and commercial banks were allowed to merge in the repeal of the Glass–Steagall separation in the USA. This had created the US banks too big to fail, which Angelides observed in 2008.

Angelides focused on the conclusions of the Commission: "But I want to talk now, briefly about our six major conclusions. The first of those conclusions, central to all our conclusions and one that runs counter to the narrative that is spun by many on Wall Street and in Washington, was that this crisis was avoidable. It was not an act of Mother Nature; it was not a matter of computer models going haywire. It was a result of deliberate policy decisions, human action, inaction, and mis-judgment... what happened at the Federal Reserve is, starting in the 1990s, there is growing evidence about widespread unfair lending practices, predatory lending practices, fraudulent lending practices." (Angelides 2011)

Federal regulators had not curbed risk and fraud because they acted under a policy of "deregulation." Angelides wrote: "Secondly, we found widespread failures in financial regulation..., there was a new ideology, driven by Greenspan and others, that we had now entered an era of 'great moderation,' that human behavior had been fundamentally tamed by mathematical models, and that the markets had become wonderfully efficient in such a way that the major financial institutions were capable of self policing themselves. The light hand of regulation was all that was needed; and, in fact, what came to be the governing ethos of our policymakers was that somehow the self-preservation instincts of private institutions would cumulatively add up to a protection of the self, of the public interest and... How wrong that ideology was." (Angelides 2011)

They found a "slowness to regulate" and "ideologically slanted economic theory for deregulation." But also the commission found there had been reasons to regulate. Angelides wrote: "Thirdly, our report describes dramatic breakdowns in corporate governance fueled by compensation systems that rewarded the quick deal, the big transaction, the big bet, without any consequence for the long term. So if you look at our report, you'll be astounded at what you see—both what CEOs knew and, even more disturbingly, what they claimed not to know. You'll see how at AIG they wrote $79 billion of credit protection on subprime securities, contracts that require that they post collateral if there's a market decline in the value of securities. But neither the CEO, the CFO, the Chief Risk Officer (nor any other senior official of that company) had any awareness that they had to place collateral up if market values declined. So when Goldman Sachs came knocking in July 2007 with the first $1.8 billion collateral call, they were stunned. By September 2008, the collateral calls from the various counterparties had grown to $30 billion, AIG was in full collapse, and the taxpayers of the United States had to come forward with $180 billion." (Angelides 2011)

The "quick deal without regard for long term" is what Hyman Minsky had called "Ponzi finance" and depends upon excessive leverage (which we will later discuss). Angelides wrote: "Fourth,...we witnessed excessive borrowing, risky investments that, coupled with a lack of transparency in the end put our financial system on a collision course with catastrophe. By 2008, the shadow banking system, the lightly regulated if regulated at all nonbank financial system, had grown to $13 trillion in assets—bigger than the regulated financial system, commercial bank, and thrift system, with $11 trillion in assets… We saw an explosion in derivatives following the conscious decision to deregulate that market and create an enormous dark market. But we also saw enormous risk at individual firms, leverage ratios of 40-to-1, and, often, true leverage ratios that were hidden. At all the major investment banks, the leverage ratios were 40-to-1 or so… A good example of this is Bear Stearns itself. Bear Stearns, $11 billion in equity at the end of 2007, $390 billion in liabilities, and borrowing $70 billion each and every night in the overnight markets, each and every day, like a small business that has $50,000 in equity borrowing $1.6 million and having to renew a loan of $300,000 each day. All it takes is a market devaluation of assets of 2 to 3 percent or any kind of liquidity disruption for the system to unravel. And it did." (Angelides 2011)

Earlier Hyman Minsky had described how excessive leverage created financial bubbles (Minsky 1975). Where was leadership who understood this? Not to be found, according to Angelides: "Fifth, and perhaps most disturbingly, we found that the key policymakers, the people we depended on to protect the public and our economy—the Department of Treasury led by Hank Paulson, the New York Federal Reserve led by Mr. Geithner, and the Federal Reserve led by Mr. Bernanke—that when this crisis hits in 2007, they were wholly unprepared for the crisis, because they no longer understand the financial system they are overseeing. They don't have a window on the $2.8 trillion repo-market; they have no sense of it because there's no information on the $600 trillion derivatives markets. As I said, the shadow banking system had outraced and outrun our regulators, so when the crisis hit, there was no plan for containment because there was and is very little understanding of the inner connections that now define our current system." (Angelides 2011)

This was the puzzle. It was not that bubbles were new or misunderstood. In 1933, Irving Fisher had described financial bubbles as a form of debt deflation (Fisher 1933). In 1975, Hyman Minsky described financial instability as arising from layering in the financial structure (Minsky 1975). Why had not the Federal regulators read Fisher and Minsky? And had they read economic history on financial panics, such as by Kindleberger and others? (Kindleberger and Aliber 2011)

So—failure of action, failure of theory, failure of sensible business practices, failure of leadership—what more? Angelides wrote: "And finally, in our report we document widespread and systemic breaches and breakdowns in ethics and accountability at all levels… One study that we reviewed in our report indicated that between 2005 and 2007 there was $1 trillion worth of mortgage loans made with proven fraud that resulted in $112 billion in losses. But all of this happened in a non-regulated, crime-facilitative environment. And finally, we catalogue striking new evidence of financial firms that bought and packaged securities, sold them to investors around the world, and knew the defective nature of those mortgage loans and never revealed them. In our report, we attribute responsibility… Minsky was right: systemic forces were at work." (Angelides 2011) (In a later chapter we will analyze this 2007–2008 Global Financial Crisis.)

Macroeconomists Divide

Yet while the commission itself had reached a consensus about the crisis, the economics profession as a whole did not reach one. For example, in 2009, Paul Krugman (a Nobel Prize economist and a widely read columnist) wrote: "Meanwhile, macroeconomists (have remained) divided in their views. But the main division was between those who insisted that free-market economies never go astray and those who believed that economies may stray now and then but that any major deviations from the path of prosperity could and would be corrected by the all-powerful Fed. Neither side was prepared to cope with an economy that went off the rails despite the Fed's best efforts… And in the wake of the crisis, the fault lines in the economics profession have yawned wider than ever." (Krugman 2009)

Why did this "fault line" in economics persist? Krugman explained this as due to "esthetics" in economic theory: "As I (Krugman) see it, the economics profession went astray because economists, as a group, mistook beauty, clad in impressive-looking mathematics, for truth. Until the (1930s) Great Depression, most economists clung to a vision of capitalism as a perfect or nearly perfect system. That vision wasn't sustainable in the face of mass unemployment. But as memories of the Depression faded, economists fell back in love with the old, idealized vision of an economy in which rational individuals interact in perfect markets, this time gussied up with fancy equations… Unfortunately, this romanticized and sanitized vision of the economy led most economists to ignore all the things that can go wrong. They turned a blind eye to the limitations of human rationality that often lead to bubbles and busts; to the problems of institutions that run amok; to the imperfections of markets—especially financial markets—that can cause the economy's operating system to undergo sudden, unpredictable crashes; and to the dangers created when regulators don't believe in regulation." (Krugman 2009)

Yet even after 2009, the split persisted. For example, in the following year, Chris Giles reported upon an economic conference held in Cambridge: "Many of the world's top academic economists agreed on Friday (9 April 2010) that the financial and economic crisis had exposed fatal flaws in their subject and ideas were urgently needed to keep economics relevant. While this represented an unusual consensus, the eminent economic brains lived up to their stereotype by disagreeing on what policies, if any, should be adopted to prevent a repetition… The participants were speaking at the inaugural conference of the Institute for New Economic Thinking, a think-tank sponsored by George Soros, the billionaire financier. They included five Nobel prize-winners (in economics). Held at King's College, Cambridge…the conference participants could neither agree on the cause of the crisis nor the necessary remedies. One disagreement hinged on whether asset price bubbles lay at the heart of the crisis. Those who thought so argued for tighter regulation…(Others, such as) Michael Goldberg, of the University of New Hampshire, said it was wrong to suggest the price swings were necessarily a bubble and that they were more likely to be fundamental to the beneficial forces of capitalism." (Giles 2010)

And on continued the division. In 2012, Howard Davies (then a professor at Sciences Po in Paris and previously the Director of the London School of Economics) wrote: "In an exasperated outburst, just before he left the presidency of the European Central Bank, Jean-Claude Trichet complained that: 'as a policymaker during the crisis...available models were of limited help'..." (Davies 2012).

Davies further concluded: "Our approach to regulation in the past was based on the assumption that financial markets could to a large extent be left to themselves, and that financial institution and their boards were best placed to control risk and defend their firms. These assumptions took a hard hit in the crisis, causing an abrupt shift to far more intrusive regulation. Finding a new and stable relationship between the financial authorities and private firms will depend crucially on a reworking of our intellectual models... There should be more teaching of economic history,... The study of economics should be set in a broader political context,... Painful experience tells us that economic agents may not behave as the models suppose they will. But it is not clear that a majority of the profession yet accepts even these modest proposals. The so-called 'Chicago School' has mounted a robust defense of it rational- expectations-based approach, rejecting the notion that a rethink is required. The Nobel laureate economist Robert Lucas has argued that the crisis was not predicted because economic theory predicts that such events cannot be predicted. So all is well." (Davies 2012)

Science and Discipline Schools

However in the history of science, whenever a discipline has split into "schools"—unable to agree and reach consensus over theory and empiricism—there emerged an attempt to reach out, beyond the boundaries of the discipline. For example, modern physical theory could never have been developed without mathematics. Also quantum mechanics was developed in physics at the atomic scale of physical phenomena, and it was incorporated into chemistry to explain molecular bonding. Chemistry and physics were both incorporated into the biology of DNA, creating "molecular biology." The history of science is replete with progress, both disciplinary and cross-disciplinary. This is our approach to revisiting economic theory, going beyond the boundaries of economics, into the wider cross-discipline of the social sciences. A financial system needs to be explained not only (and simply) in economic terms but also in concepts from sociology and political science, management science and psychology, etc. (For example, behavioral economics has been one cross-disciplinary input into modern economics.)

Economic historians themselves have been very capable of using cross-disciplinary perspectives in reconstructing economic histories. They have talked not only about economic monetary factors but also about organizational factors and political factors, cultural factors, individual-decision factors, and technology factors. These factors have been explored in many disciplines, such as sociology, political science, anthropology, management science, and management of technology.

As the historians have been cross-disciplinary in their views, many social science theoreticians have narrowly constrained their ideas within a single-discipline boundary. Disciplinary theories have partial validity in some contexts. But no disciplinary theory has complete validity in all contexts. For example, in economic theory, all markets are not perfect in all places, all societies, and all times.

This is the basic methodological challenge for the social sciences—to develop empirically valid but contextually dependent theory. What we will explore here is how to express economic theory, valid within a context dependency. And we will see how such an approach to theory enables the proper integration of the historically divided schools of economics.

References

Angelides, P. (2011, April 13–15). *Justice, reform, and rebuilding in the wake of the financial crisis*. 20th Annual Hyman P. Minsky Conference on the State of the US and World Economies. New York City (A conference organized by the Levy Economics Institute of Bard College).

Bernake, B. S. (2007, September 11). Global imbalances: Recent developments and prospects. Budesbank Lecture, Berlin, Germany. http://www.federalreserve.gov/newsevents/speechbernanke20070911a.htm. 2008.

Buck, C. (1988). *The predators' ball: The inside story of Drexel Burnham and the rise of the junk bond raiders*. New York: Simon and Schuster (Penguin paperback, 1989).

Davies, H. (2012, August 27). Economics in denial about its academic merit. *The Korea Herald*.

Fisher, I. (1933, October). The debt-deflation theory of the Great Depression. *Econometrica*.

Giles, C. (2010, April 10). Financial crisis exposed flaws in economics. *Financial Times*.

Kindleberger, C. P., & Aliber, R. Z. (2011). *Manias, panics, and crashes: A history of financial crises* (6th ed.). New York: Palgrave Macmillan.

Krugman, P. (2009, March 17). The B Word. *The New York Times*.

Minsky, H. (1975). John Maynard Keynes. New York: Columbia University Press (reprinted in 2008 by Mc Graw Hill).

Sprague, O. M. W. (1908, September). The American crisis of 1907. *The Economic Journal, 18*(71). http://www.jsotr.org/stable/2221551

Chapter 2
Empirically Grounded Theory

Introduction

Suppose financial markets are not empirically "perfect." Further suppose that "regulation" of financial markets is required for any financial market to operate toward the economic ideal of market perfection. And suppose the practice of regulation should be based upon a theory of regulation (regulatory principles) which can be empirically shown to have worked in financial history. Then what kind of regulatory theory could this be and how constructed and how verified? The goal is a cross-disciplinary theory of regulation—which can prescriptively direct financial markets toward the ideal of economic perfection. The economic ideal is for any financial market to operate with transparent financial information, rational financial behavior, effective financial performance, and integrity in economic risk. And this is a traditional idea in banking regulation.

One can see this in the perspectives of practitioners of regulatory processes. For example, Paul Volcker, former chairman of the US Federal Reserve System, wrote of his experience: "Twenty years ago, I left the world of central banking… In the world in which I grew up and had policy and regulatory responsibilities, commercial banks (and their sister deposit-taking institutions) dominated the financial structure of advanced economics. By its nature, that process carried risks and was potentially crisis-prone, particularly when the financial intermediaries were thinly capitalized. Consequently over time, modern economies developed an elaborate system of supervision and regulation,… From a competitive standpoint, there are burdens and costs in regulation. There are also advantages in access to the 'safety net' provided by official oversight and protections." (Volcker 2008)

Based upon new information technologies, dramatic change occurred in the world's financial systems: "But that was coherence and simplicity compared with the financial world of the 21st century. One symptom is the seemingly infinite variety of financial practices and instruments… (And) underneath all that financial innovation is the reality of the computer and communications revolution. That is what has made possible the speed and complexity of financial transactions and the

F. Betz, *Why Bank Panics Matter: Cross-Disciplinary Economic Theory*,
SpringerBriefs in Economics, DOI 10.1007/978-3-319-01757-0_2,

internationalization of markets. With change so rapid and diverse, it is difficult—indeed impossible—for the bureaucratic world of regulation and supervising to keep pace. Indeed, some of the incentive to innovate is the attraction of escaping official oversight. For financial operations national borders have become almost irrelevant in a world of open markets and global finance." (Volcker 2008)

One can see this view about the relation of financial practice and theory in the academic research community. For example Charles W. Calomiris and Gary Gorton wrote: "Banking panics have long been a motivating factor in the development of financial regulation and monetary policy. Ideally, public policy should reflect the lessons of history, once relevant differences between historical and contemporary environments are considered. Designing public policy is complicated not only because it is difficult to distill the appropriate lessons from history, but also because banking and capital markets continue to be transformed by technological change. That is to say, history does not end." (Calomiris and Gorton 1991)

Financial panics have been studied by historians to provide an empirical ground for economic theory and appropriate public policy in banking regulation. However as witnessed by the continuation of bank panics (particularly the global financial panic of 2007–2008 and the bank panics of the Euro dollar crisis of 2011–2112), bank panics persist. Why? Why has contemporary regulatory theory (based upon only disciplinary economic theory) not yet solved the financial system challenge?

History: Panic of 1857

Charles Calomiris and Gary Gorton provided a definition of a bank panic: "Historically, bank debt has consisted largely of liabilities which served the function of a circulating medium of exchange, bank notes and demand deposits. The contract defining this debt allowed the debt holder the contractual right to demand redemption of the debt (into currency) on demand at par… A banking panic occurs when bank debt holders at all (or many) banks in the banking system, suddenly demand that banks convert their debt claims into cash (at par) to such an extent that the banks suspend convertibility of their debt into cash…" (Calomiris and Gorton 1991)

In 1857, a bank panic occurred; and it was the first US panic on a national scale, involving both the east and west of the USA. Charles W. Calomiris and Larry Schweikart wrote: "We explain the origins of the Panic of 1857, examine its spread, and compare state banking systems' responses. We describe the decline in western land and railroad investments and the consequent stress on securities brokers and banks in eastern cities, and trace the transmission of the shock to other regions. Bank performance depended not only on regional conditions and links to eastern banks, but on the ability to coordinate behavior…our explanation for the origin of the Panic of 1857 revolves around the financing of western railroad and land speculation in eastern financial markets. The proximate cause of the panic was the bankruptcy of securities brokers who borrowed from eastern banks to finance their dealings in the stock and bond markets. To understand the panic's origins, one must begin with the economic and political history of the speculative boom and bust in investments in the West during the 1850s." (Calomiris and Schweikart 1991)

In that decade prior to 1857, large amounts of securities were issued by private companies. These were mainly stocks in railroad companies and bonds issued as loans to railroad companies. There were also bank stocks and warrants to western lands. Calomiris and Schweikart wrote: "By the mid-1850s railroads could be grouped usefully into three categories: eastern roads that served established routes; older western roads built mainly to serve local distribution needs; and newer western roads, sometimes financed through special land grants to serve as trunk lines connecting older areas of settlement and eastern markets with new areas of settlement. As early as 1854, older locally oriented roads in the West found their earnings falling and their opportunities shrinking, as a result of competition from the new trunk lines. These new lines, with their aggressive land-purchasing policies and far-reaching loans for transcontinental expansion, provided the principal speculative opportunities for railroad investors of the 1850s. Their fortunes depended on a continuing inflow of settlers and the growth of commerce on the frontier, which required confidence in the viability of expansion westward" (Calomiris and Schweikart 1991).

By 1857, financial enthusiasm had focused upon Kansas, which was the next western territory as a candidate for the next state. Allen Nevins described: "...a fever of speculation in Kansas lands was raging, men selling homes, giving up well paid positions, and even borrowing money at ten percent to purchase farms. Newspapers published along travel routes to Kansas in early 1857 described a veritable torrent of humanity. "The lure of Kansas lands led some to expect Kansas to increase by seventy thousand people that year" (Nevins 1950).

Western land was attracting immigrants and increasing rail traffic. Calomiris and Schweikart wrote: "In April settlers arrived at the rate of 1,000 per day. The link between immigrant traffic and expectations of railroad profitability is visible in the responses to this great influx. As passengers to Kansas increased, the railroads lowered rates for through traffic, indicating expectations of a lasting increase in the volume of business (and perhaps the railroads' desire to encourage immigration to stimulate development). Entrepreneurs laid ambitious plans for new railroads... (But) by late summer that optimism was shattered, the value of western land fell and the speculative railroad securities fell with it... The decline in speculative railroads' earnings and prospects forced several companies into default, including the Illinois Central, the Erie &Pittsburgh, the Fort Wayne & Chicago, and the Reading lines. Several thinly capitalized railroad companies-including the Delaware, the Lackawanna & Western, and the Fond du Lac-went bankrupt...mid-1857 represented a turning point in expectations about the profitability of westward expansion." (Calomiris and Schweikart 1991)

Thus in 1857, there was a peak of speculation in Kansas land and in railroads—just when the panic began. In addition, Kansas became the focus over the political issue of slavery. Dred Scott had filed a lawsuit for his freedom from slavery, but the Supreme Court denied it, making it a key legal decision to open up western territories as possible slave states. This reduced immigration to Kansas from people in the northern US states.

The decline in the markets of Western land and wheat and declining railroad traffic had links to the banking system. Investment in the railroad stocks and bonds had been heavily subscribed by European capital in London banks. Calomiris and Schweikart wrote: "The central puzzle of the panic is the links among the early securities markets' decline, the later decline in bank note prices and bank stocks, and the eventual suspension of convertibility. Why should a region-specific shock to western land and railroads cause a nationwide suspension originating in the East? And why the protracted delay in the reaction of bank note discount rates, bank stock prices, and bank suspension to the July-September decline in land and railroad securities?" (Calomiris and Schweikart 1991)

What linked those western markets to eastern bank failures? Calomiris and Schweikart wrote that: "Three destabilizing elements combined to transform the securities collapse into a banking panic."

> "First, the initial increase in bank risk prompted some note holders and depositors in New York State to convert their bank debt into specie. New York's free banks met this demand through sales of bonds in New York, which helped to depress bond prices further."
>
> "Second, New York banks outside New York City converted their notes into specie mainly through their city correspondents. (A regulation of June 1857 regulated city banks' trading in country notes, restricted the discount rate which city banks could charge, and limited the amount of notes that could be returned to peripheral banks without sufficient notice.) This regulation, along with rising bank risk, caused a flood of peripheral banks' notes into the city for redemption. This added to the drain of specie from New York City to its correspondents in other eastern financial centers."
>
> "Third, as New York City banks came to doubt the solvency of some prominent securities dealers, and as city banks' gold reserves fell in response to the accelerating demand for redemption of peripheral banks' notes, the city banks refused to rollover the debt of the brokers. This forced brokers to sell their bond holdings at rock bottom prices and forced many into bankruptcy. As these bankruptcies mounted, and as securities prices continued to fall, the solvency of New York City banks—whose loans to brokers and dealers often were backed by bonds—came into question."
>
> "This was the proximate cause of the run on the city banks in mid-October. Thus the declining fortunes of western railroads and declines in western land values, along with a concentration of asset risk and reserve drain in New York City banks, ultimately explain the origins of the panic." (Calomiris and Schweikart 1991)

The decline in western markets was connected to stock price declines which was connected to brokers' debts which was connected to decline of bank assets. From such empirical research into banking panic, Calomiris and his colleagues demonstrated the importance of the *context* of banking in explaining panics. Calomiris and Gorton wrote: "Empirical research has demonstrated the importance of such institutional structures as branch bank laws, bank cooperation arrangement and formal clearing houses for the probability of panic and for the resolution of crisis…banking panics are not inherent in banking contracts (bank transactions); institutional structure matters." (Calomiris and Gorton 1991)

> *One sees that a "structure" interacted with a "process"—banking infrastructure with financial speculation.*

As an example of events in the panic involving the banking infrastructure, Calomiris and Schweikart wrote: "…the Clearing House banks of New York City met on September 29 to reassure everyone that such credit would be forthcoming. This promise, however, was not kept due to a combination of the city banks' inability to do so (due to the persistent gold outflow) and their unwillingness to do so (given the rising threat of insolvency for brokers). The contraction of credit forced more and more securities houses into liquidation... When New York City banks opened for business on October 13, an unprecedented run by depositors greeted them. Before agreeing to suspend, the banks paid out between $4 million and $5 million. Wall Street literally was filled with depositors hurrying to withdraw their funds. "The banks went down before a storm they could not postpone or resist." 32 Between October 1 and October 13 deposits had fallen by $10 million. Roughly half of the specie held by city banks on October 10 was paid out on October 13." (Calomiris and Schweikart 1991)

As described by Calomiris and Schweikart, the 1857 panic was not caused by any single factor. Instead, the event occurred due to connections between *market processes* (western land speculation and railroad finances) and *banking networks* (eastern banks) and *stock exchanges* (eastern brokers). In effect, commodity (land) and industrial (railroads) markets were involved—along with an emerging national banking network, western banks and eastern banks, and an emerging national stock market, New York brokers. (The US banks and brokers connected to international finance through London banks.)

As is any societal event, the Panic of 1857 was a complicated event. It had no single cause, and many factors contributed to it: end of the Crimean War, decline in wheat prices and western land values, decline in railroad traffic and revenue, flight of gold to Europe, failure of railroads, failure of an insurance company, and Dred Scott case. All these factors contributed, but none in a simple causality. No single factor "caused" the panic; but all taken together at the time triggered the panic.

Societal and Perceptual Space for Observing History

How to explain a complicated societal event? For this, we use a method for analyzing multiple explanations in a historical event. For example, in the physical sciences, one observes and analyzes a physical event as one of motion, as shown in Figure 2.1. In historical studies of society (such as economic history), one does not observe "physical objects" but instead "societal objects." Thus physical concepts (i.e., "physical objects," "space and time," "motion," "forces," "causality") are not useful (not methodologically appropriate) to accurately describe societal history. Accordingly, there never is any "causality" in historical explanation. But there are other kinds of explanations in history. What are they? To find them, we can use a methodological analogy to a "physical observational space," which is a "societal observational space." This has been constructed from the three basic dichotomies in the social sciences: *individual–society, groups–processes, and reason–action.* (Betz 2011)

> The first basic idea in the sociological literature is the distinction between individuals and the society in which the individuals live—the dichotomy of *individual and society*.
>
> The second basic idea in sociology distinguishes how individuals associate into groups within a society and the processes a group inculcates in members—the dichotomy of *group and process*.

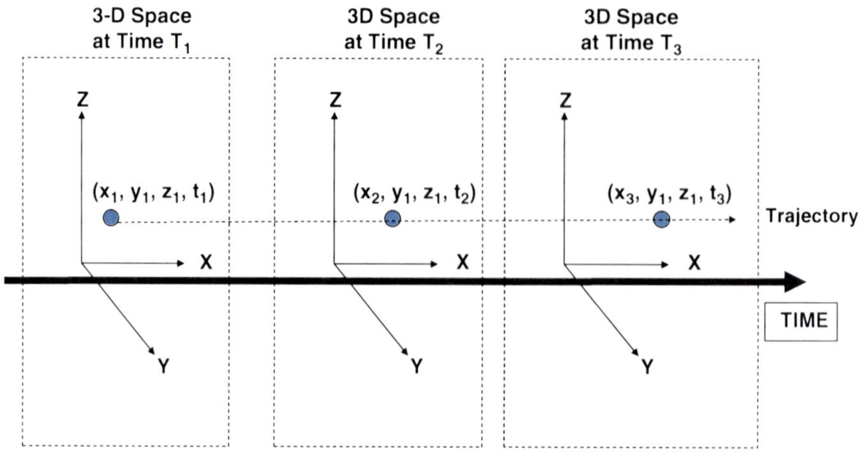

Fig. 2.1 Classical four-dimensional space-time description of motion of material object

In sociology, groups, masses, and organizations are basic units in which individuals in collect together for action. A social process is a series of actions coordinated to produce an outcome planned by a group.

The third basic idea found in the sociological literature (and in the management science literature) is about the thinking of individuals and their behavior. Individuals described as sentient (or cognitive) beings acting according to perceived reasons—the dichotomy of action and reason.

We can graphically show these three basic social science dichotomies upon a three-dimensional societal space, as shown in Fig. 2.2.

In any historical event describing an epoch of a society, the event can be described as factors and interactions of three dichotomies (in the sociological perception of the event). These dichotomies are individuals–societies and action–rationality and groups–processes. To conveniently inscribe events in the perceptual space, we will show the areas around the dimensional axes as a kind of event box—in Fig. 2.3. In this picture, we show a three-dimensional space for perceiving historic events in a society as arrows in the space. Next, we build a box around the axis arrows, in order to have surfaces for conveniently listing the factors (happenings) in the event. Since this box is three dimensional, we then open up the box to see all surfaces in one view.

In societal events, social structure and social process provide contexts for each other. To explore such contextual dependence of structure and process, we next use the societal observational space to analyze the history of the 1857 event, as shown in Fig. 2.4.

Action—Actions included railroad construction, land speculation, immigration, and wheat market prices. Rail development in western USA generated stock offerings and bonds financed in New York banks, with connections to London banks. Western land speculation and immigration generated traffic for the railroads. Wheat grown in Midwestern farms found markets in Eastern USA and in Europe. Decline of demand for wheat in Europe lowered wheat prices, and competition among railroads lowered revenues. Immigration to Kansas slowed. The US Supreme Court's

Fig. 2.2 Basic sociological dichotomies

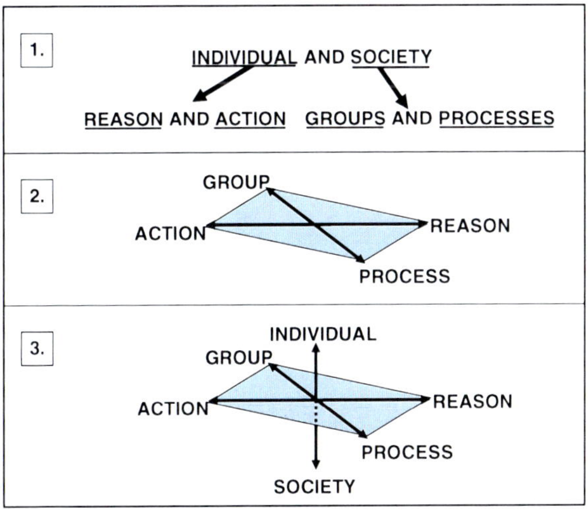

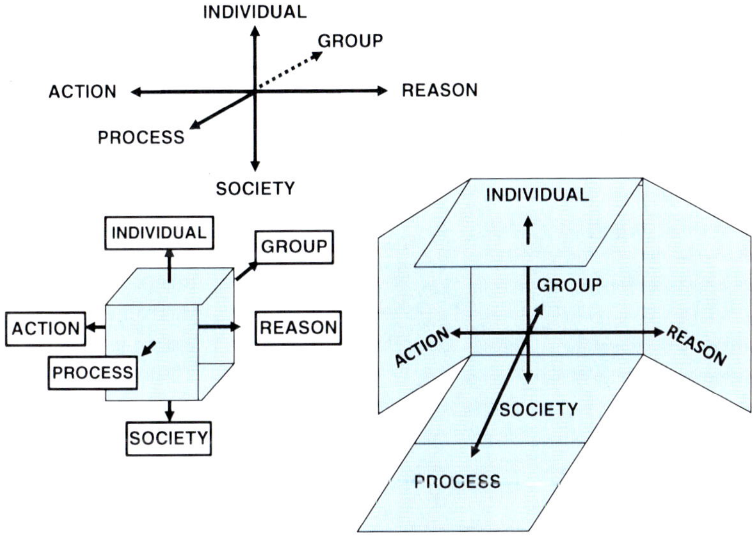

Fig. 2.3 Societal perceptual-space event box interactions of an individual and society are mediated through reason and action and through groups and processes

decision on the Dred Scott case opened Kansas to the possibility of becoming a slave state, and the land market declined. Railroads defaulted upon bonds and some went bankrupt. Some stockbrokers making markets in railroad stock collapsed, as banks called in loans and stopped withdrawal payment in species.

Reason—Financial speculation expected price rises in land and railroads and also stimulated loans taken by security brokers from banks for stock speculation.

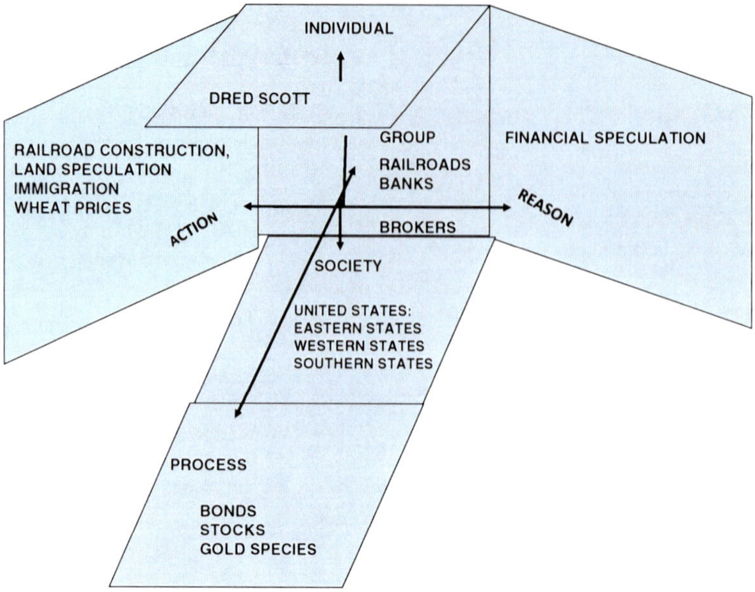

Fig. 2.4 Perceptual space of 1857 bank panic

Group—Railroads, banks, security brokers, immigrants, and London banks were some of the key groups involved in the event.

Process—Financial capital flows and firm bankruptcies were key processes in the event.

Individual—Dred Scott had filed a lawsuit for his freedom from slavery, but the Supreme Court denied it, making it a key legal decision to open up western territories as possible slave states.

Society—The society in the event was the USA: with regional focus upon Eastern, Western, and Southern states.

Explanation in a Societal Perceptual Space

Within this framework, we can now address the issue of explanation in history. We have emphasized that causality is essential to the physical sciences is a kind of explanation, but wholly inappropriate to the social sciences. One needs to ask what kinds of explanations are methodologically appropriate to the social sciences, to the observation of a societal event? And one can find this by constructing a topological graph in the societal perceptual space, as shown in Fig. 2.5.

The six-dimensional points of the space can be connected by fifteen lines as a topological graph. Each graph relationship provides a kind of explanation

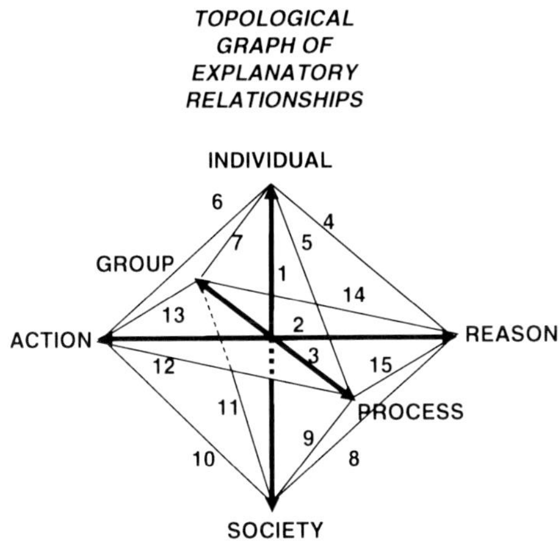

LIST OF EXPLANATORY RELATIONSHIPS

1. ETHICS
2. PRINCIPLES
3. INSTITUTIONALIZATION
4. IDEAS
5. POLICY
6. STRATEGY
7. GOVERNANCE
8. KNOWLEDGE
9. REGULATING
10. PERFORMANCE
11. INFRASTRUCTURE
12. TECHNOLOGY
13. OPERATIONS
14. IDEOLOGY
15. SYSTEM

Fig. 2.5 Explanations in a historical societal event as relationships between the principle factors

connecting two factors (Betz 2012). Topology is a field of mathematics concerning the connectedness of geometrical forms, and topological graphs display this connectivity as lines connecting points in the geometrical form. The societal dynamics event graph displays the explanations connecting principle factors in a historical event. The fifteen kinds of explanations which can occur as relationships between the principle factors are:

1. Ethics—The explanatory relationship between *individual and society* can be called the *ethical context* in the explanation of a historical event.
2. Principles—The explanatory relationship between *reason and action* can be called the *principles of order* in the explanation of a historical event.
3. Institutionalization—The explanatory relationship between *group and process* can be called the *institutionalization* in the explanation of a historical event.
4. Ideas—The explanatory relationship between *individual and reason* can be called the *ideas* which an individual uses in reasoning.
5. Policies—The explanatory relationship between *individual and process* can be called the *policies* an individual in power formulates to control social processes.
6. Strategy—The explanatory relationship between *individual and action* can be called the *strategy* in which a leader formulates the direction for action.
7. Leadership—The explanatory relationship between *individual and group* can be called the *leadership* of an individual in guiding the efforts of a group.
8. Knowledge—The explanatory relationship between *society and reason* can be called the *knowledge* which a society has to use.
9. Regulating—The explanatory relationship between *society and process* can be called the *regulation* of activities within the infrastructure of the society.

10. Performance—The explanatory relationship between *action and society* can be called the *performance* attained by processes in societal sectors.
11. Infrastructure—The explanatory relationship between *group and society* can be called the social *infrastructure* which groups provide in building and operating sectors of a society.
12. Technology—The explanatory relationship between *action and process* can be called the *technology* used in a process in producing an action.
13. Operations—The explanatory relationship between *action and group* can be called the *operations* of a group which produce a group action.
14. Ideology—The explanatory relationship between *group and reason* can be called the *ideology* as the concepts groups use to associate and justify association, the ideology of a group.
15. System—The explanatory relationship between *process and reason* can be called the *system* of controlled process in the societal event.

This list is a cross-disciplinary in the kinds of explanations used in the different social science disciplines; and it is particularly useful in describing the complexity of societal events. It provides both a generality and a logical completeness, for comparing explanations across different historical events and across different societies.

We now apply this formal explanatory framework to Calomiris–Schweikart's explanation of how the linking of western markets to the eastern banking failures occurred as the destabilizing elements which together transformed the securities collapse into a banking panic.

"First, the initial increase in bank risk prompted some note holders and depositors in New York State to convert their bank debt into specie. New York's free banks met this demand through sales of bonds in New York, which helped to depress bond prices further." (Calomiris and Schweikart 1991)

Bank risk—(4. Ideas)

Convert their bank debt into specie—(6. Strategy)

Sales of bonds in New York—(6. Strategy)

Depress bond prices—(10. Performance)

"Second, New York banks outside New York City converted their notes into specie mainly through their city correspondents. (A regulation of June 1857 regulated city banks' trading in country notes, restricted the discount rate which city banks could charge, and limited the amount of notes that could be returned to peripheral banks without sufficient notice.) This regulation, along with rising bank risk, caused a flood of peripheral banks' notes into the city for redemption. This added to the drain of specie from New York City to its correspondents in other eastern financial centers." (Calomiris and Schweikart 1991)

Converted their notes into specie mainly through their city correspondents—(3. Institutionalization)

This regulation—(9. Regulating)

Rising bank risk—(4. Ideas)

Flood of peripheral banks' notes into the city for redemption—(10. Performance)

Drain of specie—(10. Performance)

"Third, as New York City banks came to doubt the solvency of some prominent securities dealers, and as city banks' gold reserves fell in response to the accelerating demand for redemption of peripheral banks' notes, the city banks refused to rollover the debt of the brokers. This forced brokers to sell their bond holdings at rock bottom prices and forced many into bankruptcy. As these bankruptcies mounted, and as securities prices continued to fall, the solvency of New York City banks—whose loans to brokers and dealers often were backed by bonds—came into question." (Calomiris and Schweikart 1991)

Doubt the solvency—(4. Ideas)

City banks' gold reserves fell—(10. Performance)

Accelerating demand for redemption of peripheral banks' notes—(10. Performance)

City banks refused to rollover the debt of the brokers—(13. Operations)

Forced brokers to sell their bond holdings at rock bottom prices and forced many into bankruptcy—(7. Governance)

Bankruptcies mounted—(10. Performance)

Securities prices continued to fall—(10. Performance)

Solvency of New York City banks came into question—(4. Ideas)

"This was the proximate cause of the run on the city banks in mid-October. Thus the declining fortunes of western railroads and declines in western land values, along with a concentration of asset risk and reserve drain in New York City banks, ultimately explain the origins of the panic." (Calomiris and Schweikart 1991)

This was the proximate cause—(4. Ideas) (6. Strategy) (10. Performance) (3. Institutionalization) (7. Governance) (11. Infrastructure)

Run on the city banks—(10. Performance)

Declining fortunes of western railroads and declines in western land values—(10. Performance)

Concentration of asset risk and reserve drain—(11. Infrastructure)

In Fig. 2.6, we summarize all the above explanations on a societal dynamics event-space graph: "ultimately explain the origins of the panic"—(4. Ideas) (6. Strategy) (10. Performance) (3. Institutionalization) (7. Governance) (11. Infrastructure).

Thus by analyzing the Calomiris' and Schweikart's explanation for the "cause" of the 1857 in the societal dynamics topological graph, one can see that there was no one "cause" but several kinds of explanations—as relationships of the following: (4. Ideas), (6. Strategy), (10. Performance), (3. Institutionalization), (7. Governance), (9. Regulating), and (11. Infrastructure).

The concept of "Ideas" has traditionally been studied in philosophy, under the topic or reason, and also in psychology under the topic of cognition. The concept of "Strategy" is a focus of business schools, specifically in management science. The concept of "Performance" is studied both in business schools and in engineering schools—as, respectively, organizational performance and technology performance. The concept of "Institutionalization" is a focus of sociology and of political science. The concept of "Governance" is principally studied in political science and in political economy. The concept of "Infrastructure" is principally studied in sociology. Thus one sees that a cross-disciplinary framework provided many social science concepts to analyze an event in the history of economics.

This is the advantage of a cross-disciplinary approach to analyzing empirical events—a systematic identification of the kinds of explanations necessary to understand and clarify the occurrence of a historical event. Societal dynamics theory can supply more than one disciplinary view in the analysis of a society. This can assist the methodological approach of history researchers in their search for explanation of "structural and institutional" features, along with explanations of "processes."

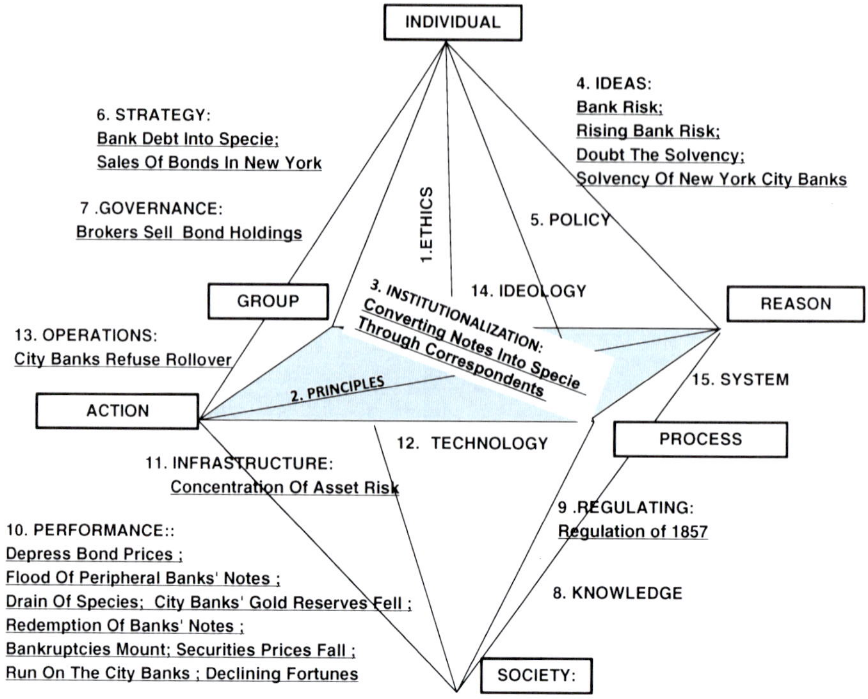

Fig. 2.6 Explanations in 1857 bank panic

Cross-disciplinary analytic framework of societal dynamics theory can assist in identifying the kinds of "structure and institutional differences" essential to explaining events of financial process—such as differences in Ideas, Strategy, Performance, Institutionalization, Governance, Regulating, and Infrastructure.

In historical studies like this one about 1857, there never is a single "cause," no single factor ever causes a historical event. Always there are several factors in history. This is especially true if one examines not just this case but all the recurrent financial panics in US history. There are several explanatory factors in each panic. Charles Kindleberger and Robert Aliber listed the US panics from the early 1800s to 2000s (Kindleberger and Aliber 2011): Panic of 1857, Panic of 1873, Panic of 1893, Panic of 1896, Panic of 1907, Panic of 1929, Panic of 1973, Panic of 1987, Panic of 1989, Panic of 2007, and Panic of 2011.

Bank panics are not simple economic events, nor are their explanations simple. But panics are recurrent. Because of their complexity and recurrence, we will examine again several of them—but in a cross-disciplinary framework.

References

Betz, F. (2011). *Societal dynamics, Springer*. In E. Carayannis (Series Ed.), *Springer innovation, technology, and knowledge management series*.

Betz, F. (2012). Control in knowledge economies. *Journal of Knowledge Economy*. doi:10.1007/s13132-012-0100-0.

Calomiris, C. W., & Gorton, G. (1991). The origins of banking panics: Models, facts, and bank regulation. In *Financial markets and financial crises* (NBER Chapters, pp. 109–174). Cambridge, MA: National Bureau of Economic Research.

Calomiris, C. W., & Schweikart, L. (1991). The panic of 1857: Origins, transmission, and containment. *Journal of Economic History, 51*(4), 807–834.

Kindleberger, C. P., & Aliber, R. Z. (2011). *Manias, panics, and crashes: A history of financial crises* (6th ed.). New York: Palgrave Macmillan.

Nevins, A. (1950). *The ordeal of the union: The Emergence of Lincoln Volume 1, Douglas, Buchanan, and Party Chaos, 1857–1859*. New York: Charles Scribner's Sons.

Volcker, P. (2008, Spring). Rethinking the bright new world of global finance. *International Finance, 11*(1), 101–107.

Chapter 3
Background: Banking and Causality

Introduction

Our quest is a cross-disciplinary theory of financial regulation, grounded upon economic history. Before we proceed further on this journey, there are two backgrounds we should share. First, what is banking? Second, what is explanation? We have seen that panics occurred in banking. Why? We have argued that explaining these panics cannot be causal. Why? We review some background, first about banking and second about causality.

Banks and Financial Systems

In a financial system, banks are the central institutions, affecting both the supply of credit and the supply of money in an economy. The nature of banking is a central concept in economic theory. But there have been two schools of thought in economics about how banks impact economies.

The first school, called "neoclassical synthesis" school (and sometimes "exogenous" school), held that banks only provide credit. Banks provide credit through loans in an economy. For example, this was nicely described by Douglas W. Diamond and Philip H. Dybvig: "Banks have issued demand deposits throughout their history, and economists have long had the intuition that demand deposits are a vehicle through which banks fulfill their role of turning illiquid claims into liquid claims… Banks are able to transform illiquid assets by offering liabilities with a different, smoother pattern of returns over time than the illiquid assets offer. Bank runs are a common feature of the extreme crises that have played a prominent role in monetary history. During a bank run, depositors rush to withdraw their deposits because they expect the bank to fail. In fact, the sudden withdrawals can force the bank to liquidate many of its assets at a loss and to fail. During a panic with many

F. Betz, *Why Bank Panics Matter: Cross-Disciplinary Economic Theory*,
SpringerBriefs in Economics, DOI 10.1007/978-3-319-01757-0_3,

bank failures, there is a disruption of the monetary system and a reduction in production." (Diamond and Dybvig 1983)

This is an important role which banks play in a financial system, as an intermediary between the liquidity of deposits and illiquidity of loans. Liquidity and illiquidity are temporal concepts. What is sellable (liquid) at one time may be unsellable (illiquid) at another time but then again sellable (liquid) later. The success in banking is in balancing a portfolio of liquid liabilities (savings deposits) against a portfolio of illiquid assets (loans).

However, a second school of economics called the "neo-Keynesian" school (and sometimes "endogenous" school) argued that banks also play an important role in affecting the money supply in an economy. The loans which banks make to provide credit come from the capital of "deposits." Savings and deposits made in a bank are assumed to be safe, because deposits can be withdrawn at any time in the form of money (liquidity). Along with the neoclassical school, the neo-Keynesian school agreed that banking "liquidity" provides an important economic connection in finance—between money and credit. They disagree about exactly how this liquidity is possible. In a modern financial system with a central bank, the neo-Keynesians see liquidity occurs not just due to private banks' transactions but also due to their relation to a public central bank.

As a "neo-Keynesian," Paul McCulley described how, in a modern financial system, a bank's profitability (private good) depends upon government's deposit insurance (public good): "Banking is a really profitable business—a really profitable business. In its most simple form, ... the bank issues demand deposits, which are guaranteed to trade at par because they've got FDIC insurance around them, and also because a bank can rediscount its assets in order to redeem deposits in old fashioned money...this is a banknote (specie). Have you ever looked at what is on this note? It says. 'Federal Reserve Note,... and also 'This note is legal tender for all debts, public and private.' This is what the public wants. They want to know that they can turn their deposit into this thing (Federal Reserve Note). And if they know they can turn it into this thing, they don't... This is a Federal Reserve liability, and actually, it's really (amazing). (As a liability) it's missing two things. It doesn't have a maturity date on it, so it's perpetual. And it doesn't have an interest rate on it. I would love to be able to issue these things." (McCulley 2010)

In the USA, a bank deposit is effectively money, good money, because it is guaranteed by the Federal government. The "public good" of deposit insurance is what gives people confidence that banks won't lose their money, making them willing to leave the money in a deposit account. Because most of the money is left in accounts on any given day, banks can lend out more money than they have in their accounts. Bank panics occur when the perception of its depositors is that the bank has become insolvent. McCulley emphasized this public good role of the Federal Reserve in avoiding bank panics. Through the Federal Reserve's role as lender of last resort and the Federal Deposit Insurance, the US government intends to prevent bank runs.

Some financial characteristics follow from this view of private and public banking relationships (private banks backed by government deposit insurance):

As liquidity, money is in both in specie and in credit. The supply of money in a nation (quantity of liquidity) depends not only upon the amount of specie (money) circulating but also on the amount of credit available. The ultimate guarantor of liquidity is the creditability of the government specie (money). This is why extreme specie inflation is perceived as the greatest threat to a financial system.

The assumption then is that with a central bank and little or no inflation, a financial system should be stable, quiet. In the USA, it is the function of the Federal Reserve to help banking have "quiet periods" in the economy. But why do "quiet periods" in financial systems end? This is the heart of the study of modern economics. Why do quiet economic periods end by the occurrence of bank runs? And this issue turns on the relationship of money (governmental function) to credit (private banking function).

L. Randall Wray summarized: "From the 1920s, a peculiarly American misunderstanding developed according to which the quantity of bank reserves issued by the Fed could somehow control bank lending and deposit creation. This was called the "exogenous money" approach. The money supply is "exogenously" controlled by the central bank through restriction of the quantity of reserves supplied. It became the starting point for Milton Friedman's monetarism—which finally ended in the disastrous Great Monetarist Experiment of the early 1980s in the US and the UK in which the central banks tried formal targeting of growth of the money supply. It didn't work, and money targets were completely abandoned by all developed nations' central banks by 1990." (Wray 2012)

Friedman belonged to the exogenous (neoclassical) school, while Wray belonged to the "endogenous" (neo-Keynesian) school. Wray wrote: "There was always another tradition, dating back to the Banking School of the early 19th century... It is called the "endogenous money" approach that insists central banks cannot control private money creation by banks through control over reserves... Modern central banks are responsible for maintaining a smoothly operating payments system, which among other things requires that bank liabilities clear "at par" (a one dollar deposit at Chase is valued the same as a one dollar deposit at Bank of America). The Fed makes sure that checks clear among banks and that depositors can use the ATM machines. That means banks must have reserves as required. So the Fed's control is based on "price", not "quantity". It can set the interest rate at which it lends reserves to banks, but cannot determine the quantity." (Wray 2012)

In contemporary economics, the two schools, exogenous and endogenous, differed on whether (1) the quantity of money can be controlled by the central bank or (2) only the price of money can be controlled. The difference was based upon two different models of money and banks. The exogenous school viewed banking as primarily creating credit, based upon deposits (as described by Diamond and Dybvig)—so that changing reserve requirements (the percentage of their deposits they could not loan out) controlled the supply of credit—in a linear manner. In contrast, the endogenous school saw the ratio of credit-to-reserve requirements as nonlinear; and only the "price" of credit could be directly controlled, not the supply.

From the endogenous view, Wray saw the operations of a bank this way: "...in practice, bank reserve requirements are calculated based on deposits created up to six weeks previously. So the quantity of reserves that banks are required to hold in systems like the one we use in the US (with required reserve ratios) is always a function of historical deposits. But, the central bank's control is price, not quantity. Modern central banks work with interest rate targets (the Fed announces its fed funds rate target), which again means that the Fed can set the "price" and then supplies reserves as needed to hit the fed funds rate target." (Wray 2012)

This is one critical difference about economic control between the exogenous and endogenous schools: the Federal Reserve can control either (1) the quantity (supply) or (2) only the "price" of money (interest rate).

The reason Wray emphasized control over "price" of credit rather than "quantity" of credit was that he viewed banks not just merely as "transformers of liquidity" but also as "balance sheets": "A bank deposit is the IOU of the bank, showing up on the liability side of the bank's balance sheet. Banks have trillions and trillions of dollars of these IOUs on their balance sheets… The IOUs are 'contingent liabilities' in the sense that the bank's creditors can insist on 'payment' or 'conversion to cash' either on demand (demand deposit) or after some waiting period (time deposit) or after some specified event. (Yet) the total amount of cash in existence is less than a trillion dollars… So, only a small fraction of the total cash is available for banks to receive in deposits in order to make loans. And yet they've got trillions and trillions of loans on their balance sheets and have issued just as many IOUs." (Wray 2012)

In this endogenous school view of a bank as a "balance sheet," the quantity of credit can be pyramided to trillions and trillions of dollars in loans. Credit is not simply in linear proportion to bank reserve requirements. Instead it can be multiplicative. How is it possible that modern banks can issue so large amounts of loans and yet have only a small amount of cash in their till on any given day?

The answer lies in the interaction between the private banks and the governmental Federal Reserve System. Wray writes: "…almost everyone who goes to the bank takes cash out! Banks supply cash; they do not receive it in order to make loans. So how could that work? Because whenever banks need cash to meet withdrawal, they do not turn to depositors, rather they call up the Fed. The Fed trucks cash, going to the banks to stock the ATMs. In turn, the Fed debits bank reserves held at the Fed (these are just the private banking system's 'checking account' held at the Fed). Now what if a bank is short reserves—will the Fed refuse to send the cash? No. The Fed lends reserves to cover the cash needs. Otherwise the bank would have to close its doors—refusing to meet demands for cash—which would scare…other depositors and lead to runs on banks… Since banks promise to supply it on demand, the Fed provides banks with all they need to meet withdrawals. It is the Fed that brings the wheelbarrows of cash to the banks—not depositors. And the Fed supplies cash not so that banks can make loans; rather, the cash is to cover withdrawals from deposits." (Wray 2012)

This operation of the Fed providing "cash" provides banks with the capacity to meet daily demands by depositors for cash withdrawals. The bank has an account with the Fed. A bank's access to Federal Reserve services is vital to the bank. When in extremis of a bank run (when all depositors want all their savings back immediately), the Fed can provide loans to the bank, acting as a "lender of last resort" to delay a banking collapse.

But this same bank's access to Fed cash can also increase the supply of money, as Wray writes: "Now the economic problem about money is not printing it (minting it) but in getting society to accept species as liquid-able money… (As Minsky said) 'anyone can create money, the problem is in getting it accepted'… What we are getting at is the degree of 'moneyness'. I am making no claim that your IOU is as good as a bank's IOU—clearly that is not the case. Banks are special. Except for government's own currency, nothing fulfills money's functions as well as bank deposit IOUs. In crisis, however, the government backstop provided to banks in the form of FDIC insurance and Fed lender of last resort promises make bank IOUs much better bets than shadow bank IOUs. So, unless you've got Uncle Sam standing behind you, your IOUs will be 'less liquid' and thus inferior 'money' in comparison to bank deposits." (Wray 2012)

In a national financial structure, money liquidity is the result of a private–public partnership, between private banks and a government central bank.

The endogenous school's view is that the financial structure interacts with the financial process. The money supply is a balance between the private good of money (as a store of wealth) and the public good of money (as an acceptable form of liquidity). In this view of modern banking, banks operate by both private and public good. This is why bank runs are such a critical feature of economic history and theory. When bank runs occur, a public good, as well as a private good, breaks down. For a private good, banks operate to enable individuals to create wealth through financial transactions. For a public good, regulatory agencies oversee the operations of banking to ensure that money provides a legitimate means of facilitating financial transactions.

A modern financial system requires a balance between private and public good for an economic system to be effective and stable. In the private good, banks convert liquid liabilities (deposits) into illiquid assets (loans); and bank runs occur when depositors perceive the bank as insolvent (bad assets). In the public good, a central bank guarantees deposits, but, in so doing, can control only the price and not the quantity of money/credit.

Thus in both exogenous and endogenous schools, there is consensus that money and credit are major "lubricants" (modes of transactions) in economic performance. But there has been a disagreement about just how money and credit interact. Quiet periods (economic stability) and unquiet periods (economic instability) are the key subjects of modern economic theory. The basic mission of regulatory theory is to ensure an honest, effective financial system and to provide a dampening down of wild swings in economic dynamics—swings from booms to busts. This is the importance of having economic theory that really works.

Background: Cross-Disciplinary Explanation

One reason we have needed to take a cross-disciplinary approach to observe bank panics is that explanation of financial systems has been contentious among economists. For example in that global banking panic of 2007–2008, the central bank policies in the USA and in England had not properly regulated financial markets. Then central bank regulators had been using the exogenous economic theory that all markets are perfect. But empirically, financial markets had been far from perfect, and bank panics have been recurrent. Using "neoclassical synthesis" exogenous economic theory, government regulators had neither anticipated nor avoided the collapse of the world's financial system.

Why had this incompleteness in economic theory existed—this assumption that empirically all markets are perfect? Why was it extensively used for policies of deregulating financial markets? In a cross-disciplinary view, we can see that, partly, it was due to the isolation of economics from important insights on society by other social science disciplines.

A critical assumption in "mainstream" economic theory had been that economic agents are rational decision makers and have perfect information. But we know from psychology that people behave as much irrationally as rationally (e.g., studies of the unconscious mind). And we know from computer science that information is never perfect. Also we know from management science that rational decision making is not simple, as market decisions are often complex (e.g., computer-algorithm trading that now dominates stock market trading). We know too from political science that politics often influences economic decision making (as occurred in the repeal of the US Glass–Steagall Act in 1999). We know from sociology that institutions and infrastructures bound individual thinking and decision making (e.g., processes of government regulatory agencies). So the whole of rational decision making within a society, even in an economic system, requires a cross-disciplinary approach for theory to match reality.

Moreover, economic theory should be based upon economic history, as history is the scientific ground for all societal theory. Although economic historians have produced splendid and detailed histories, these have not always grounded the construction of economic theory (particularly the doctrine that "markets are perfect"). Economic historians have taken broad views about the history of banks and economies; but a broad historical insight has not always crept into economic theory construction. For example, Ben Bernanke wrote: "Economists have not always fully appreciated the importance of a healthy financial system for economic growth nor the role of financial conditions in short-term economic dynamics. As a matter of intellectual history, the reason is not difficult to understand. During the first few decades after World War II, economic theorists emphasized the development of general equilibrium models of the economy with complete markets; that is, in their analyses, economists generally abstracted from market, 'frictions'—such as imperfect information or transaction costs. But without such frictions, financial markets have little reason to exist" (Bernanke 2007). Bernanke was commenting that, due to the prosperity in the US economy for two decades after World War II, this encouraged many economists to believe that markets were actually perfect—and to downplay any "problem" about any market as merely a small "friction" on the powerful drive of economic "perfection."

One of the amazing historical facts about current economic theory is that two such schools have existed and persisted—without resolving their differences. This is amazing and (as we noted) peculiar to the social sciences. This is because, methodologically, the physical/chemical/biological sciences interact cross-disciplinarily, and each bases theory construction upon experiments—empirically grounded theory. They talk to one another and, based upon experiments, reach consensus about theory.

But experimentation is difficult in the social sciences, because manipulating and controlling people for scientific study is usually unethical. However, history provides "natural experiments," describing what people actually did to each other—histories of societies and histories of economic systems. In biology, the observation of organisms in the wild has been called a "natural history." This is the approach we are taking—a "natural history" of economic systems.

Economic theory should be constructed within a cross-disciplinary framework and based on and validated by the empiricism of "natural" economic history.

What does it mean to be "cross-disciplinary" in science? It means to use the full range of scientific perspectives, all the disciplines of science, to observe nature. Science is a method to observe nature, but each observation requires a vantage point about nature—a place upon which to stand to look over nature. These vantage points are disciplines; and each discipline has a meta-framework for viewing nature. Physics uses the meta-framework of "mechanisms." Biology uses the meta-framework of "mechanisms" but also the meta-framework of "function." Such meta-frameworks are called "scientific paradigms."

We look first at explanation within the scientific paradigm of mechanisms, which is used in the physical sciences. Therein explanation is by "cause–effect"—causality. In physics, all nature can be described as mechanisms—mechanistic events and processes. In a mechanistic description of nature, a cause and an effect is an explanation which provides a mode of relationship (a temporal relationship) between two physical objects, interacting by physical forces.

In this interaction, the first logical criterion is that a cause must occur in physical time before an effect. This means that a physical cause (A) must precede in time before the physical effect B. If B has occurred, then A must have previously occurred (A is necessary to B). A second logical criterion is that whenever A does occur, then B will always subsequently occur. If A occurs, then B occurs (the occurrence of A is sufficient for the occurrence of B). Putting these two logical criteria together, a causal explanation is methodologically defined by the following:

Causality is a relationship between two objects of nature in which the occurrence of A precedes the occurrence of B and the occurrence of A is both necessary and sufficient (N&S) to explain the occurrence of B.

Historically in the philosophy of the science, this logic of explanation was understood in the physical and biological sciences—but misunderstood in the social sciences. In fact, some economists tried to find causal explanations in economics.

One well-known example was Milton Friedman's desire to make economics into a "positive science" like physics: "Positive economics is in principle independent of any particular ethical position or normative judgments…it deals with 'what is', not with 'what ought to be'. Its task is to provide a system of generalizations that can be used to make correct predictions about the consequences of any change in circumstances. Its performance is to be judged by the precision, scope, and conformity with experience of the predictions it yields. In short, positive economics is, or can be, an 'objective' science, in precisely the same sense as any of the physical sciences. Of course, the fact that economics deals with the interrelations of human beings, and that the investigator is himself part of the subject matter being investigated in a more intimate sense than in the physical sciences, raises special difficulties in achieving objectivity at the same time that it provides the social scientist with a class of data not available to the physical scientist. But neither the one nor the other is, in my view, a fundamental distinction between the two groups of sciences." (Friedman 1953)

But despite Friedman's view, there is a fundamental distinction between physical and social things; and this is in "mechanism." Economic activity is not a mechanistic activity.

For example, human bodies are mechanisms, but human minds are not mechanisms. The human brain operates as a mechanism (e.g., neurons and neural circuits), yet the human mind operates functionally (e.g., functions of vision, speech, cognition, etc.). In computers, the hardware (brain) are mechanisms (transistorized electronic circuits); but the software are functional instructions (programs). Information is functional (not mechanistic), while the hardware to process or communicate information is mechanistic. All hardware can be explained mechanistically as causality. Software can be explained functionally as prescriptive programming.

In economics, cognition and social interactions are never mechanisms but functional constructs (ideas about function and purpose). Society is not a mechanical activity; it is a functional activity. Human activity is not describable as mechanisms, and hence causality cannot be used in social science explanation. Economic systems are not describable as a mechanism; and hence causality cannot be used in economic history and in economic theory. Economics can never be a "positive" science. Economics is instead functional, a kind of "cognitive" science of rationality in human systems of utility. Economists study transactions of utility in human society—functional constructs. Information is fundamental to economic interactions and not electrons and electronics. (While now electronic trading systems are used in financial markets, yet the trading algorithms must be programmed and functionally scripted.)

This is the basic difference between the physical sciences and economics—nature as "mechanism" or nature as "functionality" (e.g., *hardware versus software*).

In contrast to Friedman, other economists have understood that economics cannot be simply a science like physics. These rejected the simplistic notion of an economic market as a kind of mechanism (controlled by an "invisible hand" over the market). Joseph Stiglitz nicely put this: "The notion economists pushed—that markets are efficient and self-adjusting—gave comfort to regulators like Alan Greenspan, who didn't believe in regulation in the first place...economic theory never provided much support for these free-market views. Theories of imperfect and asymmetric information in markets had undermined every one of the 'efficient

RELATIONSHIP	NECESSITY		SUFFICIENCY	
CAUSAL	NECESSARY (N)	&	SUFFICIENT(S)	N&S
PRESCRIPTIVE	NECESSARY (N)	&	NOT-SUFFICIENT_(S)	N&S̲
ACCIDENTAL	NOT-NECESSARY_(N)	&	SUFFICIENT (S)	N̲&S
THEMATIC	NOT-NECESSARY_(N)	&	NOT-SUFFICIENT_(S)	N̲&S̲

Fig. 3.1 Modality of explanatory relationships in science

market' doctrines, even before they became fashionable in the Reagan-Thatcher era. Bruce Greenwald and I had explained that Adam Smith's hand was not in fact invisible: it wasn't there." (Stiglitz 2010)

All markets are human functional activities of production and trade and finance. There is no mechanics in economic systems. There are processes, transactions, institutions, and contracts, but not mechanisms. There are no "forces" in economics. There is no law of conservation of energy and matter. Credit and money can be created in financial booms or destroyed in financial busts.

But if there is no "causality" in social science theory, how can the social sciences explain societal phenomena? There are other kinds of explanation, in addition to that of "causality." The kinds of explanations can be found by the logical analysis of explanation. We just reviewed the definition of a causal explanation as requiring two criteria for the explanation—necessity and sufficiency in the relationship of occurrence of A and B. One can also identity three more kinds of explanations, by taking the two criteria in logical combination. These combinations provide three more kinds of explanation: prescriptive, accidental, and thematic explanations (Fig. 3.1).

N&S—A *casual relationship* between the occurrence of A and the subsequent occurrence of B must be have necessity and sufficiency in the relation. Whenever A occurs, then B occurs if (necessity) and only if (sufficiency) A has previously occurred.

N&S—A *prescriptive relationship* between the occurrence of A and the subsequent occurrence of B must have necessity in the relation but may not have sufficiency. Whenever B has occurred, then A must have previously occurred (necessity), but also whenever A occurs, B may not follow (not sufficient). A is necessary but not sufficient for the subsequent occurrence of B.

N&S—An *accidental relationship* between the occurrence of A and the subsequent occurrence of B must have sufficiency but not necessity in the relation. Whenever A occurs, then B occurs (sufficiency) and B can occur without a previously occurring A. A is sufficient but not necessary for the occurrence of B.

N&S—A *thematic relationship* between the occurrence of A and the subsequent occurrence of B may have been neither necessary nor sufficient in the relation. Whenever B occurs, then A might not have occured (not necessary) and may not occur whenever A has occurred (not sufficient).

History and the social science disciplines can use the three explanatory relationships of prescriptive, accidental, and thematic explanations—but not causal explanations.

References

Bernanke, B. S. (2007, May 15). *Regulation and financial innovation*. 2007 Financial markets conference, Sea Island, Georgia. Federal Reserve Bank of Atlanta.

Diamond, D. W., & Dybvig, P. H. (1983). Bank runs, deposit insurance, and liquidity. *Journal of Political Economy, 91*(3), 401–419. doi:10.1086/261155. Reprinted (2000) Fed Res Bank Mn Q Rev 24 (1), 14–23.

Friedman, M. (1953). Essays in positive economics, University of Chicago Press (1953 and 1970).

McCulley, P. (2010, April). *Keynote speech at 19th Annual Hyman P. Minsky Conference on the State of the U.S. and World Economies*, The Levy Economics Institute of Bard College, New York. Available at. (http://neweconomicperspectives.org/2010/04/19th-annual-hyman-p-minsky-conference.html.

Stiglitz, J. (2010). The non-existent hand. *London Review of Books, 32*(8), 17–18.

Wray, L. R. (2012, May). *Introduction to an alternative history of money* (Working Paper No. 717). New York: Levy Economics Institute of Bard College.

Chapter 4
Dynamics of Bank Panics

Introduction

We looked at the historical event of the 1857 bank panic, but what led up to it? What is the dynamic of a financial structure which creates the historical conditions for a crisis? We noted that the two schools of economics had not achieved a synthesis of their different views on an economy, which divided them. Accordingly, economic theory had not been able to explain why the panic occurred. Next we use the cross-disciplinary approach of societal dynamics to understand how the conditions for the 1857 panic had arisen in the US society. Societal dynamics theory analyzes the history of society as a sequence of "stasis" (stable infrastructures)—each altered in time by a historical event which results in a "change" from the prior infrastructure. This sequence of stasis and change is shown in Fig. 4.1.

The disciplines of history and of the social sciences are complementary to each other in "societal time" (not physical time). The discipline of history can study a societal change event, and the disciplines of the social sciences can study and provide theory for the functional structures (systems) of a society at a given time (during a given social epoch). In societal dynamics, what the societal perceptual space provides is the analytical capability for historians to describe and explain an event of "societal change."

Thus societal dynamics theory provides a "framework" for integrating historical and social science studies. This integration is in a societal "timeline" of alternating states of "stasis" and "change events." Figure 4.2 shows this for societal change events of the bank panics of 1857, 1873, and 1893.

We apply this systems dynamics societal model to the historical case of the 1857 panic, as stasis before the panic. Earlier we described the panic event, which we now show again as Fig. 4.3.

We next put this societal stasis model into the dynamical framework of a time-ordered historical sequence in societal dynamics theory, Fig. 4.4. And preceding it, we need to add a societal model of the stasis of US financial society before the change event.

F. Betz, *Why Bank Panics Matter: Cross-Disciplinary Economic Theory*, SpringerBriefs in Economics, DOI 10.1007/978-3-319-01757-0_4,

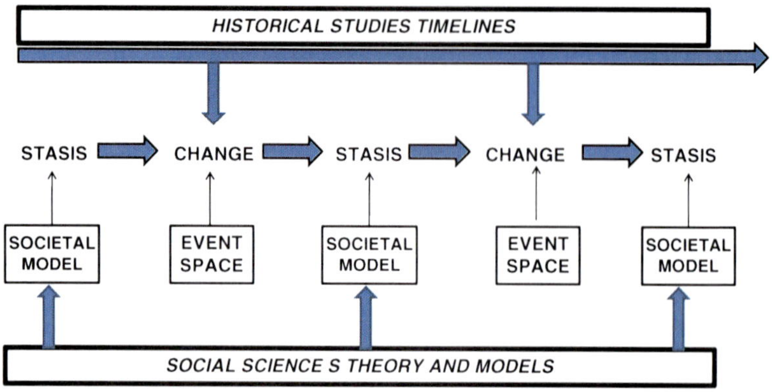

Fig. 4.1 Societal dynamics timeline sequences of stasis and change in a society's history

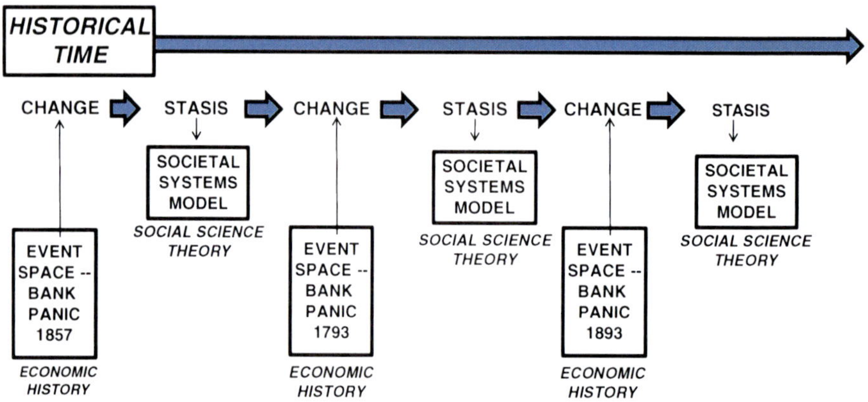

Fig. 4.2 Societal dynamics of US bank panics

Societal Systems Model

We have used the societal perceptual space from societal dynamics upon which to describe the event change of the 1857 panic. But what model can we use to describe the stasis of US society in the decade leading up to 1857 (the societal epoch from 1847 to 1857)? For this, we use a systems model of a society. A systems model of a society describes the stasis, or stability, of structures and processes in a society during a historical epoch. The model of a society is an idea, a picture, of how a society works. The systems paradigm is an appropriate framework in which to depict a societal model, since it can describe both social structures and processes. For this we use the society dynamics model (Betz 2011), constructed upon Max Weber's sociological theory (Weber 1947).

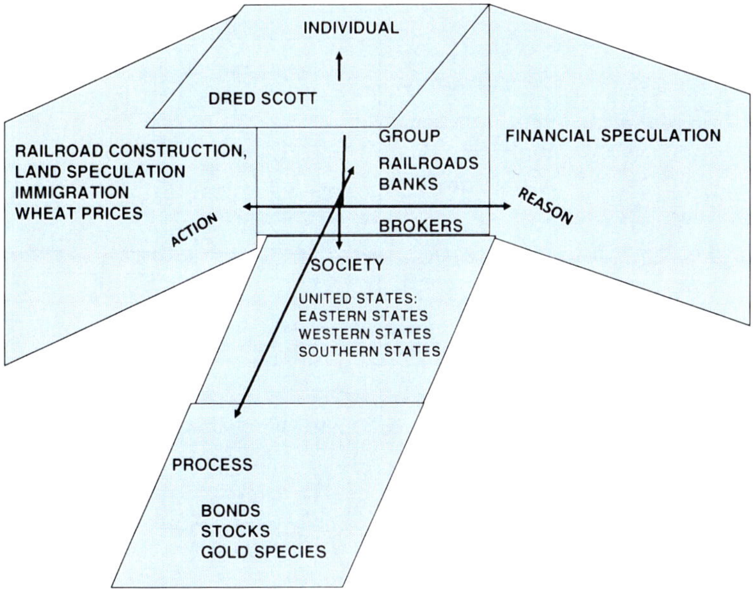

Fig. 4.3 Perceptual space of 1857 bank panic

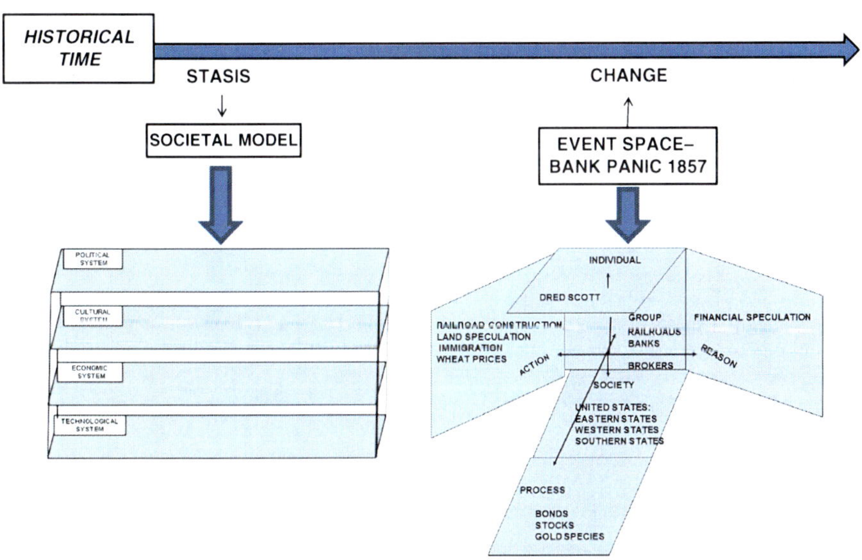

Fig. 4.4 Societal dynamics: bank panic 1857

Fig. 4.5 Societal taxonomy of interactions

	UTILITY	*IDENTITY*
RECIPROCITY	ECONOMIC INTERACTIONS	CULTURAL INTERACTIONS
AUTHORITY	SCIENTIFIC & TECHNOLOGICAL INTERACTIONS	POLITICAL INTERACTIONS

Weber wrote that for any social interaction in a society, participants can hold four kinds of expectations about that interaction: (1) utility or identity and (2) reciprocity or authority. By the dichotomy of utility or identity, Weber meant that in any societal interaction, each party to the interaction will anticipate either:

(1) *Utility in a relationship*—as a useful value for a participant in the interaction (such as buying or selling goods)
(2) *Identity in the relationship*—as an identification of one party with the other party as belonging to some same group and sharing the values of the group (such as belonging to the same family or same political party)

By the dichotomy of reciprocity or authority, Weber meant that in any societal interaction, each party will also anticipate as a basis for the interaction either:

(1) *Reciprocity in the relationship*—as a mutual and equal advantage for each party in the relationship
(2) *Authority in the relationship*—as one of the parties in the relationship for making decisions about the relationship (such one being a judge and the other a plaintiff or one being a mayor of a city and the other a citizen)

As shown in Fig. 4.5, one can construct a taxonomy of societal interactions using the two dichotomies of expectations in social interactions: with utility–identity across the top of the matrix and reciprocity–authority down the side of the matrix.

Economic interactions are the social interactions which anticipate benefits of both utility and reciprocity. Two participants each expect from their interaction both usefulness (utility) and that utility should be fair (reciprocal) in mutual benefit. For example, in an economic system, two participants in a market, as buyer and seller, expect (1) both to benefit from the sale (product for the buyer and price to the seller) and (2) that the sale should be fair (a competitive price for a quality product).

Cultural interactions are the social interactions which anticipate benefits of both identity and reciprocity. Therein two participants each expect to share a mutual identity in their interaction and also expect actions that are reciprocal in mutual benefit (fairness). For example, two participants in a church as priest and congregant both expect each to believe in the same religious faith (as members of the same church or synagogue or mosque) and share religious practice.

Political interactions are the social interactions that anticipate benefits of both identity and authority. Therein two participants each expect to share a mutual identity in their interaction but also expect actions to be decided by the one participant superior in societal authority and performed by the inferior participant. The participant superior in authority is said to hold political power over the other participant. For example, a political officeholder such as a judge in a court of law can sentence another participant in a trial (having been

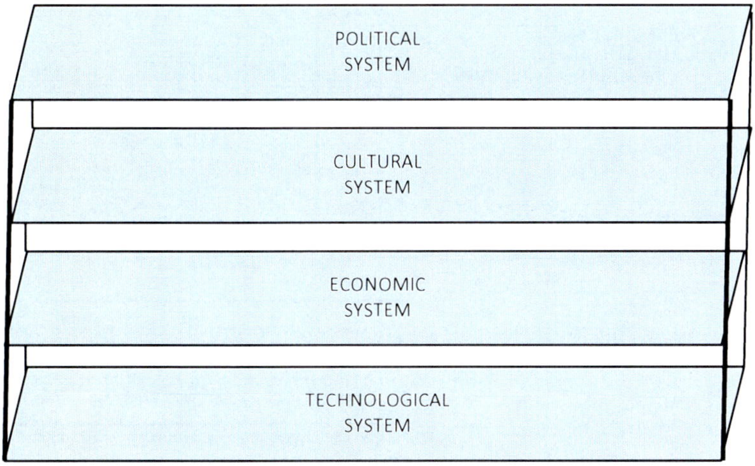

Fig. 4.6 Topological graph of societal systems

brought into court as an arrested offender) to a sacrifice of life or freedom or property. The judge has legal power over the defendant in a trial.

Science and technological interactions are the social interactions that anticipate benefits of both utility and authority. Therein two participants each expect from their interaction a usefulness (utility) and also that utility is based upon an action (technical process) which can effectively create the utility—a methodological authority which guarantees the technical effectiveness of the useful action. For example, as a business person might hire an engineer to design a factory to produce the business person's product. (One example is that of a chemical engineer hired to design chemical processes for producing chemicals.) In this interaction, the engineer's useful action in designing a factory is based upon his or her methodological authority of engineering knowledge.

One can extend this model of societal interactions as being incorporated into societal structures for the conduct of many of these interactions. The taxonomy of societal interactions can then be transformed into systems models of societal sectors, and one converts this societal system taxonomy into a topological graph, consisting of four parallel and connectable planes, Fig. 4.6.

Model of US Society Financial Speculation in the Decade Before 1857

It is in this modeling framework, we now ask the following questions. What led up to the bank panic 1857? What was the pattern in the societal model of the American society, just before 1857, which led to the panic? From the first chapter, we recall that "...the origin of the Panic of 1857 revolves around the financing of western railroad and land speculation in eastern financial markets. The proximate cause of the panic was the bankruptcy of securities brokers who borrowed from eastern

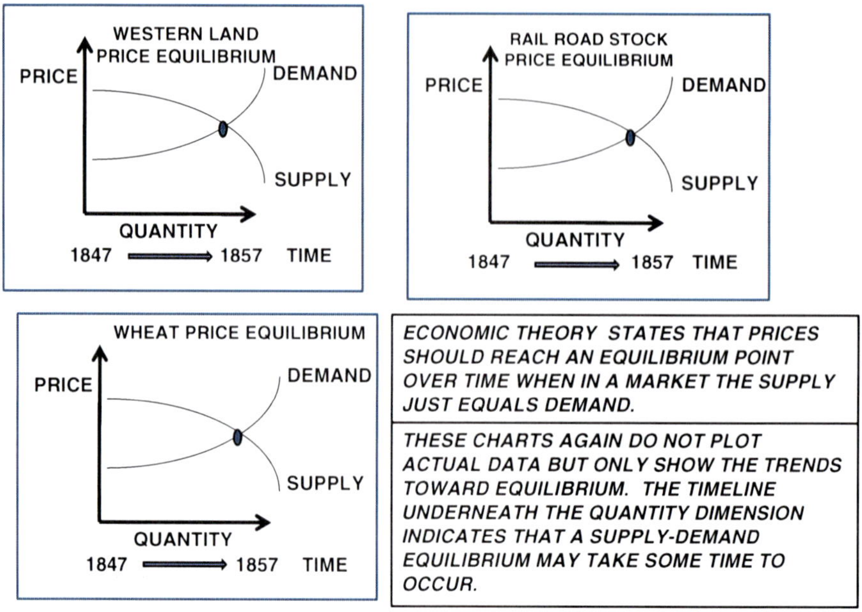

Fig. 4.7 Price equilibrium theory

banks to finance their dealings in the stock and bond markets. To understand the panic's origins, one must begin with the economic and political history of the speculative boom and bust in investments in the West during the 1850s." (Calomiris and Schweikart 1991)

And we recall that in the decade prior to 1857, large amounts of securities were issued by private companies, and their fortunes depended on settlers in the growth of the western frontier. By 1857, financial enthusiasm was focused on Kansas, the next western territory as a candidate for the next state. Western land was attracting immigrants and increasing rail traffic. With this economic growth, the prices of the assets of railroad stocks and western land had grown. But according to economic theory of supply–demand equilibrium, prices in each market should have stabilized at an equilibrium point where supply just matched demand. This is shown in Fig. 4.7.

But historically in 1857, such equilibrium pricing did not happen! Instead, a kind of "disequilibrium pricing" occurred. Instead of price equilibrium, there was an expectation by speculators for higher and higher prices. Speculators were not "betting" (trading) on the current prices (nor toward any price- equilibrium point, as assumed by economic equilibrium theory). Instead, speculators were trading (betting) upon a continuing future growth in prices—price disequilibrium.

> *This kind of speculative trading has been called "disequilibrium theory"—when pricing over time drifts away from a supply–demand equilibrium point and instead upward, toward higher prices.*

Disequilibrium Pricing Theory

We next review economic theory about "disequilibrium pricing," and for this, one must turn to the endogenous economics school, neo-Keynesians. We recall that central to the other exogenous school, neoclassical synthesis, price equilibrium was their key economic idea. They believed that all markets (including financial markets) are "perfect" in a "price equilibrium" where supply matches demand. In contrast the neo-Keynesian school argued that financial markets move instead toward "price disequilibrium." The key writers about financial markets and disequilibrium were Irving Fisher, John Maynard Keynes, Hyman Minsky, and George Soros (to all of whom we next refer). One can see the idea of "disequilibrium pricing" as a movement away from equilibrium pricing in a supply–demand model, in Fig. 4.8.

This sketches how an extrapolation to another pricing in disequilibrium can appear when market traders expect prices in the future to be higher. After a time, trading speculators push a higher pricing from an equilibrium point, until the prices become much too high and prices collapse—in a speculative "bubble." About such financial bubbles, Irving Fisher in 1933 wrote: "(In deflation)…two dominant factors (are)…over-indebtedness to start with and deflation following soon after…the big bad actors are debt disturbances and price level." (Fisher 1933)

In 1936, John Maynard Keynes underpinned Fisher's idea of a "debt deflation event" with the further idea that financial markets all differ from commodity markets (Keynes 1936). Pricing in commodity markets moves toward equilibrium, but pricing in a financial market moves toward disequilibrium.

Thus in any economy, there were two kinds of pricing processes: (1) a commodity-pricing process in the production of commodities and (2) an asset-pricing process for valuing the liquidity of productive assets. The first process occurs within the production system of an economy and the second in the financial system of the economy. In a commodity market, prices move toward an

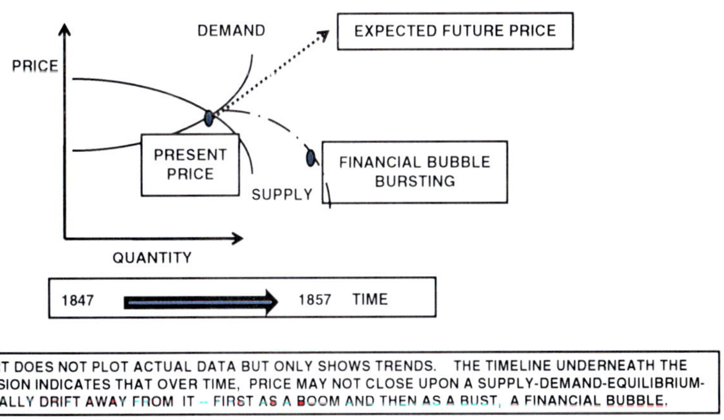

Fig. 4.8 Price equilibrium and disequilibrium

equilibrium of supply and demand. However, in a financial market, prices move toward disequilibrium—because of the nature of capital asset pricing.

In a financial market, prices undergo continual present valuations of capital assets. Therein a speculator can place a higher price on an asset (than currently justified), moving the prices upward toward a financial bubble. This pricing of an asset above a price justified upon current production revenue of the capital asset (based upon an expectation of future growth in asset price) is called "speculation." It is a speculative pricing of an asset in a present financial market, based upon future expectations of rising asset price. Keynes argued that this is the basis for the financial phenomenon of a "bubble," when speculators buy and buy, anxiously anticipating a rapid future growth in asset value.

In 1975, Hyman P. Minsky extended the Fisher–Keynes concepts of financial pricing, by introducing three different states in a financial system: (1) a conservative pricing of a financial asset, (2) a speculative pricing of a rising financial asset, and (3) a Ponzi pricing of a highly leveraged financial asset. (Minsky 1975)

Conservative financing occurs when assets are purchased at a price that the income from the capital asset can service the debt of acquiring the asset, for the interest and principle payments. Speculation financing occurs when assets are purchased at a high price so that the income can service only interest payments but not principle payments; and then repaying the debt requires refinancing. Ponzi financing occurs when the asset is purchased at so high a price that the income from the asset cannot service either interest or principle payments; and the asset must be quickly resold, "flipped."

Minsky pointed out that when a financial market expands prices into a financial bubble, then the asset prices are in a Ponzi stage, with the bubble bursting! Fisher's debt deflation commences rapidly. (Note that Minsky actually called "conservative financing" as "hedge financing." But today it is awkward to use his term this way, because currently the term of "hedge financing" means something entirely different from Minsky's use of the term. Today hedge financing is "speculation financing," and a large financial sector has grown to specialize in this called "hedge funds." I have renamed Minsky's term as "conservative financing," because it is conservative in that it is financially low risk.)

In 1988, George Soros rephrased the Fisher–Keynes–Minsky debt deflation destabilizing financial scheme, using his philosophical terms. Like his predecessors, Soros also argued that it was speculative debt that created instability in a financial system, and he called this "leveraging." Also Soros used the term "reflexivity" to indicate future expectations of speculators. Reflexivity in speculative finances describes how human expectations about a future can influence the path of the future. Soros wrote: "Reflexivity is, in effect, a feedback mechanism in which 'reality' helps shape the participants' thinking and the participants' thinking helps shape 'reality'…" (Soros 1994). A participant in the action in a society can affect the future of the society, by the decisions taken by the participant on actions in the present. For Soros, the impact upon future reality by participants' present thinking about the future and acting upon future expectation is a kind of "feedback between 'thinking' and 'reality'…'reflexivity.'"

For example, Soros wrote: "I have collected and analyzed such instances (of financial bubbles) . ... In the case of stocks, I have analyzed two particular instances which demonstrate my case perfectly; one is the conglomerate boom and bust of the late 1960s, and the other is the boom and bust of real estate investment trusts in the early 70s... The common thread in the two instances...is so-called 'equity leveraging'; that is to say, companies can use inflated expectations to issue new stock at inflated prices, and the resulting increase in earnings per share can go a long way to validate the inflated expectations." (Soros 1994)

Timing is everything in financial speculation—if one gets out of a speculation before the financial bubble bursts, one can make money, but if too late, one loses money.

Fisher, Keynes, Minsky, and Soros all emphasized that "economic thinking" within a financial system is different from "economic thinking" within a production system. In a production system, thinking is about matching supply to demand in equilibrium pricing. But in a financial system, thinking is about speculation. A speculator's "thinking about reality" partly shapes "reality," and "reality" partly shapes a participant's "thinking"—a reflexivity (interaction) between thinking about future assets and the future reality of asset prices. In a financial market, leverage is essential to speculation, and speculation is basic to financing, but good timing is essential.

"Supply and demand" are the two concepts central to the model of a commodity market of the exogenous economics school—creating equilibrium pricing in commodity markets.

"Leverage and reflexivity" are the two concepts central to the model of a financial market of the endogenous economics school—creating disequilibrium pricing in financial markets.

US Societal Stasis Prior Leading Up to 1857

Banks operate in financial markets and not in commodity markets. Therefore price disequilibrium is inherent in banking, recurrent bank panics. Historically, one can see in the 1857 bank panic that a "reflexivity" in speculative thinking had occurred from 1847 to 1857. We now use the societal systems model to show how "disequilibrium pricing" occurred. For this, we place a disequilibrium pricing model upon the economic system plane of the societal model, as shown in Fig. 4.9.

The dynamics of market speculation occurred in the plane of the economics system of a US society. On the political system plane of the US American society, government policies of providing land grants (free land) both to railroad construction and to settlers in the West stimulated immigration from east to west and from Europe to the USA (such immigration appearing on the cultural system plane). Indicated in the technological system of the society, railroads were the new technology providing land transportation in the country and in its territorial expansion.

Immigration from the cultural system provided a source of market change, increasing "demand" in the economic system. Railroads from the technological

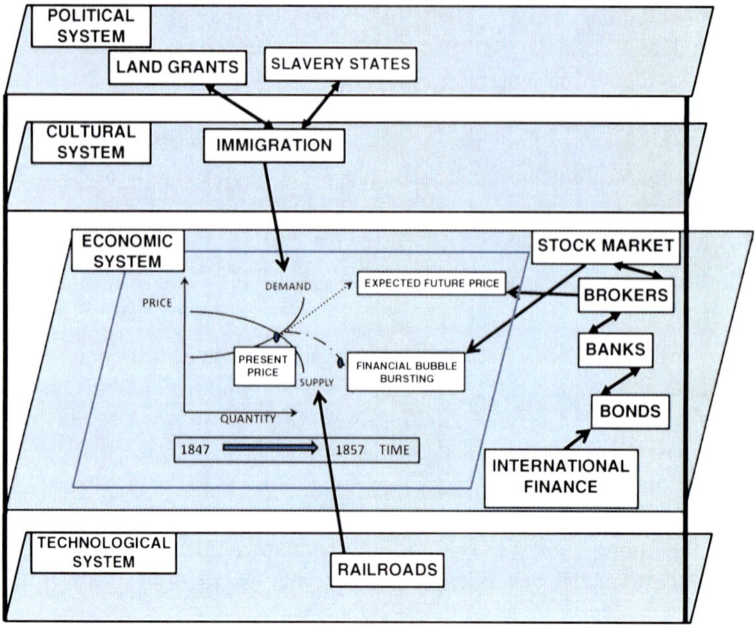

Fig. 4.9 Societal model—dynamics leading up to 1857 bank panic

system provided a source of market change, increasing "supply" in the economic system. So the economic system from 1847 to 1857 was not static but dramatically changing; and the economic system did not move toward a pricing equilibrium of demand matching supply. Instead, this perception of market change by financial speculators encouraged their "thinking" that the future reality of land prices and of railroad stock prices would be higher and higher. *This is how disequilibrium theory in financial markets describes the creation of financial bubbles.* When rail revenues and wheat prices declined, then the financial market in the Eastern USA went bust—with banks calling in loans to brokers and raising collateral margins on their speculative loans.

The societal stasis which can lead up to a bank-panic event (financial crisis) involves trends in the models of its systems, including political policies, cultural shifts, and technological trends. Leading up to the 1857 panic, these were the political policies of land grants and the cultural shift of westward immigration and the technological trend of railroad expansion. These all influenced the dynamics of markets, creating investment and speculation opportunities to which the financial markets responded (by providing investments for growth and speculations on price increases). For the 1857 panic, the speculations in land prices and railroad stock prices had been Ponzi financed by the loans and bonds from Eastern banks.

All this is analyzed within a societal model—as the stasis of a society's systems before a historical-crisis event. Then the historical crisis occurs, and that event can be analyzed within the framework of a societal perceptual space. A sequence of

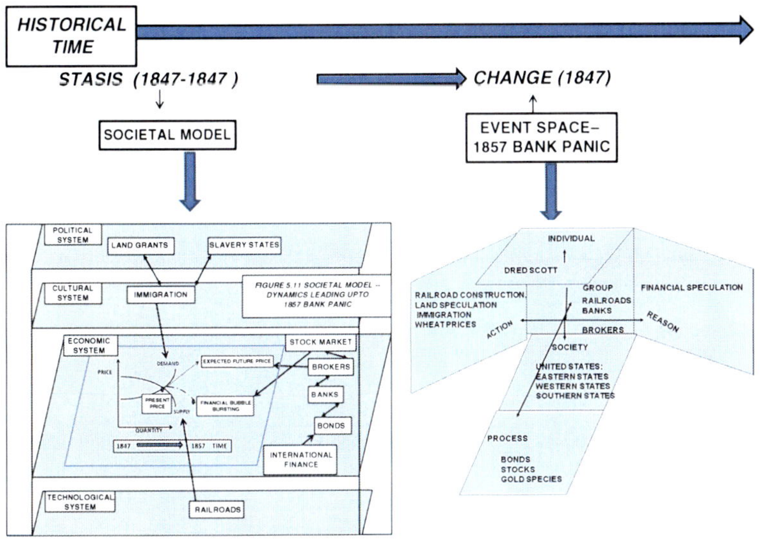

Fig. 4.10 Societal dynamics: bank panic 1857

societal stasis and event crisis can be represented on a historical timeline for the society; and Fig. 4.10 shows this sequence of stasis and change for the US society in the bank crisis of 1857.

Summary

We have noted the emphasis which the endogenous school (neo-Keynesian) have placed upon having an explicit "time dimension" in economic modeling. Also this emphasis on time in economic systems had divided the exogenous and endogenous schools of economics. The exogenous (neoclassical synthesis) school emphasized a production system with a rapid equilibrium pricing in a supply–demand model of a commodity market, and hence here time toward equilibrium was relatively unimportant. However, the endogenous (neo-Keynesian) school emphasized instead a financial system, in which time is very important as reflexive expectations about the future drive disequilibrium prices away above equilibrium prices, and hence time toward disequilibrium is very important.

Accordingly in disequilibrium price theory, there are the two key ideas: (1) "reflexivity" in price expectations and speculation decisions and (2) "financial leverage" in maximizing speculation. The cognitive action of "reflexivity" occurs between expecting market growth (thinking) and buying growth stock (action). This creates rising prices (reality), at least in the short run until finally excessive prices collapse in a financial bubble. There is also a "financial leverage" through a multiplication decision to borrow money for stock purchases, in order to maximize gain from speculation, such as loans for speculation and stocks bought on margin. Thinking in "financial reflexivity" grows the financial bubble, and "financial leverage" bursts the bubble. It is the reflexivity which creates the speculation (boom). But later when market prices decline, investments made by "loaned money" (leverage) must be cancelled or sold (and cannot be held for any future price recovery). And so it is the "leverage" collapse which creates the bust—followed by a bank panic—followed by debt deflation.

A financial bubble as a boom-and-bust societal phenomenon centers upon the ideas of both reflexivity and leverage as essential (fundamental and internal) to any financial system.

References

Betz, F. (2011). *Societal dynamics*, Springer. In E. Carayannis (Series Ed.), *Springer innovation, technology, and knowledge management series*.

Calomiris, C. W., & Schweikart, L. (1991). The panic of 1857: Origins, transmission, and containment. *Journal of Economic History, 51*(4), 807–834.

Fisher, I. (1933, October). The debt-deflation theory of the Great Depression. *Econometrica*.

Keynes, J. M. (1936). *The general theory of employment, interest, and money*. New York: Harcourt Brace.

Minsky, H. (1975). *John Maynard Keynes*. New York: Columbia University Press (reprinted in 2008 by Mc Graw Hill).

Soros, G. (1994, April 26). The theory of reflexivity. MIT Department of Economics World Economy Laboratory Conference, Washington, DC. http://www.georgesorose

Weber, M. (1947). *From Max Weber: Essays in sociology*. ISBN 0-19-500462-0.

Chapter 5
Control in an Economic System

Introduction

As we have seen in the example of the 1857 panic, bank panics occur in a common pattern. There is a price disequilibrium in a capital asset market, created by speculators' reflexivity about future prices and their use of excessive leverage—increasing prices unto a financial bubble which grows and finally bursts. Then the banks which funded the speculation suffer bank runs, as their assets fall in the "debt deflation" from the bubble. And before 2007, this pattern had been identified in the economic writings of Fisher, Keynes, Minsky, and Soros. So why was this pattern a surprise again in 2007?

We jump in history, a 100 years from 1857 panic to the panic in 2007—from the first American-wide bank panic to the first global-wide bank panic. The reason we do this is that, by the beginning of the twenty-first century, major economists in the USA had thought the problem of bank panics was solved. But they were surprised anew! A new and even more virulent bank panic occurred—the first global bank panic, enabled by the new information technology. The pattern of the panic was old. But with new technology, this was a new kind of panic. The combination of new information and financial technologies had altered the financial system.

History of a Disruptive Societal Event: The 2007–2008 Global Financial Crisis

July 2007

An article in The New York Times then summarized the crisis: "The first shoe (of the global financial implosion) to drop was the collapse in July 2007 of two hedge funds, owned by Bear Stearns, that had invested heavily in the subprime market."

F. Betz, *Why Bank Panics Matter: Cross-Disciplinary Economic Theory*, SpringerBriefs in Economics, DOI 10.1007/978-3-319-01757-0_5,

(NY Times, Dec 2008). Banks, such as Bear Stearns, had been making up bonds to be sold as a collateralized debt object (CDO). These CDOs contained some good, low-risk "prime" mortgages but often also as much as 60 % bad and risky "subprime" mortgages. The bank's funds had deliberately mixed prime with subprime mortgages in their bonds to increase the size and number of bonds. This resulted in the CDOs being contaminated with high risk. The buyers of the bonds did know this; instead they had been told the CDO derivatives were low risk, based upon AAA bonds. The fund managers said that the mixture of subprimes "spread the risk," but this was misleading as they really only increased risk—so much so that Bear Sterns would collapse when the CDO market collapsed.

March 2008

It would take eight months, from July 2007 to March 2008, for the "financial dominoes" to begin falling: "Bear Sterns kept reporting larger and larger losses on mortgage bonds. Bear Sterns was on the verge of bankruptcy, because it did not have sufficient reserve funds to satisfy Federal regulations to continue being chartered as a bank. Then in March 2008, the Fed staved off a Bear Stearns bankruptcy by assuming $30 billion of Bear Sterns' liabilities and arranging its sale to JPMorgan Chase. The price of that sale was at $10 dollars a share, when only months earlier shares had been in the $100 dollar range, so that Chase acquired Bear Stearns for a price that was less than the worth of Bear's Manhattan skyscraper." (NY Times, Dec 2008). This was only the first bank that would fail to meet its banking reserve requirements. Several more were to follow in the USA and around the world.

August 2008

Next, the two giant semipublic mortgage companies in the USA, Fannie Mae and Freddie Mac, failed. "In August, government officials began to become concerned as the stock prices of Fannie Mae and Freddie Mac, government-sponsored entities that were linchpins of the housing market, slid sharply." (NY Times, Dec 2008). Earlier the Federal government had guaranteed their bonds, but then the government nationalized both companies: "On Sept. 7, the Treasury Department announced it was taking over (nationalizing) Fannie Mae and Freddie Mac." (NY Times, Dec 2008)

September 2008

In the same month, a second major investment bank fell: "On Sept. 12, top government and finance officials gathered for talks to fend off bankruptcy for Lehman

Brothers. The talks broke down, and the government refused to step in and salvage Lehman as it had for Bear Sterns. Lehman's failure sent shock waves through the global banking system…" (NY Times, Dec 2008). Lehman Brothers could not meet bank reserve requirements, having borrowed too much to buy mortgages, which they assembled into collateralized debt objects—a CDO was a financial derivative, consisting only of interest payment without any collateral. Then that mortgage bond behind a CDO was not saleable, as then the bond no longer paid interest. Also a stock brokerage firm, Merrill Lynch, had also been buying large numbers of sub-prime mortgages to make up mortgage bonds for CDOs; and Merrill Lynch was forced to sell itself to the Bank of America. "On Sept. 16, American International Group (AIG), an insurance giant on the verge of failure because of its exposure to exotic securities known as credit default swaps (CDS as insurance on a CDO derivative), was bailed out by the Fed in an $85 billion deal." (NY Times, Dec 2008). AIG had been issuing insurance on all those CDOs, all of which AIG couldn't pay if the CDOs failed. Then all the stock exchanges in the world imploded: "…Stocks plunged, with the Standard & Poor's 500-stock index losing nearly 9 percent, its worst day since Oct. 19, 1987." (NY Times, Dec 2008)

October 2008

Governments began to intervene in the collapsing economies: "The US Treasury Secretary, Henry M. Paulson Jr., publicly announced a three-page, $700 billion proposal that would allow the government to buy toxic assets from the nation's biggest banks, a move aimed at shoring up their balance-sheets and restoring confidence within the financial system… Many Americans were angered by the idea of a proposal that provided billions of dollars in taxpayer money to Wall Street banks, which many believed had caused the crisis in the first place. US government intervention to save the US banking industry was underway…(but) it was still unclear how effective the bailout plan would be in resolving the credit crisis." (NY Times, Dec 2008). The banking crisis spread around the world: "Banks in England and Europe had invested heavily in mortgage-backed securities offered by Wall Street… Over the weekend that followed the (US) bailout's passage, the German government moved to guarantee all private savings accounts in the country, and bailouts were arranged for a large German lender and a major European financial company." (NY Times, Dec 2008). But stock markets around the world continued to plunge. The central banks of many nations cut their prime interest rates to lower lending costs. Still the credit crises hadn't ended. The governments' investments in their banks increased: "…after a week in which stocks declined almost 20 percent on Wall Street, European and American officials announced coordinated actions that included taking equity stakes in major banks, including $250 billion in investments in the USA." (NY Times, Dec 2008). The impact of the credit crisis spread from banks to stock markets to exchange rates and even the price of oil: "The volatility in the stock markets was matched by upheaval in currency trading as investors sought shelter in the yen and the dollar, driving down the currencies of developing countries and even the euro and the British pound. Oil-producing countries were hit by a sudden reversal of fortune, as the record oil prices reached over the summer were cut in half by October because of the world economic outlook" (NY Times, Dec 2008). A global recession was anticipated: "But as the prospect of a severe global had begun, then Ben S. Bernanke, the Federal Reserve chairman, said there would be no quick economic turnaround even with the government's intervention', and the Dow plunged 733 points." (NY Times, Dec 2008)

November 2009

In November 2008, the US government elections were held; and a new president, Barack Obama, was elected: The credit crisis emerged as the dominant issue of the presidential campaign in the last 2 months before the (US presidential) election. The weakening stock market and growing credit crisis appeared to benefit Mr. Obama, who tied Mr. McCain to what he called the failed economic policies of President Bush and a Republican culture of deregulation of the financial markets. Polls showed that Mr. Obama's election on Nov. 4 was partly the fruit of the economic crisis and the belief among many voters that he was more capable of handling the economy than Mr. McCain." (NY Times, Dec 2008)

Analysis of the Event in a Societal Perceptual Space

In Fig. 5.1, we analyze the event in the general societal factors of the following: *individual–society, group–process, and action–reason.*

Group

Banks and hedge funds were the main groups in the event. For this, there are three kinds of banks: commercial, investment, and trading banks. Commercial banks aggregate the savings of many depositors to make loans to borrowers. The profit margin in this kind of banking is not large—the difference between the interest rate collected from the borrowers and the interest rate paid to the savers. Investment banks assemble investors for investments in commercial enterprises, such as establishing a new business, expanding a business, acquiring or merging or selling businesses, and for issuing public stock in a business. Profits per project (investments) in an investment bank are usually much larger than profits per project (loans) of a

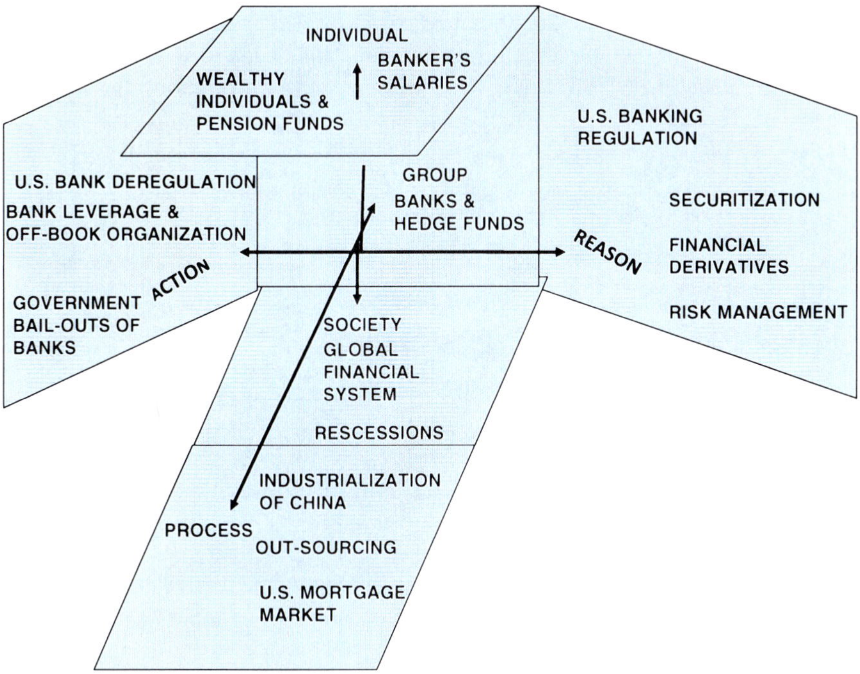

Fig. 5.1 2007–2008 Global financial crisis

commercial bank. Trading firms facilitate trading in commodities or money or stocks, earning commissions on trades or in trading on their own account (with their own money). Profit per project (a trade) in a trading bank is usually much, much smaller than the profit per project (an investment) of an investment bank; but it can be multiplied by leverage (borrowing money for a trade). Most large investment banks now also include trading activities. In 1999 in the USA after the passage of the Gramm–Leach–Bliley Act, investment banks were allowed to merge with commercial banks. That incentive was (1) for executives in investment banks to have access to depositors' savings for financing their trading activities and (2) for executives in commercial banks to reward themselves at the higher level of bonuses which executives in investment banks earned.

In addition, hedge funds were formed in the USA as trading firms which trade <u>with</u> investors' money, instead of trading <u>for</u> investors. In the 1980s and 1990s, some hedge funds made risky investments in financial markets and compiled a record of high financial returns. Then many US institutions (such as pension-fund managers or university endowment-fund managers or managers of the investments of wealthy clients) began investing in hedge funds and hedge funds ballooned. By 2007, assets in hedge funds had grown to nearly two trillion dollars, whereas the whole US banking system then had assets of about ten trillion dollars—so the hedge fund industry held 17 % of US capital assets. If this 20 % began to fail, then the whole banking industry might be brought down. This occurred with the failure of two hedge funds in the investment bank of Bear Sterns—triggering the financial debacle of 2007–2008.

Action

Deregulation of the US Banking Industry

US investment and commercial banks were allowed to merge in 1999; as then US regulatory law of the Glass–Steagall Act of 1933 (previously separating investment and commercial banks) was repealed in the Gramm–Leach–Bliley Act. With this merger of investment and commercial banks, the Federal government was, in effect, guarantying commercial banks' deposits—even when the investment side was gambling with the depositors' savings in making trades. In 2007–2008, when merged investment–commercial banks failed because of high-risk trading, the Federal government was still responsible for all the savings accounts. Also in 2004, the Security Exchange Commission (SEC), the US government agency responsible for regulating the business practices of public stock companies, relaxed the bank-capital rule of how much should be the ratio of loaned capital-to-liquid capital. Also to help banks increase their money leverage, accounting practices in the USA adopted a standard of allowing banks to move loans for which they were responsible "off their books"—pretending to not to account for liabilities to which banks were really liable. The result was that when large amounts of bad loans failed, the highly leveraged banks did not have sufficient liquid capital to meet SEC standards and were in danger of losing their banking licenses. The Federal government bailed them out by purchasing stock in their banks.

Lack of Regulation of Hedge Funds

The "shadow banking industry" of hedge funds remained unregulated by the US government (and we will explore this concept in a later chapter). And the emerging derivatives market also was not regulated. In 1997, the Federal Chairman of the US Federal Reserve argued against any regulation of the derivatives market. The US Congress and President enacted the Commodity Futures Modernization Act of 2000, in which the derivatives market was allowed to continue unregulated.

Reason

Securitization

In an industrial society, capital is increased in three ways—through investments in productive activities, through speculative trading, and through appreciation of owned assets (such as property, gold, and art). Securitization was a financial idea to facilitate speculative investment in the trade of debt. Because in the US residential mortgages were usually long term, such as 30 years, they were too long for most investors. Fannie Mae had been set up by the US government to buy these long-term residential mortgages and finance its purchases by issuing 10-year bonds guaranteed by the US government. Since private banks would not have any US government guarantee, they invented "securitization." This meant the banks and hedge funds purchased mortgage loans and bundled them into a mortgage bond, which they called a collateralized debt object (CDO). Then they did not sell the bond but only interest from the bond, as a 10-year financial contract of interest payments (called a financial "derivative"). Since the derivatives were not based upon any collateral (the house collateral for each mortgage remained in a bond (CDO), they would reassure the buyers of the derivatives with insurance on each derivative (called a "credit default swap," CDS). The insurance firm AIG sold the insurance CDSs. The derivatives were then sold over the Internet to pension funds domestically and to foreign banks and wealthy investors internationally. There were five flaws in the scheme:

Firstly, the bonds, which the banks "securitized" into a CDO, were afterwards worthless as an asset. The banks had paid out money to buy the mortgages (which composed a bond) but then had to wait 30 years to recover the bond principle through the mortgage payments—all that while receiving no interest from mortgage payments since the interest payments had been securitized (sold off) as derivatives. Hence the bonds were not resalable. The banks only made money once as a commission in selling the derivatives of the CDO, and afterwards the bonds they still held were illiquid, unsalable—for 30 years.

Secondly, since the bonds cost more money than the commissions earned in securitizing a CDO, the bank could not make enough money for a CDO itself to be profitable to them (profits = sales—costs). So how did the hedge funds of a bank which sold the CDO derivatives make money? The hedge funds bought the bond from a bank but with borrowed money. Until a bank sold a bond to a hedge fund, the bank was stuck with a worthless bond. So to make a short-term profit, hedge funds borrowed short-term money from banks to buy the long-term bonds. The CDOs were financed with short-term loans,

(continued)

(continued)

but the CDO's bond principle could not be collected fully for 30 years. This is called "borrowing short and lending long." It is a well-known (but bad) financial principle in banking—a very bad principle. Never borrow short and lend long! But hedge funds did this, and the banks loaning a hedge fund its "leveraged loan" were still "on the hook" for the original cost of the bond. Why would hedge funds do this? Why would banks do this? They did it for short-term commissions in the sales of the CDO derivatives. Also they must have hoped that the long-term "tomorrow" would never come. But "tomorrow" did arrive soon and in 2008. Then hedge funds could not refinance their CDO-borrowed money (leverage) and collapsed. The banks loaning the hedge funds the leverage money also collapsed. First, a Bear Sterns hedge fund collapsed, and then Bear Sterns collapsed. Next, a Lehman Brothers hedge fund collapsed, and then Lehman Brothers collapsed.

Thirdly, the banks and hedge funds sold fraudulently rated derivatives. They had assembled bad bonds (CDOs), which had deliberately mixed bad subprime mortgages (high risk) with good prime mortgages (low risk). They called the CDO a low-risk investment and bought low-risk ratings (AAA) from bond-rating agencies. But later the investors who had purchased the mortgage-securitized derivatives learned that the so-called "low-risk" derivatives were really "high risk," full of subprime "very high-risk" mortgages. All the CDOs then became financially "toxic," and the derivatives market collapsed.

Fourthly, the so-called insurance "CDSs" which the firm AIG had issued were worthless—because AIG could not pay off all the billions of dollars of CDS insurance contracts they had sold. AIG was about to be bankrupt, until the US Federal government "bailed out" AIG.

Fifthly, the banks had sold so many billions of dollars of derivatives that when the derivatives market had suddenly became worthless, many of the major banks of the world had such large illiquid liabilities that they could not meet government-required minimum amounts of liquid capital—and so were in jeopardy of collapse. Then banks could not loan, even to each other; and all financial transactions between banks in the world temporarily ceased. The financial system of the world stopped.

In sum, the problems were as follows: worthless securitized assets, unpaid-for assets, fraudulent risk ratings, worthless insurance contracts, and large illiquid liabilities. In sum, along with fraudulent representation, there was just extremely bad, bad banking.

Risk Management

When a bank makes a loan, the way to reduce risk is to own an asset more valuable than the loan, if the borrower fails on the loan. This is called collateral on the loan. But if a derivative does not have collateral, then insurance on the debt is essential. But how can one judge the proper insurance on a CDO if it is composed of mortgages of different risk? Obviously, one cannot except by adding in a weighted manner the risk on each mortgage. Bankers did not do this. Instead, fund managers made up a mathematical model to estimate risk, a "risk management model." But any mathematical model is true only when based upon proper empirical data (garbage in, garbage out). Bond raters did not gather empirical data, relying instead upon what their customers told them. They were being paid by hedge fund managers to give high ratings to the securitized CDOs. George Soros commented: "The super-boom got out of hand when the new products (derivatives) became so complicated that authorities (bond raters) could no longer calculate the risks and started relying on the risk management methods of the banks themselves. Similarly, the rating agencies relied on the information provided by the originators of synthetic product. It was a shocking abdication of responsibility." (Soros 2008)

Individual

Banker's Salaries and Bonuses

In the USA before the 1990s, most executive compensation was in the form of salaries and perks. But in the late 1980s, executive compensation moved increasingly to bonuses. The reason for this was threefold. First, control of corporate boards passed from shareholders to corporate executives through proxy voting. Second, capital gains were at the time taxed at half the rate as dividends, so corporations could stop paying out dividends. (US tax laws distorted financial incentives—resulting in unintended consequences.) This gave executives large amounts of corporate "retained earnings" with which to buy other companies—thereby "purchasing" corporate growth and raising stock prices. Third, through such corporate acquisitions (and any other means executives could think of), executives focused exclusively upon the short-term future of the corporation in order to soon maximize the value of their stock bonuses. If, in the long term, a corporation failed because of excessive focus upon the short term, then only shareholders and lower-ranking employees would lose savings and jobs. In such an eventuality, short-term bonuses would have already made the executives multimillionaires.

(continued)

(continued)

In banking, this executive bonus policy encouraged executives of banks to ignore any long-term risks their employees were taking in making loans. Loan commissions increased revenue to fuel executive bonuses. This is why some banking executives allowed their hedge funds to engage in the bad banking practice of borrowing short and lending long. As mentioned earlier, when, in February 2008, hedge funds of the investment bank Bear Sterns were unable to obtain renewed loans, the funds failed. Bear Sterns, which had lent them $6 billion dollars, also failed. This triggered the Global Financial Crisis.

Wealthy Individuals with Sovereign Oil Companies

From 2006 to 2008, world oil prices quintupled from $30 dollars a barrel to $150 dollars a barrel. The rapid rise in prices was due to market speculation that commodity prices would increase due to the market demands of China's rapid industrialization and India's economic growth due to information technology. Sovereign oil companies (owned by governments) controlled 70 % of the world's oil—Russia, Saudi Arabia, Nigeria, Kuwait, Iran, Libya, Nigeria, Venezuela, etc. In the economies of these sovereign companies, large wealth was being accumulated by individuals, which needed places for investment. Ben S. Bernanke spoke about the times: "Large and growing amounts of foreign funds (capital) flowed into the USA. This created a demand for various types of financial assets… Foreign investors had these funds to lend, either because they had a very high personal savings rate or because of high oil prices… A 'flood' of funds reached the USA financial markets" (Bernake 2007). The US dollar was still seen as a safe international currency. Until 2007, the USA was viewed as a safe haven for investments.

Process

Industrialization of China

The rapid economic growth of China required great capital investments, which were provided internally by the government banks. Some external capital was flowing into China; but it was small compared to the enormous export profits earned by the state industries of China, as outsourcing suppliers for American and European global companies. China had a communist government and state-majority-owned industry; and capital from the rest of the world

(continued)

(continued)

saw political risk in investing in the government-owned enterprises. So while the industrialization of China required large capital investments, this was not provided by the global financial market—which instead "flooded" money into the US financial market. Opportunities for financial investment in industrial growth in Western economies were also being limited by this "outsourcing" of hard-good production to China, slowing industrial growth in goods production in America and Europe. Some economists, such as Samir Amin (2010), argued that this lack of industrial growth failed to provide opportunities for productive investment and US financial markets turned to fabricating speculative investment.

US Mortgage Market

Lacking a basis for investments in industrial growth, US banks and hedge funds turned to the US mortgage market. Traditionally, the US residential mortgage market had been dominated by the quasi-governmental but private corporation, Fannie Mae, which bought long-term residential mortgages from banks and issued shorter-term bonds to pay for them (with the bonds guaranteed by the US government). This worked well until executives at Fannie Mae decided they wanted to quickly and dramatically increase revenue and, in consequence, receive large bonuses quickly becoming wealthy. Fannie Mae began to buy subprime mortgages. Morgenson and Rosner wrote: "For years, Fannie Mae's compensation structure had been a conservative one, with executive pay linked to a wide range of performance measures…but after Johnson took over the company, Fannie Mae's executive pay structure changed. Compensation became tied almost to earnings growth… As Johnson increased sales, executive pay would raise from 1993 to 2000 from $8.5 million to $35.2 million, quadrupling executives' pay." (Morgenson and Rosner 2011, p. 23)

To purchase subprime mortgages in large volumes, James Johnson, the CEO of Fannie Mae, encouraged business with a major subprime mortgage lender, Countrywide Financial. Johnson retired from Fannie Mae, but subsequent CEO's continued the strategy. In 2008, after the Federal government took over the bankrupt Fannie Mae, the last CEO was fired.

Society

Using the new information technologies, the economic systems of many nations of the world were tied together, forming a global financial market. Failure of this global financial socio-technical system brought economic processes in national economics to a halt and tipped these economies into recession.

Control in a Societal Socio-technical System

We can use this analysis to understand how "control" failed. Explanations can be ordered into three sets, which focus respectively upon control of managed systems, control of socio-technical systems, and control of self-organizing systems (Fig. 5.2).

We look at these issues about control to obtain empirically based answers to three important questions. How did all this occur—all that misbehavior of managers in banking, hedge funds, accounting, and rating firms and also that misbehavior of officials in regulatory agencies? Why was all the misbehavior allowed? How did their "misbehaving" actions bring down the world's banking system? These are questions about "control" in a society.

One of the theoretical social science assumptions which the economic profession has proposed about "control" in any market (even in a financial market) is that all markets are "perfect," needing little or no regulatory control. But the empirical evidence is that a kind of theoretical "automatic" control of an economic system is seldom true.

All industrialized societies have institutionalized infrastructures in which social activities–processes occur and are institutionalized as a "system" in a society, a "socio-technical system." This term was introduced into the organizational literature by Eric Trist, Ken Bamforth, and Fred Emery, then of the Tavistock Institute in London (Trist and Murray 1993). We now focus on why this socio-technical system of finance did not work properly in the economic system of the world (Fig. 5.3).

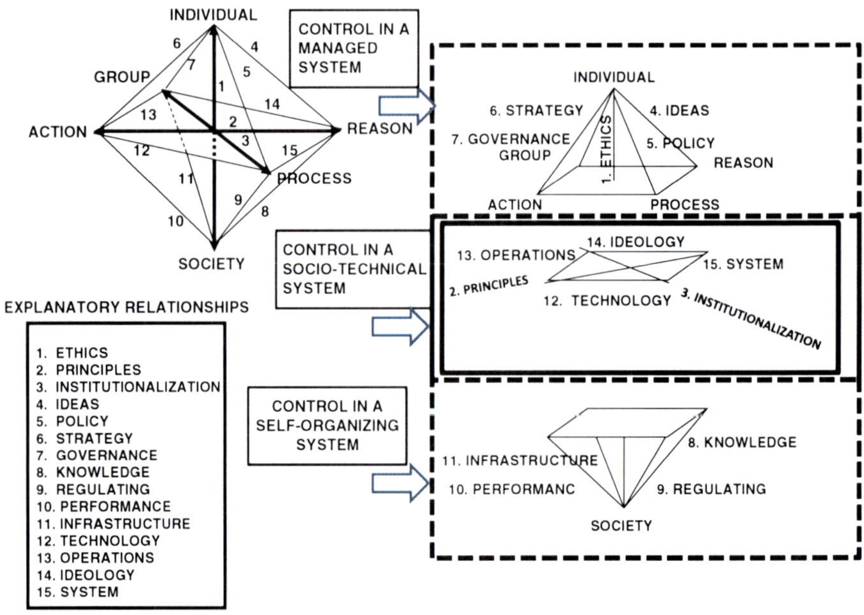

Fig. 5.2 Types of control in a society

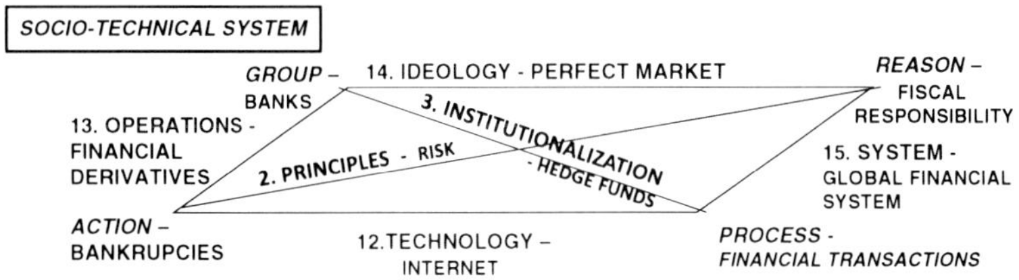

Fig. 5.3 2007 Failure of the global financial system as failure in 'control' of a socio-technical system

The (15.System*) of the* financial socio-technical system consisted of a global banking system:

- Operated with financial derivatives *(13) operations*
- Sold in the information *(12) technologies* of computers and Internet

The group performing these derivative operations consisted of banks in different countries, which sold the derivatives in financial transactions, process:

- But the investments were not safe because they violated a basic principle of risk management, low-risk *(2) principles,* by including high-risk subprime mortgages in the derivatives.

The action of selling the derivatives resulted in bankruptcies of banks, into which governments had to intervene to save their economies:

- *Economic theory was used as a rationale (14.Ideology) to justify these operations, arguing that all markets are perfect and require no regulation (ideology justifies the interest of a particular group, whereas theory should be objective and independent of any group).*
- *The (3) institutionalization of hedge funds into the financial/banking system created a wholly unregulated part of the US banking system, some of which turned to selling fraudulent strategic investment vehicles (SIVs) based upon short-term financing for leverage.*

But how exactly did this socio-technical system fail? Banks and hedge funds are organizations directly managed by an individual leader (a president or a chief executive officer, CEO). Government agencies are directly managed by an elected or appointed official individual (director or executive secretary). In the financial socio-technical system, the banks and hedge funds conducted financial transactions within a financial regulatory infrastructure run by government regulatory agencies. The actions (and inactions) of directly managed banks (and regulatory agencies) together indirectly controlled the performance of the financial socio-technical system. Failure of responsible management (greed and fraud) in banks and hedge funds contributed to a highly leveraged, poor-quality derivatives market, which froze up (stopped financial transactions); and then some hedge funds and banks failed. This occurred within a financial infrastructure of poor regulation—wherein regulatory

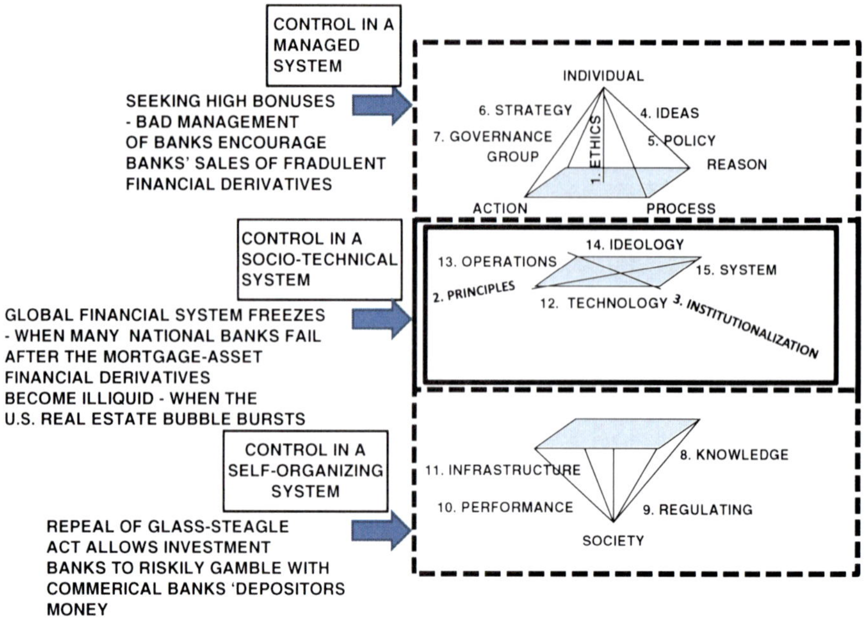

Fig. 5.4 Systems failures in 2007 global financial crisis

officials (with bad and irresponsible judgment) failed to have/enforce proper regulations—which should have the controlled financial abuse (Fig. 5.4).

In a society, socio-technical systems are never directly controlled—but only indirectly controlled—by means of direct control in organizations and institutions.

A systems dynamics analysis of a historical event helps the examination of control issues in a historical societal event by sorting explanations about control (success or failure) into three kinds of controls: socio-technical system control, managed system control, and self-organizing system control.

Control in an Organization

Next how can one explain the actions of the organizations and the behavior of their leaders (including misbehavior)? In sociology, a modern society is composed of individuals, groups, and organizations. In organizational theory, an organization is viewed as a formalized group. In management science theory, organizations are viewed as a system, a managed system. We use these two views to see an organization as a formally organized group (operations) acting under a managed form (authority): an *operational structure* of an organization provides its *socio-technical-system* form, and an *authority structure* of an organization provides its *managed system* form. As shown in Fig. 5.5, the full understanding of the proper control of an organization must use all these explanatory relationships.

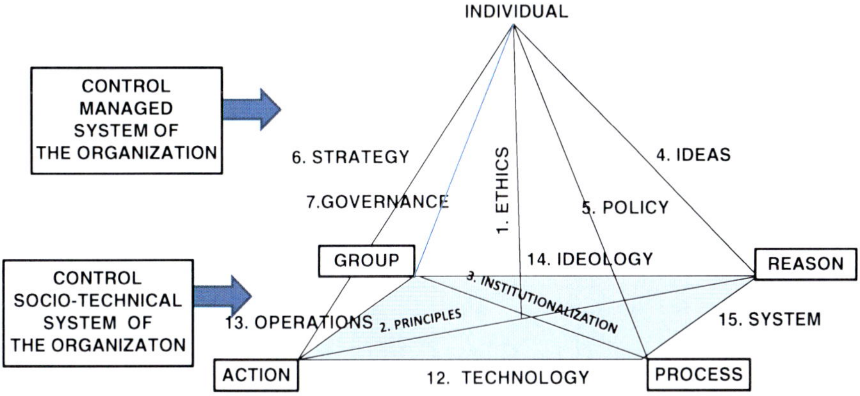

Fig. 5.5 Control in an organization

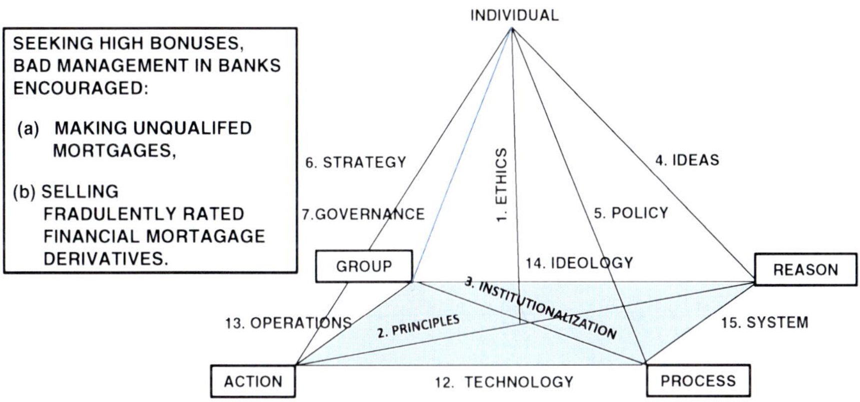

Fig. 5.6 Ethical failures of banking and regulatory leadership caused banking failures which triggered the 2007–2008 failure of the global financial socio-technical system

Greed and corruption by leaders is a principle explanation of why many socio-technical systems fail. Control by leadership in organizational managed systems depends upon the quality of character of the leader and in the quality of governance of the organization. This happened in 2007–2008 when banking executives' focus upon greed created the conditions for the failure of the global society (Fig. 5.6).

After 1989, a very large executive-to-employee salary ratio became common in US corporations. For example, before the financial collapse in 2006, the head of Goldman Sachs, Lloyd Blankfein, earned $54.4 million, which included a cash bonus of $27.3 million. During the financial collapse in 2007, Blankfein still earned a $54 million compensation, with a base salary of $0.6 million and a cash bonus of $27 million and stocks then worth $15.5 million and stock options of $10.4 million (http://www.en.wikipedia, Blankfein 2012).

The large bonus policy continued in banking, despite the global financial crash. For example in 2010, the chief executive officer (CEO) of JPMorgan Chase earned $17.5 million, compared to an average bank employee salary of $0.177 million—for a CEO-to-employee salary ratio of 100 to 1 (Dash and Craig 2011).

Control in a Self-Organizing Society

Finally, we turn to explaining the failure of control in the self-organizing societal aspect of the world's financial market. In the sociology literature in the mid-twentieth century, Talcott Parsons was a well-known advocate of a *structure–function* approach to societal description (Parsons 1937). Societal dynamics theory is based upon this structure–function method. Accordingly in Fig. 5.7, the explanation of control of a society uses explanations of self-organizing-systems (structure) and socio-technical systems (function).

Social infrastructure/processes of a society occur as a self-organizing-system; and functioning of the society's infrastructure/processes occurs as a socio-technical-system. All these explanations were needed to explain the socio-technical system of money and credit in the banking system (Fig. 5.8).

As earlier noted, the Gramm–Leach–Bliley Act repealed the separation of commercial and investment banking, and this allowed a merged commercial–investment bank to trade using depositors' funds. One of the executives who lobbied for this change was Sanford Weill. At the time, Weill was Chief Executive of Travelers Group (an insurance company) and wished to merge it with a commercial bank Citibank. The ideology of the Gramm–Leach–Bliley Act was "deregulation"—banks need little regulation as the banking market performs as a self-regulating "perfect market." Weill then became CEO of the merged company as Citibank. Morgenson and Rosner wrote: "Happily for Weill, he had friends in positions of

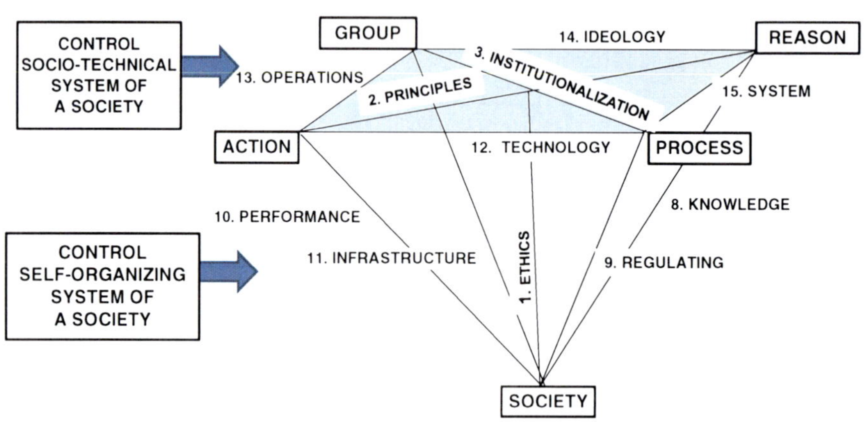

Fig. 5.7 Control in a society

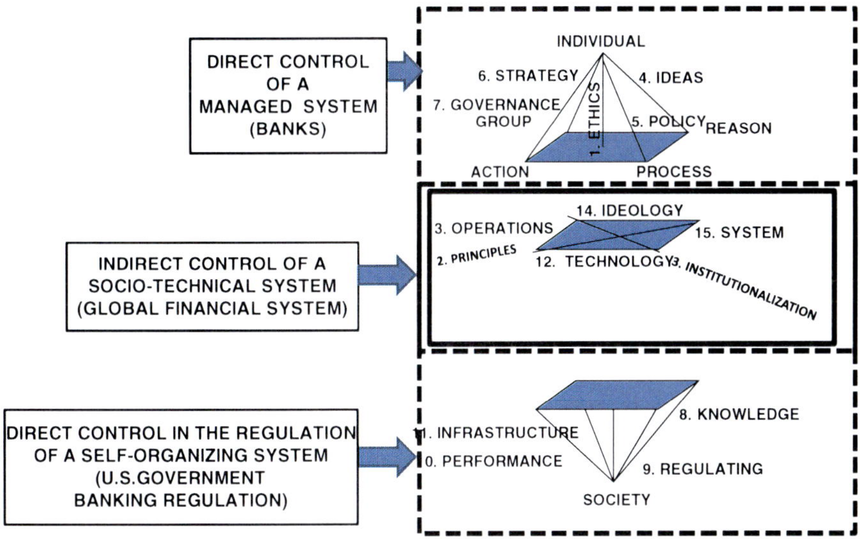

Fig. 5.8 Control in the systems of a society

power to help him overcome these legal obstacles. Robert Rubin (was) the Secretary of Treasury, and former head of Goldman Sachs… Rubin left Treasury to return to corporate America. He landed a cushy job as vice chairman of Citigroup… Over the following decade Rubin pocketed more than one hundred million dollars as the bank sank deeper and deeper into a risky morass of its own design… Glass-Steagall's demise…opened the door to greater risk taking among banks." (Morgenson and Rosner 2011, p. 108)

Also in the US financial regulatory framework, Fannie Mae was changed by law in 1968 to a private corporation, yet still having the Federal government back their bonds. Next, in 1992 (after losses at Fannie Mae occurred), the Federal Housing Enterprises Financial Safety and Soundness Act created another governmental regulatory agency, the Office of Federal Housing Enterprise Oversight (OFHEO) to regulate mortgage banking. Then OFHEO, in a desire to spread home mortgage access to lower-income groups, ordered a new goal for Fannie Mae: to purchase at least 30 % of new mortgages as home loans to low–moderate-income groups. But to do this, subprime mortgages would have to be made. For approval of such mortgages, loan underwriting standards would have to be lowered. For this, Fannie Mae used this ideology of "increasing access to housing loans" to justify lowering its lending standards: "…Fannie Mae spent $7 billion between 1994 and 1997 on 'underwriting experiments'…code words for loosening underwriting-standards and lending to people whose incomes, assets, or abilities to pay fell far below the traditional homeowner…" (Morgenson and Rosner 2011, p. 35)

Despite the laudable goal of assisting low-income groups, leadership in Fannie Mae abused this by purchasing subprime mortgages, which just could not be paid. No matter how low an income, a borrower still has to have sufficient and steady income to afford to make monthly mortgage payments. But mortgage lenders then proceeded to disregard any fiscal responsibility—even the most basic of the "ability to pay"—in their enthusiasm to lend a mortgage and gain a commission. And the executive leadership in Fanny Mae encouraged this abuse by buying any and all subprime mortgages—all in order to justify their large executive bonuses, even despite financial risk to the organization: "To strengthen its (Fannie Mae's) ties with the growing Countrywide, Johnson went about courting Mozilo… The two men did share a love of golf… Johnson showcased Mozilo at corporate retreats… Mozilo returned some of these favors. He allowed Johnson frequent flights on Countrywide's corporate jet and provided Johnson with cut-rate loans on the many properties the Fannie Mae chief owned." (Morgenson and Rosner 2011, p. 54)

Also to facilitate the rapid processing of subprime mortgages, lenders (such as Countrywide) resorted to a new metric introduced by credit-rating agencies (such as Equifax Inc). A credit score then substituted for the larger effort needed to learn whether or not a borrower was actually financially eligible for a loan: "Models like those used by Equifax had already begun to find a real foothold with smaller mortgage brokers and lenders. While it once had taken hours to process a loan application…(processing time became so brief that)…production increased to fifty or so loans a day." (Morgenson and Rosner 2011, p. 57)

Countrywide made large volumes of subprime mortgages, irrespective of risk, and sold them to Fannie Mae. Countrywide was happy to lower lending standards. Morgenson and Rosner wrote: "Certainly, Countrywide jumped on the lax lending bandwagon . Countrywide acknowledged that the debt-to-income ratios of borrowers could not be calculated because of a lack of documentation." (Morgenson and Rosner 2011, p. 192)

Some members of the US Congress also assisted in the lowering standards for broadening home ownership. Morgenson and Rosner wrote: "In an April 2003 hearing sponsored by the Committee on Financial Services, Maxine Waters, a Democrat from California, implored the housing finance industry to eliminate down payments…" (Morgenson and Rosner 2011, p. 192)

Countrywide responded by issuing subprime mortgages with no down payments and also began making "adjustable-rate mortgages" and "balloon payment mortgages." To help influence government's favor for lowing standards and in backing Fanny Mae, Mozilo also cultivated friendships. Morgenson and Rosner wrote: "…Countrywide mimicked Fannies' influence-peddling… Records from 2004 show Countrywide granting twelve special loans to members of (former Senator Robert Bennett's) staff… Countrywide also hired children of politicians and others in power…" (Morgenson and Rosner 2011, p. 188)

In 2000, private investment banks enthusiastically joined this subprime boom. Morgenson and Rosner wrote: "Wall Street marched right behind, accelerating and expanding enormously the previous Fannie Mae and Countrywide march toward jeopardy." (Morgenson and Rosner 2011, p. 235)

By 2008, the volume of subprime mortgages exploded to \$1.6 trillion dollars. These subprime mortgages were the "toxic" mortgages which collapsed the financial market. But the scheme of mortgage-based financial derivatives was still not enough to make big money in the securitization process. Also financial "leverage" occurred in the purchasing of the subprime mortgages. Hedge funds borrowed money short term to buy the long-term mortgages. Banks loaned short-term money to hedge funds.

At the time, these leverage loans were made possible by the "cheap money" policy of the Federal Reserve under Greenspan. Morgenson and Rosner noted: "All this is highly esoteric, of course. But the result was that Citigroup and other financial institutions were allowed to set up special investment vehicles, or SIVs, that raised money by borrowing from investors for short periods and investing the proceeds in investments with longer terms. The SIV would pocket the difference between the income generated by the mortgage and the amount paid out to investors who bought its obligations." (Morgenson and Rosner 2011, p. 235). This was the leveraging strategy that Wall Street followed.

Yet this leveraging strategy was only a short-term financial tactic and never a long-term financial strategy. Morgenson and Rosner wrote: "This game worked while the mortgage mania was raging; but in 2007, when losses in subprime mortgages began to spook the markets. Investors fled SIVs in general and Citi's in particular… Suddenly, Citi was left with mortgages…(which) had to be either sold or brought back onto Citi's balance sheet at massive losses." (Morgenson and Rosner 2011, p. 235)

Thus the failure of the indirect control of the world's financial socio-technical system of the world was due to two failures of direct control: executive control in banks and regulatory control in government agencies:

- There was failure of ethical leadership in the managed organizational systems of the banks.
- There was failure of ethically responsible leadership in the governmental regulation of the self-organizing system of the financial market.

In 2008 when the socio-technical financial system collapsed, the Federal government "bailed out" the Wall Street banks. Later Morgenson and Rosner wrote: "Of all the partners in the homeownership push, no industry contributed more to the corruption of the lending process than Wall Street. If mortgage originators like NovaStar or Countrywide were the equivalent of drug pushers hanging around a schoolyard and the ratings agencies were the narcotic cops looking the other way, brokerage firms providing capital to the anything-goes lenders were the overseers of the cartel." (Morgenson and Rosner 2011, p. 263)

Discussion

We have used systems dynamics theory to provide a structure–function description of a societal historical event. As we earlier noted, Talcott Parsons argued for a structural–functional school in sociology (Parsons 1968). A *social structure* is the *infrastructure* in a society and *function* is *what the infrastructure provides*. An economic system in a society consists of an infrastructure in which economic production and trading of goods and services occur—providing an economic function for the society. At that time the anthropologists, Franz Boas and Claude Levi-Strauss, were advocating a similar approach, but applied to nonindustrial societies and called a "*culture*" (Boas 1911; Levi-Strauss 1955). For them, all human cultures had similar "underlying patterns of thought" in which social interactions (*structure*) were guided by practical meanings (*function*).

What societal dynamics theory contributes to structural–functional methodology is an analytical technique to systematically apply a general structural–functional analysis to an historical event.

Economic systems have become dependent upon proper control and use of financial services (and information and communication technologies in financial services). We have seen how the failure of control of the financial socio-technical system was due to ethical failures.

The managed and socio-technical system of banking organizations failed in proper ethical control, when executive greed dominated fiscal responsibility and the unethical behavior of a few spread widely to the many:

1. The managed and socio-technical system of government regulatory agencies failed in responsible ethical control over the financial infrastructure.
2. The self-organizing system of economic financial market failed when the market was flooded with fraudulent and high-leveraged financial derivatives.
3. The socio-technical system of the global financial system failed when massive amounts of capital were invested and lost in the worldwide distribution of the financial derivatives.

The managed and socio-technical system control of an organization depends on how leading individuals in an organization provide the following: private good in the (1) ethical leadership and effective (6) strategy and efficient (5) policies—for the organization's functional (10) operations of its (15) system of production.

The (10) performance of a socio-technical system of a self-organizing system depends upon effective (10) operations and proper (9) regulating for public good in the (1) ethical behavior in the (11) infrastructure of a society's structural–functional system.

Briefly put—in an unregulated *financial system, if there are suckers to be taken, they will be taken.*

References

Amin, S. (2010). *Global history: A view from the south*. Oxford: Pambazuka Press.

Bernake, B. S. (2007, September 11). Global imbalances: Recent developments and prospects. Budesbank Lecture, Berlin, Germany. http://www.federalreserve.gov/newsevents/speechbernanke20070911a.htm. 2008

Blankfein, L. (2012). http://www.en.wikipedia, Blankfein 2012.

Boas, F. (1911). The mind of primitive man. ISBN 0-313-24004-3. (Online version of the 1938 revised edition at the Internet Archive).

Dash, E., & Craig, S. (2011, January 22). Big paydays return with big profits at wall street banks. *The New York Times*, B4.

Levi-Strauss, C. (1955). Tristes Tropiques (A world on the wane). English translation by John Weightman and Doreen Weightman.

Morgenson, G., & Rosner, J. (2011). *Reckless endangerment: How outsized ambition, greed, and corruption led to economic Armageddon*. New York: Henry Holt and Company.

Parsons, T. (1937). *The structure of social action*. Boston: McGraw Hill (1967 edition, Free Press).

Soros, G. (2008, January 22). The worst market crisis in 60 years. *Financial Times*.

Trist, E., & Murray, H. (Eds.). (1993). *The social engagement of social science, volume II: The socio-technical perspective*. Philadelphia, PA: University of Pennsylvania Press.

Chapter 6
The Great Depression

Introduction

As Ben Bernanke (Chair of the US Federal Reserve System in 2012) commented: "To understand the great depression is the Holy Grail of macroeconomics. Not only did the Depression give birth to macroeconomics as a distinct field of study, but also—to an extent that is not always fully appreciated—the experience of the 1930s continues to influence macroeconomists' beliefs, policy recommendations, and research agendas." (Bernanke 1995)

The economic historians Charles P. Kindleberger and Robert Z. Aliber summarized some of the arguments: "The monetarist view of the Great Depression is set out in a monumental work by Milton Friedman and Anna Schwartz (Friedman and Schwartz 1963). They maintained that the sharp decline in economic activity in the first half of the 1930s was the result of policy mistakes by the Federal Reserve; they focused upon the decline in the money supply from August 1929 to March 1933... Peter Temin challenged this monetarist view from a Keynesian point of view (Temin 1976). He asked whether the decline in the money supply followed from the decline in spending or whether instead the decline in spending followed from the decline in money supply; he used sophisticated econometrics to choose between the two views... Temin concluded that there is no evidence that changes in the money supply between the stock market crash and the British departure from the gold standard in September 1931 caused the depression... Temin's analysis did not provide an explanation of the depression event though it was a strong challenge to the monetarist view..." (Kindleberger and Aliber 2011)

Our objective is to see how the explanations about the US Great Depression by the differing schools of economics can be seen as complementary explanations—within a cross-disciplinary meta-framework for analyzing the economic historians' studies about the crisis event.

F. Betz, *Why Bank Panics Matter: Cross-Disciplinary Economic Theory*, SpringerBriefs in Economics, DOI 10.1007/978-3-319-01757-0_6,

Bank Runs and the Great Depression

G. Richardson reviewed the scholarship about the banking runs which triggered the depression: "Scholars ask three big questions about the banking system during the Great Depression. Why did bank suspensions surge at certain points in time? How bank suspensions affect commercial and industrial activity? Could Federal Reserve intervention have prevented (or did its actions trigger) this crisis?" (Richardson 2007). These are structural questions about the banking industry: timing, impact, and intervention.

First in order to understand the importance of timing, one can plot the timing of the bank panics with the decline of industrial production, as shown in Fig. 6.1. Therein one can see that three bank runs (in 1930, 1931, and 1932) each preceded three declines in industrial production. The bank panic of 1930 began an economic recession, but two more years of bank panics (1931 and 1932) turned the recession (business cycle) into a depression (altered stasis of society).

Bank Panics 1930–1933

The first bank panic in 1930 followed soon after the stock market crash at the end of 1929. Another panic followed in 1931. Richardson wrote: "As Friedman and Schwartz (1963) contended, illiquidity played a role in the surge in bank

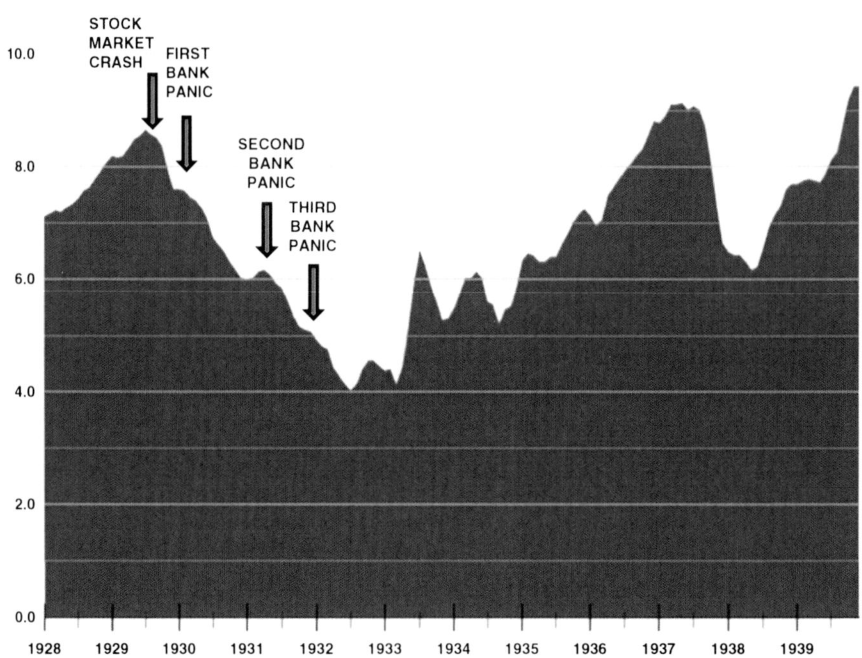

Fig. 6.1 Graph of an index of United State's industrial production from 1928 to 1939

suspensions in June of 1931. In that month, runs occurred on banks in Illinois. Examiners reported that heavy withdrawals were the primary cause of almost all of these suspensions. Frozen assets and limited cash reserves contributed to many closures, but none of the banks possessed portfolios which had deteriorated near the point of insolvency." (Richardson 2007)

The "point of insolvency" did occur in the next year. Continuing depositors' fears about bank solvency set off another bank panic in 1932. Richardson wrote: "As Calomiris and Mason (1997) maintain, the Chicago banking panic of June 1932 was due to depositors' confusion about bank asset quality. Examiners reported that for the preponderance of the banks which entered receivership, the primary cause of suspensions was the problem of doubtful and worthless assets… Declining asset values were the principal cause of bank suspensions. Most banks which closed their doors did so permanently. All were insolvent." (Richardson 2007)

Bank insolvency had resulted from worthless assets, as the stocks held as loan collateral became more worthless with each year, 1930, 1931, and 1932. Bad banking practices had set in motion the chain. Bank assets became illiquid, resulting in bank insolvency. The bad practices were risky loans made to stockbrokers who had allowed customers to purchase stock on margin. "Margin loans" by banks leveraged the investments in stocks toward a financial "bubble." Bad banking practices had triggered the depression.

Irving Fisher described this kind of connection: "Any deviation from equilibrium of any economic variable theoretically may, and doubtless in practice does, set up some sort of oscillations. The important question is: Which of them have been sufficiently great disturbers to afford any substantial explanation of the great booms and depressions of history? I venture the opinion…that the big bad actors are debt disturbances and price-level disturbances… Over-investment and over-speculation are often important; but they would have far less serious results were they not conducted with borrowed money. That is, 'over-indebtedness' may lend importance to over-investment or to over-speculation disturbances." (Fisher 1933)

"Over-indebtedness" was created by the bank loans for margin stock purchases. When the stock price fell, the stock owner could not hold onto the stock (without putting up more money responding to an increase in the "margin call"). They lost the stock and all the money they had invested into the purchase. Next in line, the stockbroker was "over-indebted," from obtaining a loan from a bank to purchase the "margined" stock.

Next then a bank was "over-indebted"—which had made a large number of margin loans to brokers. When the stock market crashed in 1929, many margined-stock owners lost all the wealth they had in the market, and some stockbrokers went bankrupt. It was the margined stock (held as collateral) in the banks' assets which triggered more bank runs. Finally, when in March 1933, bank runs were continuing across the nation. President Roosevelt called a "bank holiday," temporarily shutting down all the banks to stop the runs. The infrastructure of the banking system of the USA had collapsed.

History: US Stock Market Crash 1929

The economic historian Harold Bierman Jr. summarized: "The 1929 stock market crash is conventionally said to have occurred on Thursday the 24th and Tuesday the 29th of October. These two dates have been dubbed "Black Thursday" and "Black Tuesday," respectively. On September 3, 1929, the Dow Jones Industrial Average reached a record high of 381. At the end of the market day on Thursday, October 24, the market was at 299, a 21 % decline from the high... By all accounts, there was a selling panic. By November 13, 1929, the market had fallen to 199 (48 % drop). By the time the crash was completed in 1932, with an unprecedentedly large economic depression, stocks had lost nearly 80 % of their value." (Bierman 2010)

Bierman described the "trigger": "While no consensus exists (in 2010) about its precise causes,...one of the primary causes was the attempt by important people and media to stop market speculators. A second probable cause was the great expansion of investment trusts, public utility holding companies, and the amount of margin buying—all of which fueled the purchase of public utility stocks, and drove up their prices. Public utilities, utility holding companies, and investment trusts were all highly levered using large amounts of debt and preferred stock. These factors seem to have set the stage for the triggering event. This sector was vulnerable to the arrival of bad news regarding utility regulation. In October 1929, the bad news arrived and utility stocks fell dramatically. After the utilities decreased in price, margin buyers had to sell and there was then panic selling of all stocks." (Bierman 2010)

Public expectation of rising prices had driven the stock market higher and higher in 1925–1929. When it collapsed, the leveraging of stocks purchased on margin made the prices fall steeply, destroying wealth: "Margin buying during the 1920s was not controlled by the government." (Bierman 2010). Leveraging was added in the finance of the investment trusts: "By 1929, investment trusts were very popular with investors. These trusts were the 1929 version of closed-end mutual funds." (Bierman 2010)

Leveraging also occurred in holding companies of public utilities. Bierman wrote: "Public utilities were a very important segment of the stock market, and even more importantly, any change in public utility stock values resulted in larger changes in equity wealth. In 1929,...any change in a public utility's underlying value would result in a larger value change in the market and in the investor's value... The holding company typically owned 100 % of the operating companies' stock and both entities were levered." (Bierman 2010)

Thus in the 1920s stock market, there had been three forms of financial leverage: (1) margin buying of stock by individuals, (2) leveraged buying of companies by investment trusts, and (3) leveraged buying of utility companies by utility holding companies. Their financing all required bank loans, with only a small amount of actual money invested.

Thus the financing of equity growth in the late 1920s was in the form of vast amounts of leverage which would leave banks exposed when the stock market crashed. For example, in the utility holding companies and investment trusts: "When the large amount of leverage is combined with the inflated prices of public utility stocks, holding company stocks, and investment trust stocks, the problem is…dramatic… A $1,000,000 asset is supporting $1,761,000 of debt; and the investor's $38,000 of equity is very much in jeopardy." (Bierman 2010). This is a debt-to-equity ratio (leverage) of 46—forty-six dollars of debt for every one dollar of cash invested.

One can see that the excessive amounts of leveraged financing in the late 1920s had built an unstable US financial structure. *It was a large inverted pyramid of debt resting on only a small amount of cash investment. All this inverted pyramid of debt was financed by loans from banks, leaving the banks financially exposed if the market crashed. In 1929, the US stock market crashed.*

Societal Perceptual Space Analysis of 1929 Stock Market Crash

We analyze this event in a societal perceptual space, as shown in Fig. 6.2.

Individual—Prominent individuals in the USA expressed public concern about an overpriced stock market in the spring and summer of 1929.

Society—The society of the event was the nation of the USA.

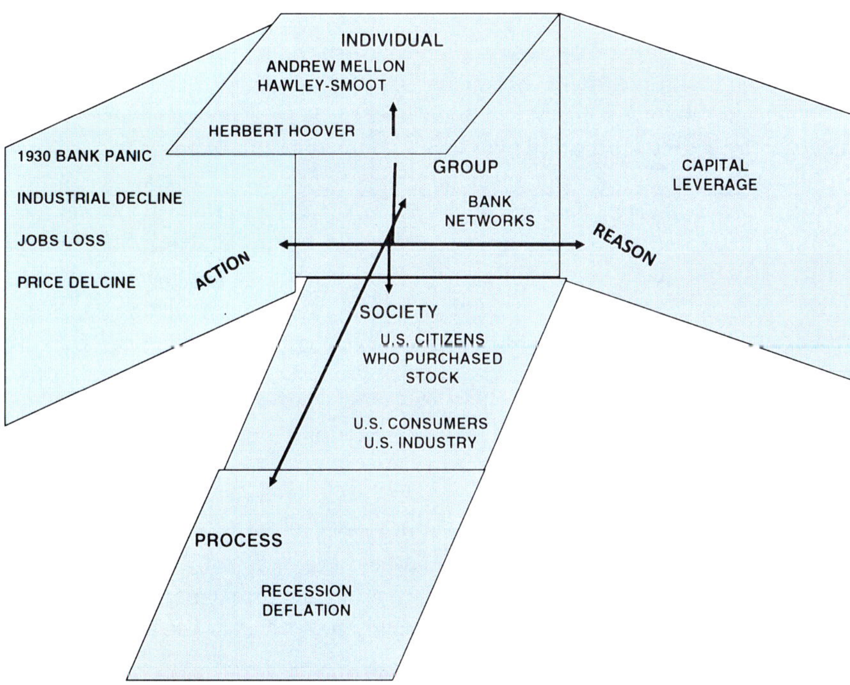

Fig. 6.2 Perceptual space of 1930 bank panic

Action—The action of the event was the steep decline of the New York Stock Exchange Market in October 1929.

Reason—Stock speculation was the reasoning which had driven the stock prices higher and higher.

Group—Groups involved in the event were banks, stockbrokers, investment trusts, and utility holding companies. And also involved were the state public utility commissions, concerned about utility company profits.

Process—The financial process of "leverage" was important to the height of the price rise in the New York Stock Market. Stock purchases have been financed by the (1) banks which had provided stock issues and margin loans, (2) investment trusts which had purchased companies on leverage, and utility holding companies which acquired utility companies on leverage.

Earlier we had noted how Hyman Minsky identified the importance of leverage to financial speculation, describing three levels of leverage conservative finance, speculative finance, and Ponzi finance (Minsky 1982). Minsky argued that speculative finance was used in a rapidly growing financial market, moving toward a bubble. Ponzi finance occurred just before the financial bubble burst (Minsky 1982). We also recall that George Soros reemphasized the importance of leverage in financial bubbles and also introduced his concept of "reflexivity" in the expectations of financial speculators. (Soros 1988)

About "expectations" (reflexivity) in the 1929 event, Bierman wrote: "It is possible that Hoover's aggressive campaign against speculation, helped by the overpriced public utilities hit by the Massachusetts Public Utility Commission decision and statements and the vulnerable margin investors, triggered the October selling panic and the consequences that followed. An important first event may have been Lord Snowden's reference to the speculative orgy in America. The resulting decline in stock prices weakened margin positions. When several governmental bodies indicated that public utilities in the future were not going to be able to justify their market prices, the decreases in utility stock prices resulted in margin positions being further weakened, resulting in general selling. At some stage, the selling panic started and the crash resulted." (Bierman 2010)

About "leverage" in the event, Bierman wrote: "A levered investment portfolio amplifies the swings of the stock market. Some investment securities have leverage built into them (e.g., stocks of highly levered firms, options, and stock index futures)." (Bierman 2010)

In this event of the 1929 stock crash, public perception of a rising stock market drove the speculative nature of the market, (a) creating a reflexivity (feedback to reality) in the future pricing of the market; and (b) the steepness of the fall in prices and the non-recovery of the prices occurred because of the leveraging of loans in the purchase of stocks and in the building of holding companies and investment trusts. We can sketch the dynamics leading up to the event in the societal stasis model in Fig. 6.3.

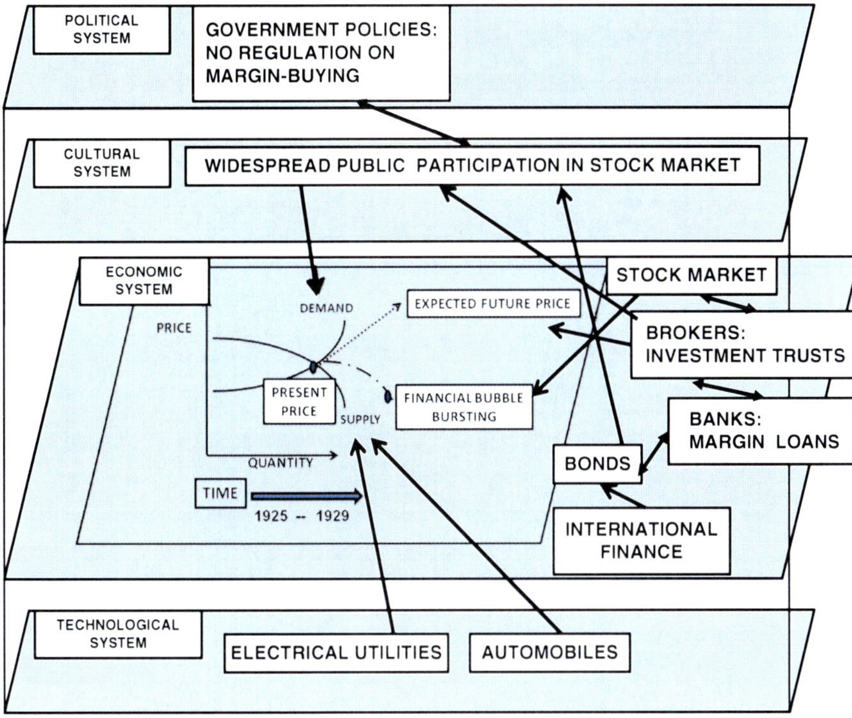

Fig. 6.3 Societal stasis—leading toward the 1929 U.S. stock market crash

On the political plane, the government policy (of no regulation for limiting the margin percentage on "margin loans" by banks) allowed the leverage in market speculation to become very great. In a steep price decline, stock positions had to be liquidated when more money was required by margin calls.

On the cultural plane, the banks in the 1920s had been actively formulating and selling public stock issued by corporations, broadening public participation in the market. The creation of investment trusts facilitated indirect public participation in the stock market. The creation of public utility holding companies and their stock issues also increased indirect public participation. Banks also widely solicited investments in foreign government bonds. For example: "From the marble Morgan halls (J. P. Morgan Bank) emerged $6 billion in securities underwritings between 1919 and 1933… A third was railroad bonds, another third foreign bonds, and the last third corporate bonds" (Chernow 1990). The cultural change was that the American middle classes began investing in stocks and bonds, which previously had been only invested in by the wealthy.

On the technological plane, rapid industrial expansion occurred in the USA after the end of the First World War and lasting through the 1920s. For example, Randall Parker wrote about that period: "The decade of the 1920s also saw major innovations in the consumption behavior of households. The development of installment

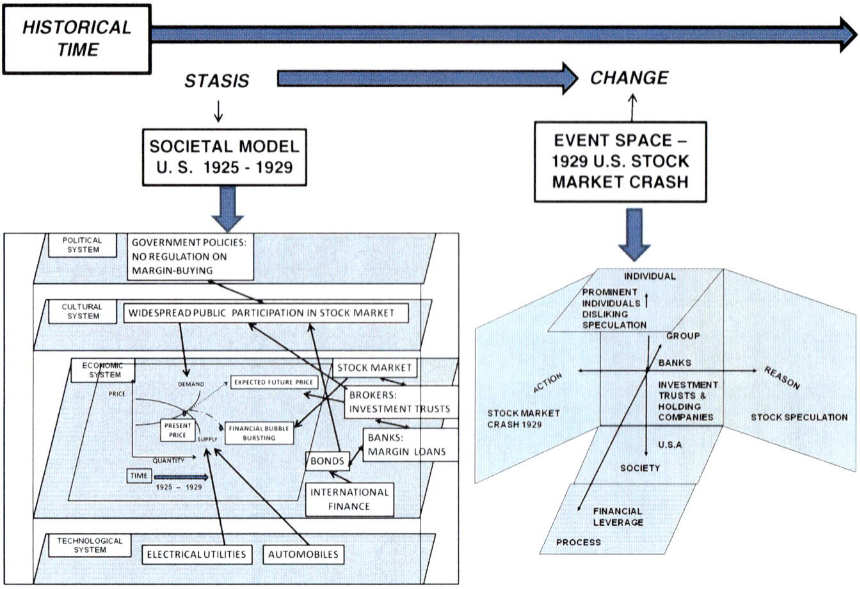

Fig. 6.4 Societal dynamics: 1929 stock market crash

credit over this period led to substantial growth in the consumer durables market. Purchases of automobiles, refrigerators, radios and other such durable goods all experienced explosive growth during the 1920s as small borrowers, particularly households and unincorporated businesses, utilized their access to available credit." (Parker 2010)

On the economic plane, stock prices from 1925 through 1929 climbed toward a speculative disequilibrium point in the summer of 1929, when public perceptions of an overpriced stock market and decline in utility stocks triggered a sharp decline in prices in October—a stock crash.

In Fig. 6.4, we illustrate the societal dynamics of the stasis of American society in the 1920s (a stasis of industrial expansion and economic growth) that ended suddenly in 1929, after the beginning of the stock market collapse (which would extend through 1933).

Bank Fragility: Process and Structure

We have seen that banking fragility was not caused by the depression. Instead bank fragility triggered the depression. In 2007 with access to new access to data archived in the Federal Reserve System, G. Richardson reviewed the history of the 1930–1933 banking process: "Illiquidity bedeviled banks throughout the depression. Heavy withdrawals played a primary or contributing role in nearly half of all suspensions.

Asset problems also bedeviled banks throughout the Great Depression. Slow, doubtful, or worthless assets played a primary or contributing role in over half of all suspensions. The initial banking panic in the fall of 1930—with its cluster of temporary bank suspensions, bank runs, and collapsing correspondent networks—appears to have been a credit crunch inspired by the collapse of financial conglomerates and propagated by the public's flight from deposits to currency." (Richardson 2007)

The "slow, difficult, or worthless assets" of the banks were margin loans. In 1929, as the stock prices declined, margin loans were called, and stockbrokers went bankrupt. Banks which had issued the loans then held vast amounts of stock as collateral—illiquidity. These illiquid (unsellable) stocks continued to decline in value—as the stock market continued to decline in 1930 and 1931 and 1932. All the wealth initially put into the stocks purchased on margin became illiquid assets of banks. Liquid wealth was transformed into illiquid assets—a loss of wealth.

As the asset values of stock collateral declined, banks had to call in other loans made to other banks and to other customers and businesses. This "chain reaction" occurred in the collapse of correspondent (bank) networks. The failed margin loans triggered a sharp decrease of credit in the USA. At the same time, the tight-money policy of the US Fed in late 1928 also decreased the money supply. The economic school of "monetarists" was correct in their explanations that contracting money and credit was the mechanism (process) which spread the stock crash into bank panics into industrial depression.

In addition to bank "fragility" arising from the financial process of speculation and leverage, there was also "fragility" arising from the institutional structure (of how banks connected to banks and other financial institutions). For example, about structure, Richardson wrote: "A trend of consolidation in the commercial banking industry (as small banks in rural areas left the business, often liquidating involuntarily and after suffering large losses) existed prior to the depression, continued during the contraction, and intensified as the downturn deepened. The collapse of the Caldwell conglomerate triggered the initial banking panic in the fall of 1930. Correspondent networks propagated the panic during the initial weeks, when almost all of the banks which suspended operations were financially or geographically connected to the Caldwell conglomerate. Bank runs radiated outward from these focal events…" (Richardson 2007). The explanation of the deflation was a process (contraction of money/credit) and structure in how the banking system was organized. Both *process and infrastructure* (function–structure) together are needed to explain the occurrence of the depression.

Connection Between the Stock Market Decline and Bank Insolvency

Thus the stock market had continued to decline in 1930, 1931, and 1932. Stock positions in the market which had been purchased on margin were wiped out. The continuing decline in bank assets (from margined stock held as collateral) created

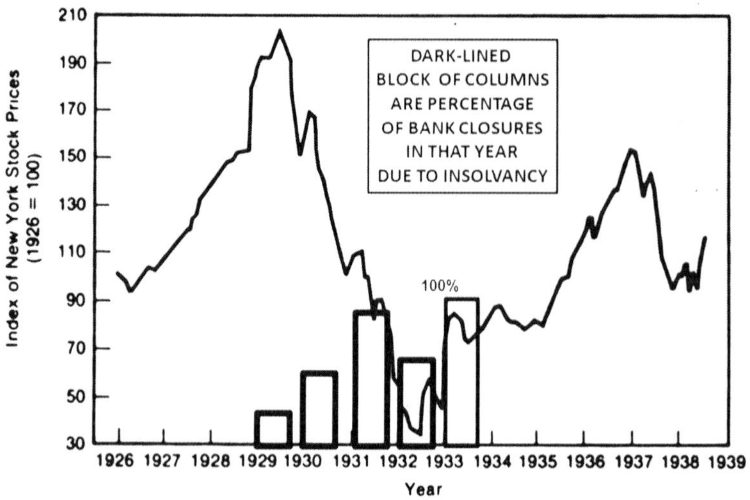

Fig. 6.5 Bank failures due to bank insolvency superimposed upon stock market prices. Source of bank closures data (Richardson 2007)

the sequence of bank runs. One can plot the percentage of bank failures due to insolvency and compare this to the drop in stock market prices, Fig. 6.5. The stock prices are shown over the different years, and superimposed are numbers of bank closures in the critical years 1929 through 1933 (columns). In the superposition of the stock prices and bank closures, one can see the coincidence between the decline of share prices and the decline of bank assets (triggering bank closures).

The percentage of bank failures due to insolvency increased each year from 1929 to 1933, as the stock market had continued to decline. First there was the stock market crash in 1929, triggering the 1930 bank failures—which began the depression. The next year in 1931, bank runs occurred again. Randall Parker wrote: "In May, the failure of Austria's largest bank, the Kredit-anstalt, touched off financial panics in Europe. In September 1931, having had enough of the distress associated with the international transmission of economic depression, Britain abandoned its participation in the gold standard. Further, just as the United States' economy appeared to be trying to begin recovery, the second wave of bank failures hit the financial system in June and did not abate until December. In addition, the Hoover administration in December 1931, adhering to its principles of limited government, embarked on a campaign to balance the federal budget. Tax increases resulted the following June, just as the economy was to hit the first low point of its so-called 'double bottom' …" (Parker 2010)

This second wave of bank runs had additional and serious impacts upon the economy. Parker wrote: "The results of these events are now evident. Between January and December 1931 the industrial production index declined from 78 to 66 (15.4 % and the consumer price index fell 9.4 % and the nominal supply of M1 (money) dipped 5.7 %... By December, the money supply, and the price levels were all on negative growth paths, dragging the economy deeper into depression." (Parker 2010)

The third bank run in 1932 finally collapsed the economy. Parker wrote: "The economic difficulties were far from over. The economy displayed some evidence of recovery in late summer/early fall of 1932. However, in December 1932, the third and largest wave of banking panics hit the financial markets; and the collapse of the economy arrived with the business cycle hitting bottom in March 1933." (Parker 2010)

All the bank panics traced back to the 1929 stock market, which had left a large amount of stock collateral in the banks from their earlier margin loans. When bank assets declined in value below bank liabilities, the banks became insolvent. When the market hit bottom in 1932, the market had lost 83 % of its value. (Later in 1933 and 1934, some recovery occurred; but even then the market still had lost 40 % of its value.) A vast amount of wealth was lost; and a vast amount of capital was gone from the American economy in the 1930s.

There is this difference between physics and economics. In physics, matter and energy are conserved in all physical events. Not so in society. Society is not describable in a "positive science" (like physics). In a society, there is no law of the conservation of money and wealth. Money and credit and wealth can be created and can be destroyed. Money and credit are not mechanisms but functionalities. And this is why bank panics matter—the abrupt loss of capital in an economy. Capital is not always transferred from a loser to a winner in an economic transaction. Instead in a bank panic, capital can be absolutely lost—no winners, but all losers. Money is functionally a social agreement, and social agreements can be broken by all and to all when a social structure for agreements collapses.

History: US Depression 1930s

As industrial production fell, unemployment increased, and consumption decreased; and by 1933, the US depression was set and frozen. President Franklin Roosevelt succeeded President Herbert Hoover, and Roosevelt closed the banks for a "bank holiday" and ordered the US Federal Reserve System off the "gold standard" (promising to redeem dollars in gold bullion). The economy began a slow and modest recovery. But another recession occurred in 1938, when President Roosevelt cut government spending. In 1941, US rearmament began, and government spending grew. And in December, the USA entered World War II. The country never really recovered from the full depression until the beginning of World War.

When banks no longer could make loans and issue credit (either by cutting back on loan business or simply by failing), then businesses and industries which depended upon bank credit for their operations also had to cut back on business or failure. Business "downsizing" and business failures resulted in job losses, increasing national unemployment. This is shown in Fig. 6.6, wherein unemployment rose from the summer of 1929 at 5 % to 10 % in 1930 and to 20 % in 1930 and was 22.5 % in 1935.

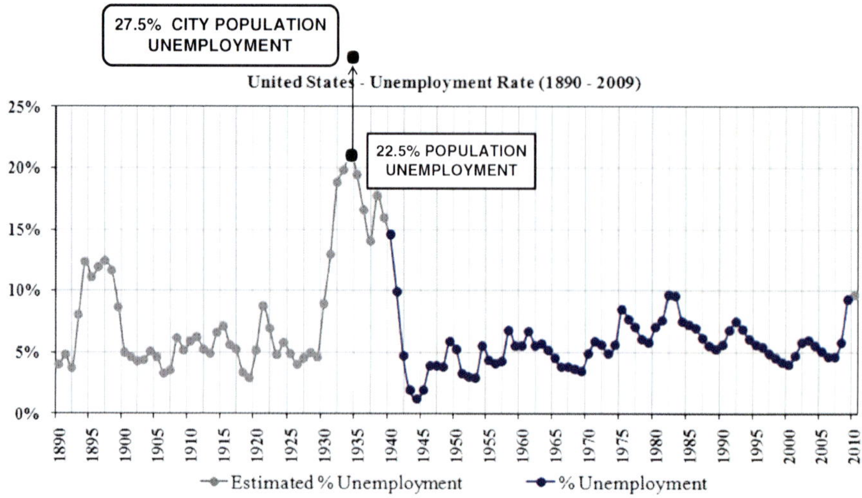

Fig. 6.6 *Source*: http://.en.wikipedia.org, U.S. Unemployment from 1890 to 2010

But the impact upon employment of people in cities was even more severe. Up until 1930, 79 % of the population had earlier been employed in industry. When unemployment reached 22.5 % in 1932, this meant that about 27.5 % of the city folk were unemployed (assuming the farmers remained employed on the farm, if they had not lost their farm).

This was a big structural change in a society—to have more than a quarter of the city folk out of work. This stasis change after 1929 altered the US economy into a state of "structural unemployment"—when at least one-quarter of a working population is unemployed in a nation.

As jobs were lost, consumer consumption fell when families of the unemployed had no income to purchase necessities. Then prices in commodities also fell as consumption fell. This followed in the pattern of the classical supply–demand equilibrium pricing theory of economics. One can see this for agricultural prices, as shown in Fig. 6.7.

After the stock market crash in the fall of 1929 down to February 1933, there is a steady decline in agricultural prices, down by nearly 62 %. It is likely that during this time, "supply" (agricultural production) may not have changed much, since then most farming was still family farming. Farming families needed to grow as much product as they could to support their families, especially during those years of declining prices (deflation). Agricultural supply was probably fairly constant over the early years of the 1930s, and the price decline was due to a decline in demand. (There was a Western drought in the late 1930s, which decreased supply, but this did not occur until 1937.)

Increasing unemployment lowered demand for consumer products, as unemployed families lost income to buy consumer necessities. The economic historian Frank G. Steindl expressed the cultural significance of that unemployment: "The

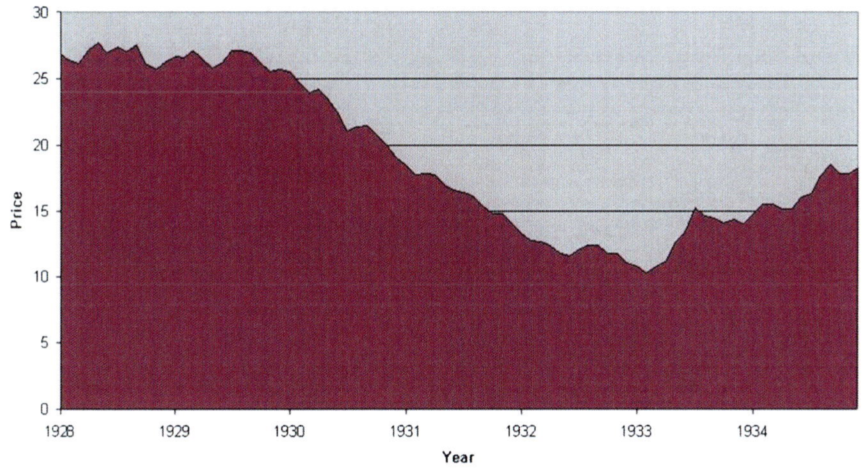

Fig. 6.7 *Source*: http://en.wikipedia.org/wiki/File:US_Farm_Prices_%281928-1935%29.JPG, 2012

Great Depression has two meanings. One is the horrendous debacle of 1929–1933 during which unemployment rose from 3 to 25 % as the nation's output fell over 25 % and prices over 30 %, in what also has been called the Great Contraction. A second meaning has the Great Depression as the entire decade of the thirties, the anxieties and apprehensions for which John Steinbeck's The Grapes of Wrath is a metaphor…" (Steindl 2012)

Stasis Change: US Society Before and After 1929

In Fig. 6.8, we model the stasis of society in the USA in the 1920s, before 1929.

We see the structures of the society from 1925 to 1929:

- On the economic plane, there was a rising stock market (rising capital), rising industrial production (rising economy), and stable agricultural prices (supply–demand equilibrium pricing); the Federal Reserve had held interest rates to banks low to make bank credit easy to obtain at low interest rates.
- On the cultural plane, there was low unemployment in the cities (relatively full employment) and a movement of the people from farms to cities (with most population, 79 %, living in the cities).
- On the technological plane, technologies of automobiles and electrical power utilities were being developed and implemented.
- On the political plane, in 1929 President Herbert Hoover acted to discourage speculation, ordering the Fed to reverse its stimulus policy and raise its interest rates to banks.

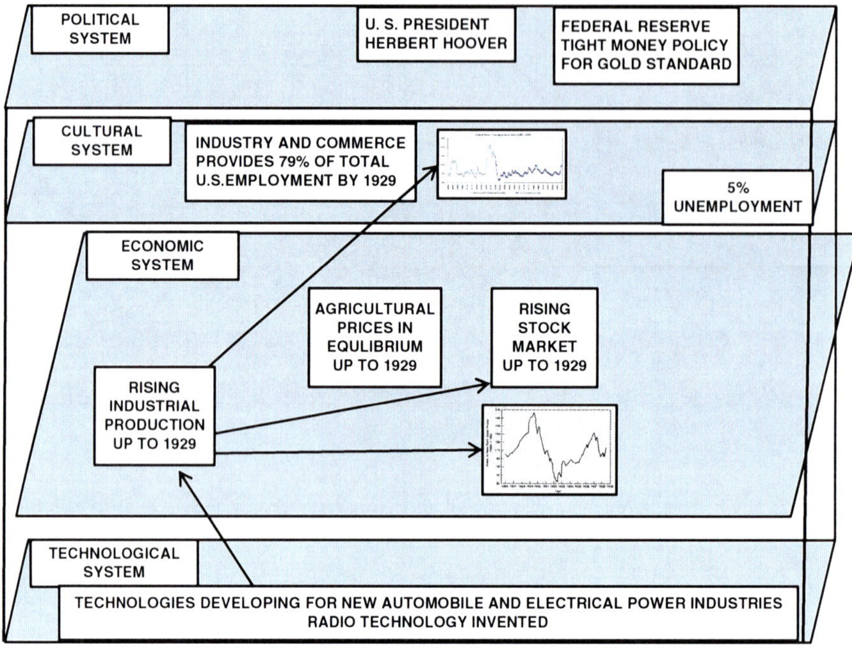

Fig. 6.8 U. S. society from 1925 to 1929

It was the succession of bank panics and the accompanying industrial contraction together fatally altered the structure of US society. Instead of a bank panic triggering an economic recession, the three panics triggered an economic depression. In an economic recession, the economic structure remains the same, but a business cycle occurs from expansion to contraction to expansion again. But in an economic depression, societal structure alters and the normal business cycle does not run as before.

Irving Fisher had earlier made this distinction: "The old and apparently still persistent notion of 'the' business cycle, as a single, simple, self-generating cycle (analogous to that of a pendulum swinging under influence of the single force of gravity) and as actually realized historically in regularly recurring crises, is a myth. Instead of one force there are many forces. Specifically, instead of one cycle, there are many co-existing cycles, constantly aggravating or neutralizing each other, as well as co-existing with many non-cyclical forces. In other words… there are always innumerable cycles, long and short, big and little… Any historical event is the resultant of all the tendencies then at work… There may be equilibrium which, though stable, is so delicately poised that, after departure from it beyond certain limits, instability ensues…such a disaster is somewhat like the 'capsizing' of a ship which, under ordinary conditions, is always near stable equilibrium but which, after being tipped beyond a certain angle, has no longer this tendency to return to equilibrium,

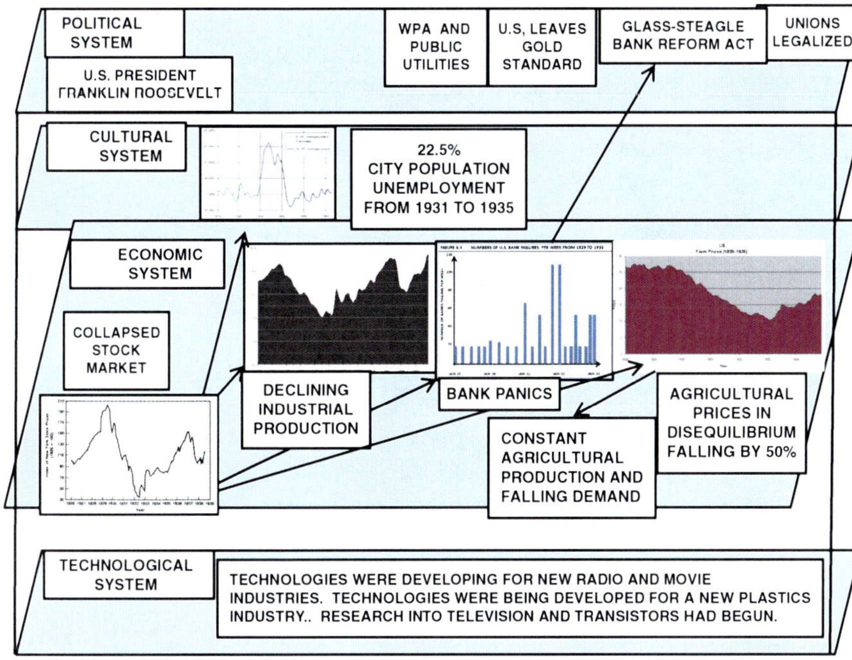

Fig. 6.9 U. S. society 1930–1940

but, instead, a tendency to depart further from it." (Fisher 1933). Like this simile, the economic US ship of state had capsized by 1933. It was not to be righted again until the war years of 1941–1946. But by then that "ship" was a different US society. We can describe this kind of transition a change of stasis in the society. Depressions are serious changes in the state of a society—not merely a business cycle of a recession. That level of unemployment in a society alters its socioeconomic structure and its consumption patterns. Next in Fig. 6.9, we can model the same society but from 1930 to 1940, seeing a different societal structure.

We see the structures of the society from 1930 to 1940:

- On the economic plane, there was a collapsed stock market and a series of bank runs (lost capital), declining industrial production (depressed economy), and much lower agricultural prices (supply–demand disequilibrium pricing).
- On the cultural plane, there was high unemployment in the cities (one-quarter of the population out of work).
- On the technological plane, new technologies of plastics were being developed but not yet industrially implemented. Technologies and new industries of radio and movies were being developed. Research into television and transistors had begun.
- On the political plane, after 1933, Franklin Roosevelt was the new president. A bank holiday was called, and then new bank regulation was enacted (Glass–Steagall Act) separating investment banking (bond and stock issuance and trading)

from commercial banking (savings deposits and loans). US species (money) left the "gold standard" (dollars were no longer redeemable by gold from the Federal government). Works projects were begun (WPA) to provide some jobs. Federal utility dams were built to provide electricity to rural areas (e.g., Tennessee Valley Authority in the east and Hoover Dam in the west). Labor unions were legally recognized by the government (National Labor Relations Act).

Results

In Fig. 6.10, we compare these two societal models before and after the change event of the 1929 stock market crash. Therein one can picture societal models changed by the historic event.

There were three big social structural changes between American society before and after 1929:

- The population structure changed among the social classes (21 % farmers and 66 % employed city folk and 5 % unemployed city folk to 21 % farmers and 44 % employed city folk and 27 % unemployed city folk). This great increase in the unemployed working class greatly decreased demand for goods and services and also destroyed many families (a quarter of the entire US population affected). This is a huge societal change—in cultural structure (classes) and in economic structure (consumer demand).
- The capital structure (societal wealth) declined at least 83 % of stock values from 1929 to 1933. Societal wealth (economic wealth) exists in the form of species (money), credit (loans), and liquid assets (sellable stocks, bonds, property). Loans were called in the bank runs of 1930, 1931, and 1932.

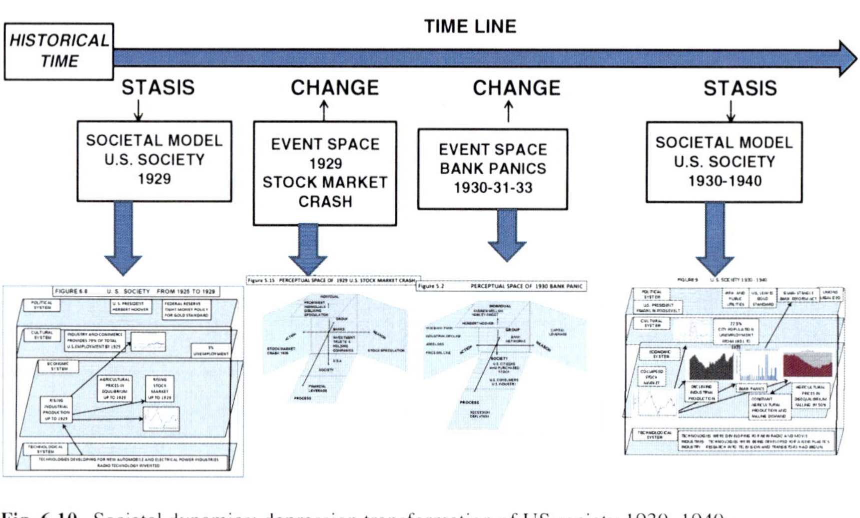

Fig. 6.10 Societal dynamics: depression transformation of US society 1930–1940

- This reduction of wealth impacted the industrial structure in America; as from 1930 to 1932, banks had to call loans. These loan calls reduced credit to businesses. Some businesses lacking credit went bust (bankrupt); others survived by reducing production and firing workers. The industrial production "index" (Fig. 6.7) fell from 8.5 in 1929 to 5.5 in 1933, recovering a bit to an average of 6.0 from 1934 to 1936. Thus from 1929 into 1936 industrial production had declined in the United States by 30 % (nearly a third less in output and in jobs).

From a cross-disciplinary perspective of economics (production) and sociology (classes) and anthropology (culture), the 1930s US depression was not merely a large economic recession; it was a structural depression. In severe economic deflation, a societal structure changes into an "industrially depressed state" (a structure characterized by lost wealth, excess industrial capacity and underproduction, large unemployed class, political instability).

Conclusion

Some scholars have argued that the banks failed because the economy contracted and others that depositors' expectations turned to fear and withdrew deposits "en masse." Which was it? Was bank failure caused by economic collapse? Or was bank failure caused by expectations collapse? What if both? Money credit was the "process" connecting banking runs to industrial decline; and bank margin loans to brokers were the "structure" connecting the stock market to bank fragility.

There was no single "cause" to the depression. Human society is not a mechanism. It was stasis changing events which altered the US society—the 1929 stock market crash and three successive years of bank panics in 1930, 1931, and 1932. Central to this stasis change was an unstable financial subsystem—*a "fragility of the banks"* and an *"instability of credit"—both in process and in structure of the US financial system.*

What societal dynamics theory contributes to the structural–functional (*structure and process*) approach is an analytical technique to systematically apply a general structural–functional analysis to any historical event. This analysis provides a strong argument for the social sciences to talk to each other. The long-running conflict in the economic discipline between the schools of economics can be resolved in the meta-framework of a cross-disciplinary perspective.

This meta-framework of this analysis has enabled the explanation of the US Great Depression—not in terms of causes but as changes in societal stasis due to events which change society (change events). This historical perspective differentiates explanations into those of "triggering events" (change events) of economic history and into those of altered states of a society, stasis in a societal model. The value of applying a broader cross-disciplinary framework to the analysis of history is to better connect economic theory with economic history.

References

Bernanke, B. S. (1995, February). The macroeconomics of the Great Depression: A comparative approach. *Journal of Money, Credit, and Banking, 27*(1).

Bierman, H. J. (2010). *The 1929 stock market crash.* Cornell University, Economic History Association. http://eh.net/encyclopedia/article/Bierman.

Calomiris, C. W., & Mason, J. R. (1997, December). Contagion and bank failures during the Great Depression: The June 1932 Chicago banking panic. *American Economic Review, 87*(5), 863–883.

Chernow, R. (1990). *The house of Morgan: An American banking dynasty and the rise of modern finance.* New York: Grove Press. ISBN 0-8021-3829-2.

Fisher, I. (1933, October). The debt-deflation theory of the Great Depression. *Econometrica.*

Friedman, M., & Schwartz, A. J. (1963). *A monetary history of the United States, 1867–1960.* Princeton, NJ: Princeton University Press.

Kindleberger, C. P., & Aliber, R. Z. (2011). *Manias, panics, and crashes: A history of financial crises* (6th ed.). New York: Palgrave Macmillan.

Minsky, H. P. (1982). *Can 'it' happen again? Essays on instability and finance.* Armonk, NY: M.E. Sharpe Inc.

Parker, R. (2010, February 5). An overview of the Great Depression. Economic History Association. http://eh.net/encyclopedia/article/parker.depression

Richardson, G. (2007). The collapse of the United States banking system during the Great Depression, 1929 to 1933. New Archival Evidence. *Australasian Accounting Business and Finance Journal, 1*(1). http://ro.uow.edu.au/aabfj/vol1/iss1/4Richardson

Soros, G. (1988). *The alchemy of finance.* New York: Simon & Schuster (paperback: Wiley, 2003; ISBN 0-471-44549-5). ISBN 0-671-66338-4.

Steindl, F. G. (2012, February 5). Economic recovery in the Great Depression. Economic History Association. http://eh.net/encyclopedia/article/Steindl.GD.Recovery.

Temin, P. (1976). *Did monetary forces cause the Great Depression?* New York: W.W. Norton.

Chapter 7
Topological Economic Theory

Introduction

We recall that one of the problems with banking regulation has been its post-facto rather than preemptive mode—fixing bank panics after they occur rather than preventing them. And we recall that this was particularly true of the 2007 global bank panic. Binyamin Appelbaum wrote: "The Fed (Federal Reserve System) began 2007 still deeply immersed in complacent disregard for problems in the housing market. Fed officials knew that people were losing their homes. They knew that subprime lenders were blinking out of business with every passing week. But they did not understand the implications for the broader economy… August 2007 was the month that the Fed began its long transformation from somnolence to activism." (Appelbaum 2013)

What was the soporific which had put the Fed to sleep? We have noted that it was "mainstream economic theory"—which had assumed all markets were perfectly self-regulating, even financial markets. This soporific was not only in US regulatory policy but also in British. Sir Meryn King (Governor of the Bank of England in 2007) later said: "With the benefit of hindsight, we (Bank of England) should have shouted from the rooftops that a system had been built in which banks were too important to fail, that banks had grown too quickly and borrowed too much, and that so-called 'light-touch' regulation hadn't prevented any of this." (Giles 2012)

Now we need to examine more deeply how this regulatory soporific had developed from economic theory—particularly from 1930 (the Great Depression) to 2006 (the great sleeping). Because of this, there has been a need to reformulate disciplinary economic theory—theory from both exogenous and endogenous schools. We will now do this, using a cross-disciplinary analytical framework, and there are three reasons for this broader approach.

Firstly, as we have noted, the economics discipline itself has been divided, divided into two argumentative schools, and these have been unable to unite, even after the empirical failure of mainstream economic theory in 2007. When intellectual schools are unrepentantly divided, it is often because each thinks upon different

F. Betz, *Why Bank Panics Matter: Cross-Disciplinary Economic Theory*, SpringerBriefs in Economics, DOI 10.1007/978-3-319-01757-0_7,

assumptions. Moreover, such differing assumptions may not be reconcilable purely within the discipline. It may take a larger meta-framework (outside of and around a discipline) to make clear the relationship of one school's theory to the other. The reason is that the validity of their respective assumptions may rest upon information or knowledge studied in other disciplines. A cross-disciplinary meta-framework can allow the placement of the different theories of the disputing economic schools within the larger framework of a complete society.

Secondly, all scientific theory must be grounded in experience. The use of societal dynamics theory as an analytic framework for historical studies can enable the direct comparison between economic history (the empiricism of economics) and economic theory (the rationalism of economics). By looking at histories of US bank failures, we have seen how societal dynamics provides a meta-framework for historical studies.

Thirdly, quantitative expression in economics made significant progress but not in expressing economic institutional insights. We add here more mathematics—topology theory—in order to facilitate the expression of institutional factors within quantitative economic theory. (Topology is an area of mathematics concerned with connectedness).

History: Division in Economic Theory in 2009–2012

We recall that going back in time from 2012 to 2009 (the recent years following the financial crisis of 2008), one could find the historical evidence not only of theory failure and also of a continuing failure of the economics discipline to agree upon how to construct valid theory. In science, of course, when theory fails to explain empirical reality, then theory is changed. But matters were not so straightforward in the recent history of the economics discipline. Instead of immediately rushing to change economic theory, there continued a contentious debate among economists. Was a market empirically perfect or only ideally perfect? Mainstream economic theory had constructed an economic model of supply–demand–price–equilibrium, which was based upon the assumption of a perfect market. But the fact was that the financial market had been far from perfect.

We recall that Howard Davies thought major change was required in economics: "Such reworking of economic models should be based upon history and more broadly based… There should be more teaching of economic history,… The study of economics should be set in a broader political context,… But it is not clear that a majority of the profession yet accepts even these modest proposals. The so-called 'Chicago School' has mounted a robust defense of it rational- expectations-based approach, rejecting the notion that a rethink is required. The Nobel laureate economist Robert Lucas has argued that the crisis was not predicted because economic theory predicts that such events cannot be predicted. So all is well." (Davies 2012)

Also we noted that Chris Giles had reported in 2010: "Many of the world's top academic economists agreed on Friday (April 9, 2010) that the financial and economic crisis had exposed fatal flaws in their subject and ideas were urgently needed to keep economics relevant. While this represented an unusual consensus, the eminent economic brains lived up to their stereotype by disagreeing on what policies, if any, should be adopted to prevent a repetition... One disagreement hinged on whether asset price bubbles lay at the heart of the crisis. Those who thought so argued for tighter regulation... (Others, such as) Michael Goldberg, of the University of New Hampshire, said it was wrong to suggest the price swings were necessarily a bubble and that they were more likely to be fundamental to the beneficial forces of capitalism." (Giles 2010)

Also we noted that Charles J. Whalen had written: "The financial crisis that ran from late 2007 through early 2009 did more than traumatize the world economy; it drew widespread attention to some major shortcomings of conventional economics." (Whalen 2012)

And we had quoted Paul Krugman, who wrote in 2009: "It's hard to believe now, but not long ago economists were congratulating themselves over the success of their field. Those successes—or so they believed—were both theoretical and practical, leading to a golden era for the profession... Few economists saw our current crisis coming, but this predictive failure was the least of the field's problems. More important was the profession's blindness to the very possibility of catastrophic failures in a market economy... There was nothing in the prevailing models suggesting the possibility of the kind of collapse that happened last year in 2008... Macroeconomists (remain) divided in their views. The main division was between those who insisted that free-market economies never go astray and those who believed that economies may stray now and then (but that any major deviations from the path of prosperity could and would be corrected by the all-powerful Fed). Neither side was prepared to cope with an economy that went off the rails despite the Fed's best efforts... And in the wake of the crisis, the fault lines in the economics profession have yawned wider than ever." (Krugman 2009)

Mainstream economic theorists had not anticipated financial crises and could not explain them. The reason for this was in methodology—a split among economists about how to explain economics. The mainstream economics school (called a "neoclassical synthesis" school) explained an economy principally as a production system, perfectly balanced in supply and demand. The contending school called "neo-Keynesians" (or "Post-Keynesians") argued that a financial system was equally important with production systems in an economy and that these two kinds of markets (commodity and financial) operated differently—and neither perfectly. Next we briefly review the partial models of an economy by the two schools of economics, neoclassical synthesis and neo-Keynesian.

Neoclassical Synthesis School

We recall that the central model in the neoclassical synthesis school is the supply–demand curve of equilibrium pricing in an economy, Fig. 7.1.

When the price of a commodity is charted as the quantity of the supply of the product (dotted line), then the price will decrease in an economy as the supply

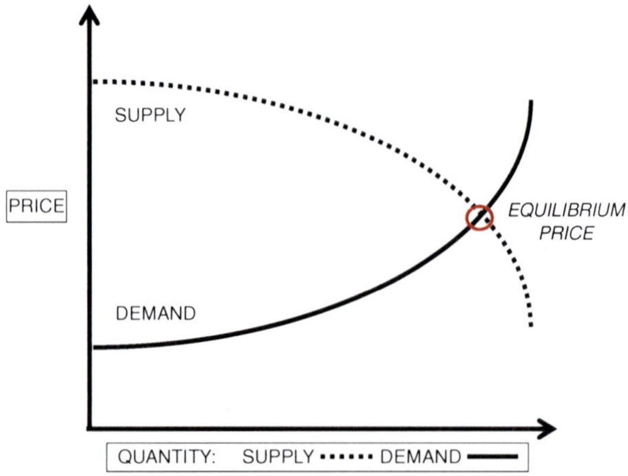

Fig. 7.1 Economic equilibrium pricing of a product when supply equals demand

increases. Because of business competition, more goods flooding a market will force prices down. Also if the demand for a product (solid line) increases, then the price will increase (as more consumers buy a limited amount of product). The optimal pricing of a product (commodity) in an economy will occur when supply equals demand. This is the equilibrium price, as supply and demand meet in quantity. If a market behaves like this, it is perfect. No control over pricing is necessary, as a supply–demand equilibrium in the market sets the optimal price.

This was the theory that financial markets were perfect which was used to deregulate banking in the USA. In 1999, the Glass–Steagall separation of investment and commercial banking was repealed. And this allowed the creation of integrated banks—which proved "too big to fail" and then needed bailing out by the Federal Government in 2008. (As a note, the "'Classical" part of the name of the school assumes that all markets are perfect and need no government regulation, while the "Synthesis" part is their acceptance of the need for regulation of inflation by a national central bank.)

Neo-Keynesian School

Neo-Keynesians argued that the neoclassical synthesis school economists had too narrowly viewed an economy as only a production system. As we earlier noted, Ben Bernanke wrote: "Economists have not always fully appreciated the importance of a healthy financial system for economic growth or the role of financial conditions in short-term economic dynamics…" (Bernanke 2007)

About this, Hyman Minsky commented: "As Ben Bernanke points out the dominant microeconomic paradigm is an equilibrium construct…that determine relative prices… (The assumption is that) money and financial interrelations are not relevant to the determination of these equilibrium variables… But if the basic microeconomic model is opened to include yesterdays, todays, and tomorrows…" (Minsky 1993)

We recall that Minsky argued that introducing a time dimension into economic models was very important to the reality of an economy. Minsky drew upon John Maynard Keynes: "In the *General Theory*, Keynes sought to create a model of the economy in which money is never neutral (to pricing). He did this by creating a model…in which the price level of financial…assets is determined in (financial) markets…Each capital and financial asset yields an income stream, (which) has carrying costs and possessing some degree of liquidity…The price level of assets is determined by the relative value…(of) income…and liquidity…" (Minsky 1993). Time dependence in a Keynes' model of a financial system lies in the concepts of a "present income" and a "future liquidity" of a "capital asset."

A capital asset is an investment which creates income and can later be sold. It produces an income stream (present income) and also can be sold in the future (future liquidity). The time dimension is from ($\mathbf{T}_1$) of a present income to ($\mathbf{T}_2$) of future liquidity. This present-to-future ($\mathbf{T}_1$ to $\mathbf{T}_2$) temporal process occurs in a financial system as a transaction of "credit–debt." Minsky wrote: "Every capitalist economy is characterized by a system of borrowing and lending… The fundamental borrowing and lending act…is an exchange of 'money-now' for 'money-in-the-future'. This exchange takes place…in a negotiation in which the borrower demonstrates to the satisfaction of the lender—that the money of the future part of the contract will be forthcoming… The money in the future is to cover both the interest and the repayment of the principle of the contract." (Minsky 1993)

A financial market makes the credit–debt contracts sellable, *over time*, as "future liquidity." Thus in a financial subsystem, three things are essential: (1) credit–debt transactions as a fundamental financial process, (2) a capital asset market for liquidity of the asset, and (3) money as a medium of value exchange. We can picture (diagram) a financial process, as in Fig. 7.2.

A financial capital asset transaction occurs over time, beginning with a loan for an asset purchase, followed by rents (income stream) from the productivity of the capital asset, which are used for payments of the loan until the sale of the asset. Financial agents provide a purchase loan to the purchaser of the asset, receiving in turn from the purchaser loan payments on the debt over time from T_1 through T_3. Financial markets price the capital asset for purchase at time T_1 and later for sale at time T_4.

Debt makes a financial process operate. Yet one aspect of debt can destabilize the process, and this is "leverage." We recall that for profit, a financial system uses debt to finance the purchase of capital assets. Profits can be increased through financial leverage. This is the financial rational of "leverage"—more "present debt" toward greater "future wealth." However, when present debt is too large, too highly leveraged, it might not create future wealth but bankruptcy. Excessive "leverage" increases the risk toward bankruptcy and not future wealth. We recall that Irving Fisher had called this financial state of excessive leverage as "debt deflation" (Fisher 1933) and later Hyman Minsky called it "Ponzi finance." (Minsky 1982)

Paul McCulley also emphasized this: "At its core, capitalism is all about risk taking. One form of risk taking is leverage. Indeed, without leverage, capitalism could not prosper… And it is grand while the ever-larger application of leverage puts

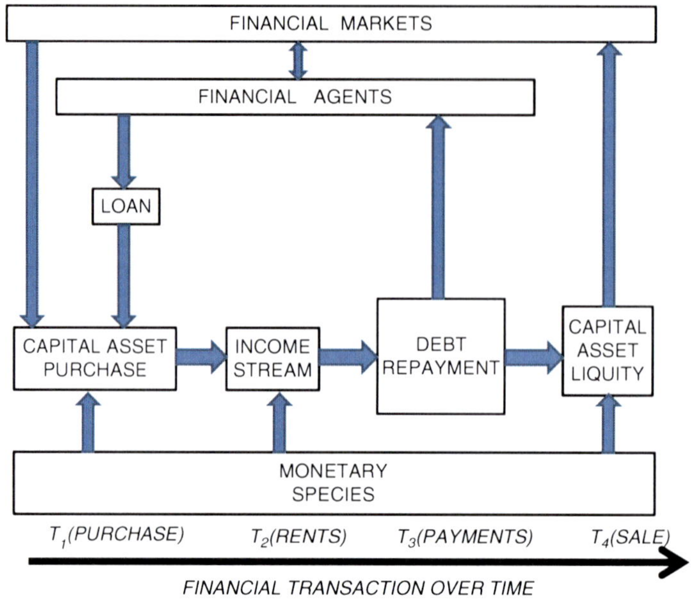

Fig. 7.2 Keynes/Minsky financial process

upward pressure on asset prices. There is nothing like a bull market to make geniuses out of levered dunces…(speculation) begets ever riskier debt arrangements, until they have produced a bubble in asset prices. Then the bubble bursts…" (McCulley 2009). *Leveraged "present debt" can increase "future wealth," but excessive leverage can lead to bankruptcy.*

Earlier in Chap. 4, we saw that a time dimension needs to be added, for a highly-leveraged asset price speculation which rises to a financial bubble. In Fig. 7.3, we add a third dimension of time (to the two dimensions of price and quantity), to depict how the price-demand curve for a financial market can change, over time, due to the price disequilibrium of the financial bubble. This shows a supply-demand curve at two different times, T_1 and later T_2.

If no speculation occurs in an asset market (financial market), then the equilibrium prices at T_1 and T_2 could be the same. But if speculation in the future price for time T_2 occurs in a financial market at time $T_{1,}$ then a price bubble can begin. When a price bubble begins (fueled by leveraged speculation in the future price of an asset), then disequilibrium pricing of the asset can increase and increase—until the financial bubble bursts.

Because of the phenomena of financial bubbles, economic instability is seen by neo-Keynesians as *inherent* to economic financial models. For this reason, the neo-Keynesian School has also been called an "*endogenous* school of economics"—instability is *indigenous*, inside an economy, through the disequilibrium pricing of asset markets in a financial bubble. They called the neoclassical synthesis school an *exogenous* school of economics because they believed all instability was *external* to an economic system (of perfect markets).

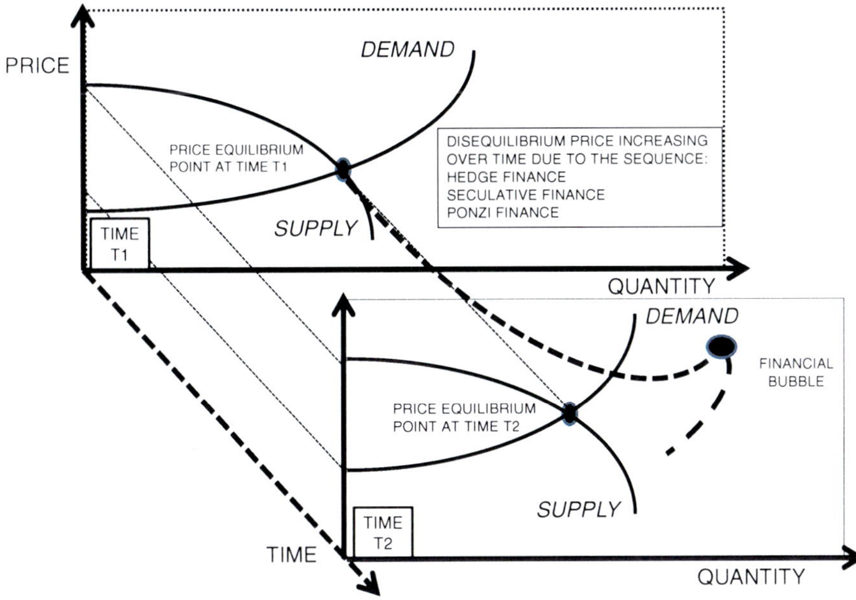

Fig. 7.3 Three-dimensional (price, quantity, time) supply–demand–price–equilibrium chart—over time

Cross-Disciplinary Model of an Economic System

Thus the neoclassical synthesis school focused upon the production subsystem (in which the present price of a commodity is the key factor of control in a production subsystem), while the neo-Keynesian School focused upon a financial subsystem (in which future price of a capital asset is the key factor of control in a financial subsystem). The modeling challenge is to use both these economic models (theories) in a complementary framework. For this, we use the societal dynamics topological model of the stasis of a society, as the major systems in an industrialized society can be classified into four kinds of subsystems (economic, cultural, political, and topological). And these can be topologically presented as stacked planes, as in Fig. 7.4. Therein, we can now place the exogenous school's model of an economy (as a production system) within this larger societal context—as the production subsystem of the economic system. Also one can place the endogenous school's model of an economy (as a financial system) within this larger societal context—as the financial subsystem of the economic plane.

An economy is composed of production, distribution, and consumption of goods and services. The production subsystem produces the goods and services from material/energy resources and financed by a financial system. These goods/services are consumed within a market. Accordingly any economic system can be partitioned into four subsystems of production, market, finance, and resources. This cross-disciplinary

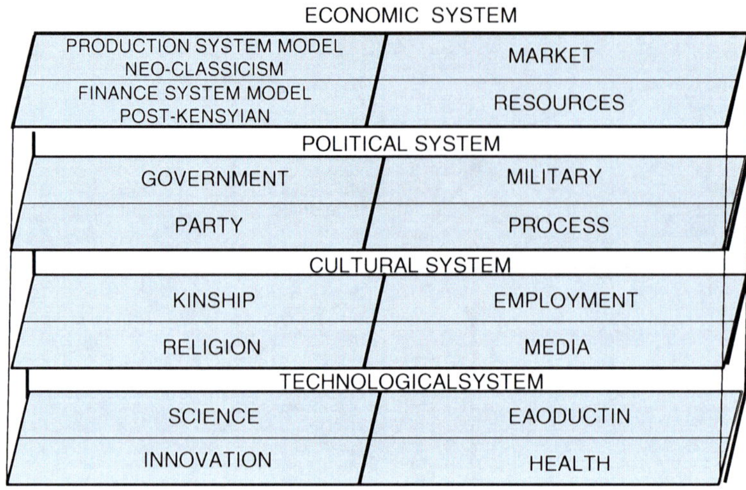

Fig. 7.4 Topological model of society as interacting systems of economy, politics, culture, and technology

meta-framework of societal dynamics can facilitate seeing the economic theories (models) of two schools of economics—exogenous (neoclassical synthesis) and endogenous (neo-Keynesian)—as complementary within the larger context of a societal system. One can place the economic models from the economics literature within this societal meta-framework as Fig. 7.5.

What this topological meta-framework shows is how the models from the two schools of economics, exogenous and endogenous, relate to each other as complementary models of production and financial subsystems, both in the framework of a society's economic subsystem.

What still needs to be discussed is how data is fed into the models and what information results and how information can be transmitted from one model to another. For this, it is important to note that we are not trying to construct one integrated model of a whole economy. The models from the economics disciplinary literature do not permit this because, as we have just reviewed, some of the economists themselves (particularly the neo-Keynesian) see their models of an economy as "partial" models: (1) as modeling pricing equilibrium in commodity-production processes and (2) as modeling disequilibrium pricing in financial processes. What this meta-framework approach to relating models provides is an effective way to use different partial models of several processes—without having to try to create one tightly integrated and complete model of a situation with a complex set of processes.

A modeling meta-framework assists relating partial models in a complex societal situation.

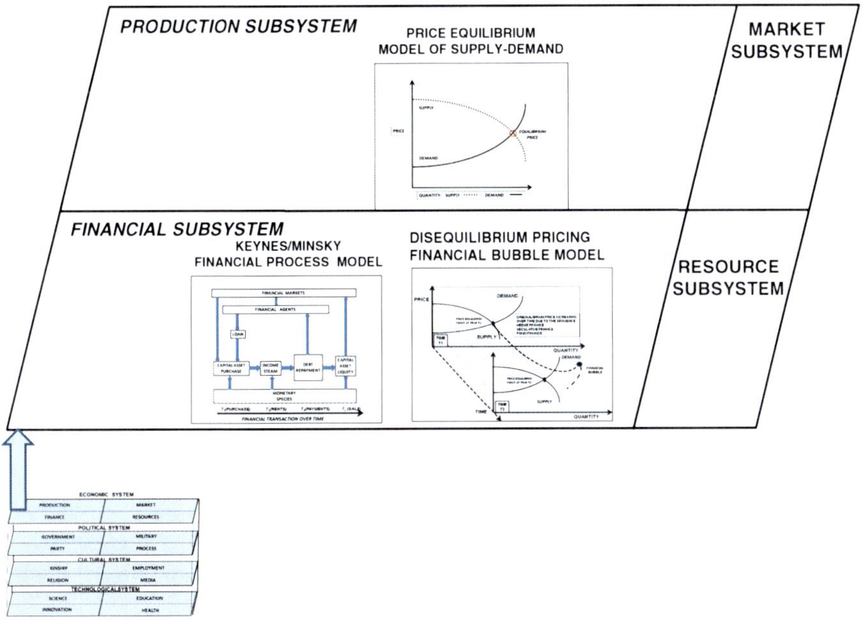

Fig. 7.5 Economic system plane of a societal model

Cross-Disciplinary Model of Production in an Economy

To understand how to connect the partial economic models from the endogenous and exogenous schools, we will next draw upon other models from other social science disciplines, aiming toward a connectable model of a societal economic subsystem—a cross-disciplinary economic system.

Because the economics discipline distinguishes micro from macro economics, we first add cross-disciplinary partial models for microeconomics. For this we turn to management science for a model of a productive economic agent, which is to say, a business that produces goods or services. This is a standard model in management science, called an "enterprise model," and first popularized by Michael Porter (1985), Fig. 7.6. A productive organization can be depicted as adding value to resources and labor obtained from its environment by transforming these into products sold back to the environment as customers. This is an open system model of a firm, receiving inputs of resources and labor from its environment and transforming this into value-added products sold back into the organization's environment.

We start a cross-disciplinary economic model by placing this firm model from management science first unto the production subsystem of an environmental system, as in Fig. 7.7.

The advantage of placing this model of an enterprise firm within a societal system model is to show where and how a microeconomics model fits within larger

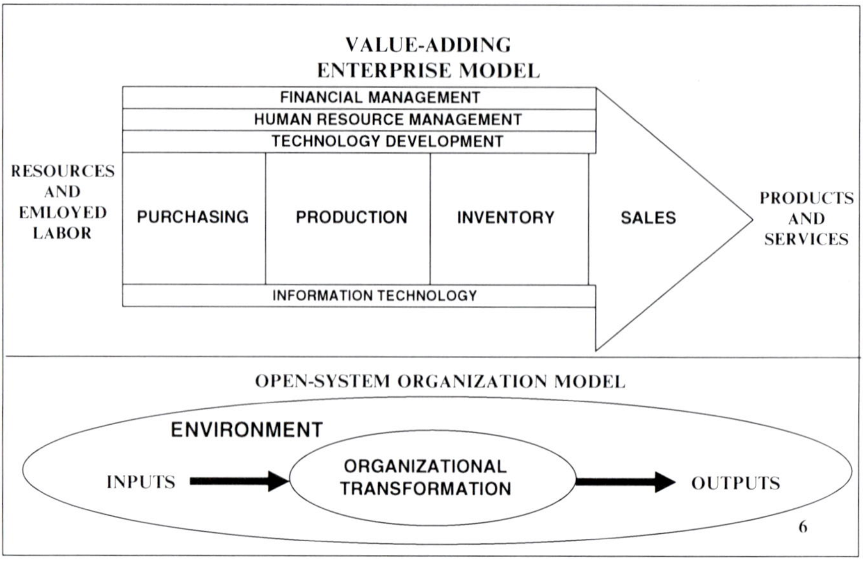

Fig. 7.6 Model of a business enterprise

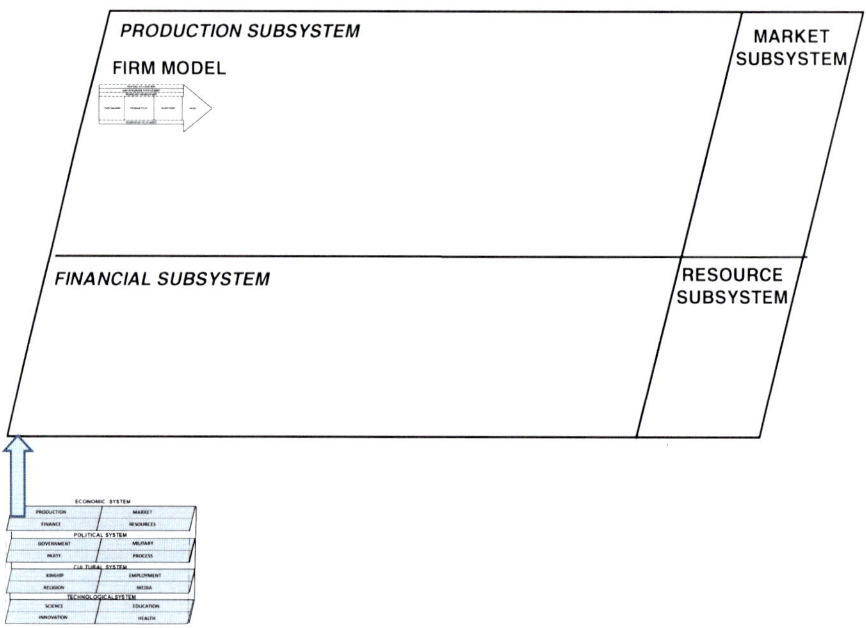

Fig. 7.7 Economic system plane of a societal model

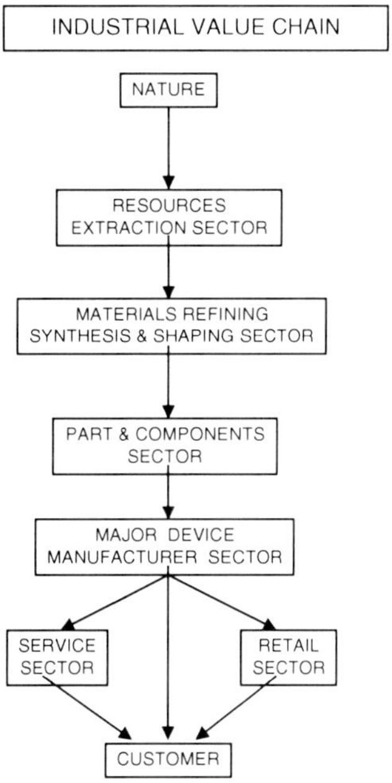

Fig. 7.8 Industrial value chain diagram

economic system modeling. Yet this model applies only to an individual firm. A Jay Forrester-type systems dynamics model can model the production system of a firm (Forrester 1961). A production planning scheme schedules production (such as Kanban just-in-time scheduling) (Ohno 1988). Thus at a microeconomics level, each enterprise model applies to each production firm and cannot be integrated nor added up into a production system.

Next in the literature of management science, Michael Porter (1985) and later Lowell Steele (1989) placed individual firms within particular industrial structures of an "industrial value chain," Fig. 7.8.

Industrial value chains of hard goods begin with some kind of resource-acquisition industrial sector. The next sector is usually a materials-processing sector. Resource-acquisition and materials-processing sectors usually organize separately because the technologies and investments and operations differ markedly between acquisition and processing operations. Materials-processing sectors usually supply materials to part-producing sectors. (For example, the automobile industry is supplied by many different kinds of part-producing firms, such as tires, wheels, brakes, battery, and electronics.) The next industrial sector is a major-device fabricator sector. (For example, in transportation applications, key major devices are automobiles for land, airplanes for air, and ships for sea.) Sometimes major devices are retailed directly to customers (such as cars) or sometimes integrated into a service-providing industry (such as airlines). Major-device industries or service industries often retail through a distribution system. Thus in any industry (goods), there is a chain of businesses taking resources from nature, transforming these into

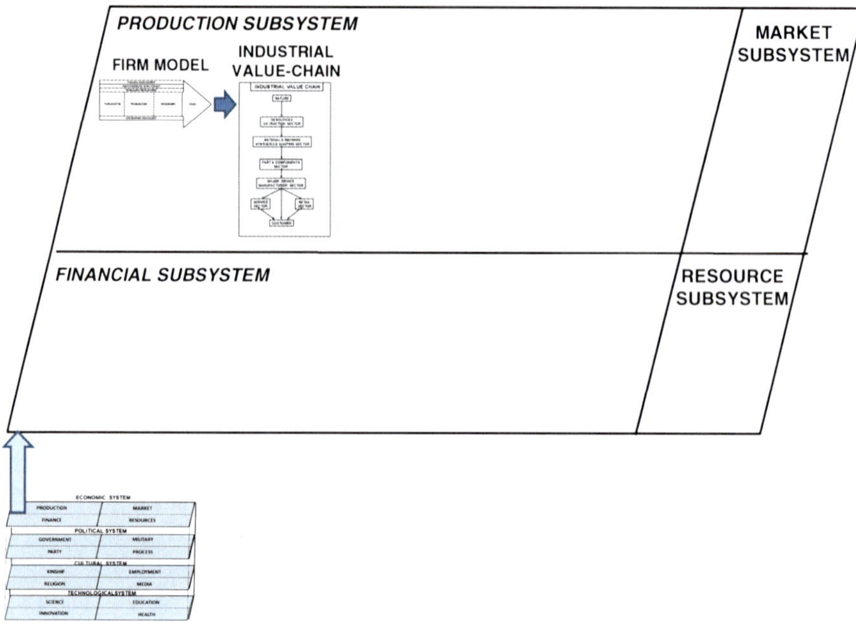

Fig. 7.9 Economic system plane of a societal model

materials or energy or services and providing these to parts manufacturers who act as component vendors to major-device producers, who then sell devices as products/services to customers (retailers or service providers).

We can place this industrial value chain model after the value-adding firm model, to show wherein a business exists in an industrial sector, Fig. 7.9.

With the arrow, we indicate a "relatedness" between the models of a firm and an industrial chain. But this arrow is not a causal connection. The arrow indicates a functional relation, not a causal relation. Data from the firm model can not necessarily feed data directly into the industrial value chain model. There are no causal connections within societal models because societal models are related by function and not by causal mechanisms. Hence data between models in societal systems cannot be causally fed from one model to another. The functional direction of the arrow indicates that a particular firm functionally belongs to a particular industrial sector, depending upon where the firm's products are produced in the value chain of an industry. Functional related data are empirically generated independently in modeling studies.

The reason one needs to add a model of an industrial value chain is that this is a way to aggregate the production results of all the firms within an industrial sector. The firm models do not aggregate to an industrial value chain but constitute the businesses within sectors, as in Fig. 7.10.

Thus the equilibrium pricing model of supply–demand is applicable only to a specific set of productions (commodity) within a specific sector of an industrial

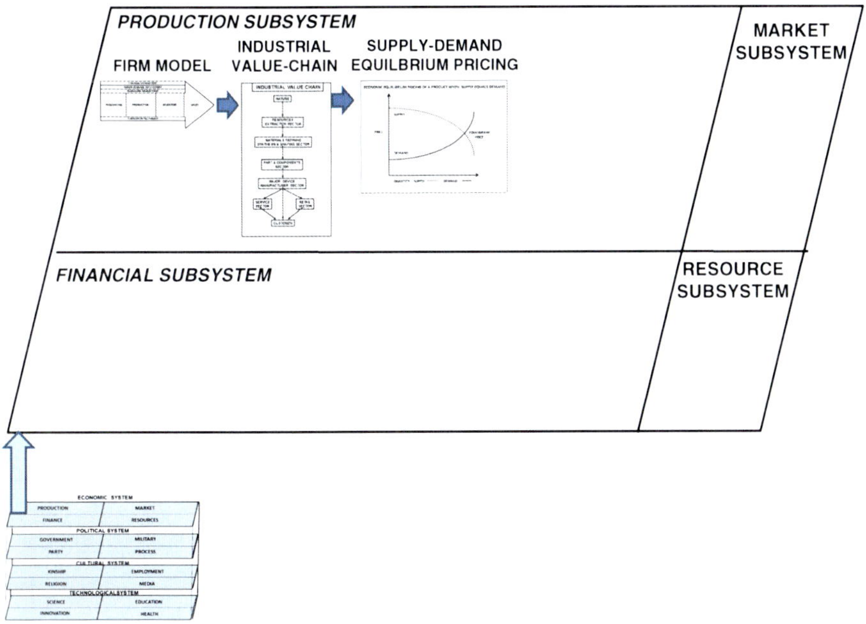

Fig. 7.10 Economic system plane of a societal model

value chain. The first arrow indicates that a firm model belongs functionally to a specific industrial sector, and the second arrow indicates that the commodity supply–demand curve is functionally specific to an industrial sector.

This placement of the exogenous school's supply–demand model upon a societal model topological plane shows that data must be specific to an industrial chain for the supply–demand model to be empirically real (real supply–demand data in and valid price information out).

So far, we have been placing models of economic agents appropriate to a small-scale description of the production system of an economy, a microeconomic scale at each industrial sector. How can one next "add up" economic data about all industrial sectors (and all industrial value chains) into an economic accounting of production of a whole economy, a macroeconomic model?

The answer to this is another economic model created by Wassily Leontief (1986), which he called an "input–output" economic model, as shown in Fig. 7.11. Leontief's input–out industrial equation says that the production of products $\mathbf{P}_I$ in the I-th industrial sector gets sold to consumers $\mathbf{C}_I$ of the products and to industrial customers $\mathbf{X}_{IJ}$ in the J-th industries. The remainder of the products $\mathbf{P}_I$ are exported $\mathbf{E}_{IK}$ to K-th countries. Leontief's industrial input–output model is particularly useful for understanding how technological innovation can impact industrial production and economic growth. In a knowledge economy, an earlier investment at time $\mathbf{T}_1$ in a technology invention will appear economically at a later time $\mathbf{T}_2$—as an

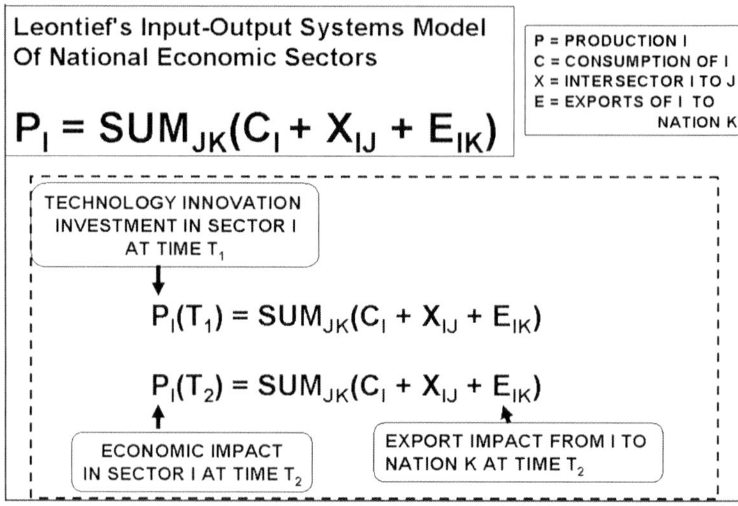

Fig. 7.11 Lieontief input-output economic model

innovation in improved production or in new products/services—which will increase revenue (income) for an I-th industry in its $\mathbf{P}_\mathbf{I}$ products at that later time $\mathbf{T}_2$.

The data for such an aggregate account comes from revenue data reported each firm and grouped by commodities produced. Again we note that in each partial model, data does not flow necessarily from one model to another but must be gathered independently. *Partial models of economic activity may not be simply aggregated (summed) but are functional relation.*

Next we add this input–output model of the production economy to the economic system plane within the production subsector, Fig. 7.12.

The third arrow indicates that all the supply–demand equilibrium pricing curves of the industrial value chains and their sectors can be functionally aggregated as revenue data in a Leontief input–output accounts model of a national economy. The advantage of placing this Leontief economic model of total industrial production alongside the previous models of industrial value chains and enterprise firms within these industries is to show precisely how to go from microeconomic theory to macroeconomy theory—from the microscale of the firm to the macroscale of the economy. In this cross-disciplinary modeling meta-framework of a whole society, one can see how the models of *neoclassical school of economics* (supply–demand and input–output national accounts) fit together.

Furthermore, this cross-disciplinary meta-framework placement of the partial models shows how the "business cycle" works. At the microeconomics level, a firm produces a commodity product (or service) based upon expected sales in the near term. The production accumulates within a product-inventory storage—from which products are shipped when sold. If the production firm anticipates a growth in sales, it increases production. But if the firm anticipates a decline in sales, it decreases

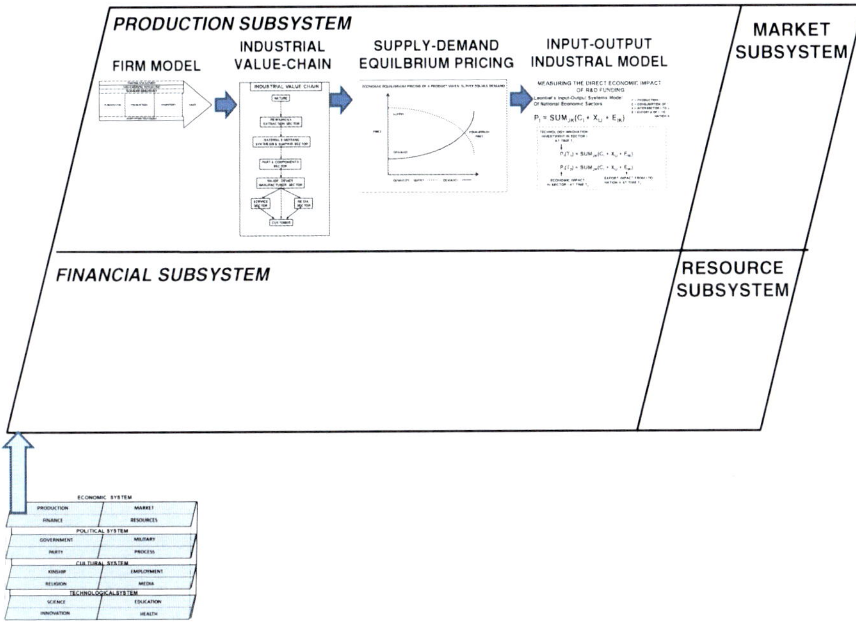

Fig. 7.12 Economic system plane of a societal model

production. In thinking about future sales, a firm anticipates the state of the economy. If the economy is growing, the firm can anticipate sales growth, but if the economy is declining, the firm can anticipate a decline in sales. When the firm perceives the economy is growing, it can add employees to increase production. But when the firm perceives the economy is receding, it can lay off employees, to decrease production and reduce costs. This is a connection between the microstructure of an economy at a firm level (microeconomics) and the macrostructure of an economy at the economic system level (macroeconomics). This is not a "mechanism" but a "perception" about the future—an expectation as a "reflexivity." This is why there is no "invisible hand" in the market place. Instead there is an invisible "reflexivity" by production agents (firms) toward an economic future. The difference between the economic concepts "invisible hand of the market place" and "reflexivity in speculation" is (1) that the first is the idea of *automatic control of pricing in a commodity market* and (2) that the second is the idea of *human anticipation impacting future prices through financial speculation*.

The concept of "reflexivity" in economic activities consists of expectations about the future. Financial agents' expectations about an economic/financial future induces the agents to buy (expecting prices to go up) or to sell (expecting prices to go down). Industrial managers' expectations about an economic/financial future induces the managers to increase production (expecting demand to grow) or decrease production (expecting demand to shrink).

This concept of "reflexivity" about an economic future explains a "business cycle." It is the "expectation about future sales at the microlevel of the firm that connects to 'fluctuations in demand and supply' at the macrolevel of the economy." When managers at the firm level perceive the economy is growing and anticipate higher sales, they hire employees. The consumption by these employees then adds to the growth of demand at the macrolevel. In contrast, when managers of firms perceive the economy is shrinking, they lay off employees. The reduction in income of the unemployed then decreases demand. Thus at the microeconomic level, growth (or shrinkage) of product inventories of individual businesses (firms) connects to the macroeconomic level expansion (or decline) of economic activity—through the connection of levels of employment to levels of demand. (This was the basis of Keynes' argument in 1933 why the US economic depression could not be fixed until new employment was financed by the government—which it eventually was when World War II began for the USA).

Cross-Disciplinary Model of a Financial Subsystem

Now we turn to adding the models of financial subsystems of the endogenous school onto the economic systems plane of the meta-space societal systems model. We begin placing partial models of finance in the financial subsystem sector of the economic system plane, Fig. 7.13.

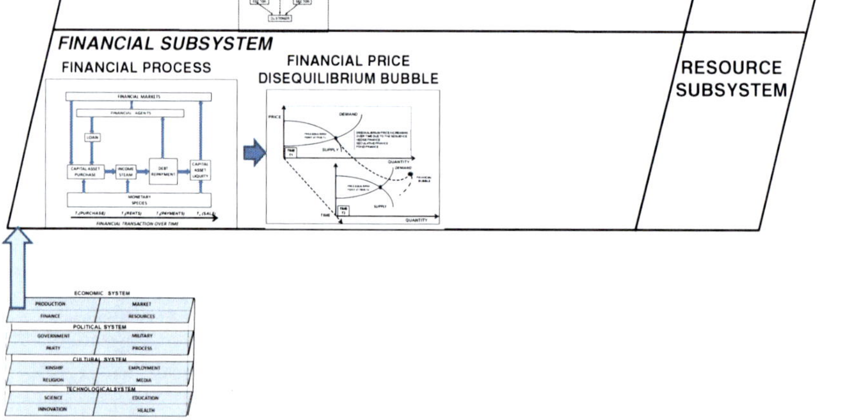

Fig. 7.13 Economic system plane of a societal model

The arrow between a financial process model and a financial bubble models indicates a functional relation in a financial market when speculation and excessive leverage is funded by loans to the market speculators.

The positioning of the economic partial models on the economic plane indicates that the production/commodity markets operate differently from the financial markets. A commodity market proceeds to a price equilibrium, whereas a financial market can proceed toward a price disequilibrium through financial speculation and leverage. Data into the model of a financial process depends upon the market being modeled, stock markets, investment markets, housing markets, commercial real estate markets, etc. When growth in a market occurs, speculation can increase and with excessive leverage create a financial bubble. In such a case, disequilibrium pricing can be modeled for the period of the bubble (such as the housing bubbles of the early 2000s).

Functional Connections Between Production and Financial Subsystems

Now we can ask about the functional connection between the two subsystems of production and finance in an economic system. A capital asset can provide financing for production capacity, and this is the connection between the production and financial subsystems in an economy. If an investment opportunity appears to a financial market which reflexitively anticipates increase in demand, then the price of the capital asset (producing the commodity) is valuable and may be financed. This is how the Minsky model of a financial system connects to the classical model of a production system. In Fig. 7.14, an investment opportunity is seen in the growth of a particular product $\mathbf{P_I}$ in a national accounts model.

Speculators invest in production capacity to serve market growth, using loans to leverage financing. If the financing is conservative, then the growing demand for the product $\mathbf{P_I}$ will be met in a price equilibrium by growth in the supply. But when too much speculation happens in investments for supply growth (with too much leverage), then a financial bubble occurs in a temporary price disequilibrium and resulting debt deflation.

Discussion

We have used six partial models, standard to the economics literature and to the business literature. These are firm model, industrial value chain, supply–demand equilibrium pricing, input–output industrial model, financial process model, and financial price disequilibrium Bubble. These models have been placed topologically in a meta-model framework of a societal system, in order to display their functional relationships to one another. The first four models are appropriate in depicting operations within the production subsystem of an economic system, and the latter two are

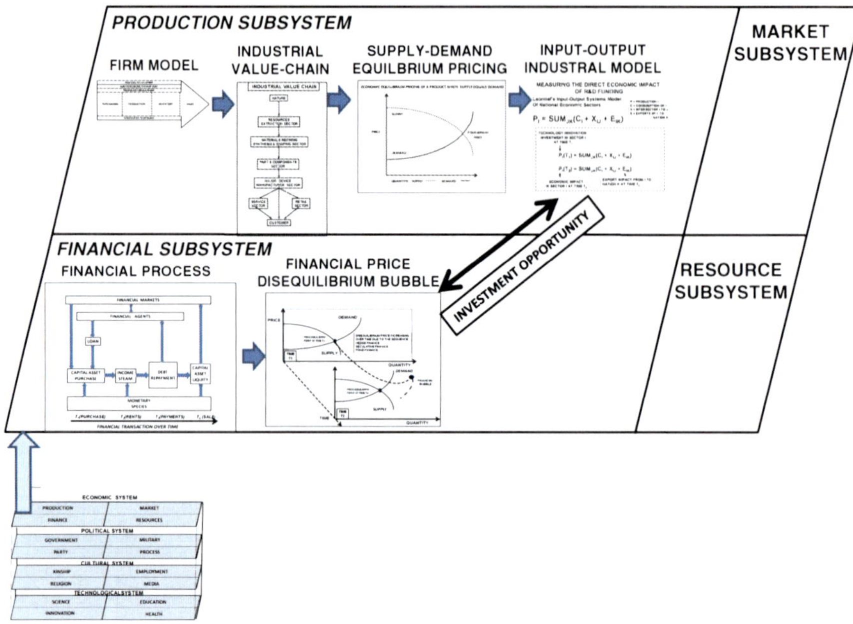

Fig. 7.14 Economic system plane of a societal model

appropriate in depicting operations within the financial subsystem of an economic system. The two economic subsystems of production and finance are functionally related by the investment opportunities perceived by the financial markets.

All these relationships between these societal partial models are functional and not causal. Therefore data specific to each model needs to be empirically developed from research and statistics, functionally defined. Data do not necessarily feed automatically from one model to another, because societal models are not causally connected but functionally related. If societal models were mechanistic with causality, then the partial models could be integrated into one large causal model. (But this is only possible in the physical sciences (e.g., special relativity mechanics and Newtonian mechanics or the correspondence principle between quantum mechanics and Newtonian mechanics). Social science models are functional models and not mechanism models. Hence data for each economics partial model must be functionally defined properly for each model.

The connectedness between societal partial models is by the flow of information from one model to another. Information flows connect together the whole of a societal model, but information must be functionally translated from one part to another. For example, data for firm models come from specific functional depictions of enterprise (production) systems of a firm and strategic plans of a firm. Data for industrial value chain models must come from specific functional depictions of a value chain and volume production and attendant revenue annually generated by all firms in an industrial sector (as statistics often generated by industrial associations). So in turn, each model must have its own data generated by functional depictions of each sector and markets. What the cross-disciplinary meta-model framework does is to show how societal partial models are related functionally. Partial models in a society's systems provide an important methodological approach for empirical accuracy and verification of a model, but partial models must be assembled toward complete societal models.

The cross-disciplinary meta-framework of societal dynamics provides the analytical framework for the functional assembly of partial models.

Also this cross-disciplinary framework provides a way to reconcile the conflicts between different schools in a social science discipline. We have seen how assembling together the economically partial models of production subsystems and financial subsystems does show how to reconcile the two historically conflicting economic schools of "neoclassical synthesis" and "neo-Keynesian." The economics discipline can be resolved as a modeling challenge. Moreover, all scientific theory must be grounded in experience. The use of societal dynamics theory as an analytic framework for historical studies can enable the direct comparison between economic history (the empiricism of economics) and economic theory (the rationalism of economics). By looking at history of the theoretical conflict in economics, we have shown how societal dynamics can provide a meta-framework for historical studies.

Since disciplines observe only slices of a societal system, disciplinary models can be only partial models—parts of a larger societal system. A cross-disciplinary framework facilitates the integration of disciplinary partial models.

References

Appelbaum, B. (2013, January 18). Days before 2007 crisis, fed officials doubted need to act. *New York Times.*

Bernanke, B. S. (2007, May 15). *Regulation and financial innovation.* 2007 Financial markets conference, Sea Island, Georgia. Federal Reserve Bank of Atlanta.

Davies, H. (2012, August 27). Economics in denial about its academic merit. *The Korea Herald.*

Fisher, I. (1933, October) The debt-deflation theory of the Great Depression. *Econometrica.*

Forrester, J. (1961). *Industrial dynamics.* Waltham, MA: Pegasus Communications.

Giles, C. (2010, April 10). Financial crisis exposed flaws in economics. *Financial Times.*

Giles, C. (2012, May 2). King admits failing to 'shout' about risk. *Financial Times.*

Krugman, P. (2009, March 17). The B Word. *The New York Times.*

Leontief, W. (1986). *Input-output economics* (2nd ed.). Oxford: Oxford University Press.

McCulley, P. (2009, February). Saving capitalistic banking from itself. PIMCO.

Minsky, H. P. (1982). *Can 'it' happen again? Essays on instability and finance.* Armonk, NY: M.E. Sharpe Inc.

Minsky, H. (1993). Comment on Ben Bernanke, 'Credit in the Macro-economy'. Hyman P. Minsky Archive, Paper 361. (http://digitalcommons.bard.edu/hm_archive/361)

Ohno, T. (1988). *Toyota production system.* Portland, OR: Productivity Press.

Porter, M. (1985). *Competitive strategy.* New York: The Free Press.

Steele, L. W. (1989). *Managing technolgy.* New York. McGraw Hill.

Whalen, C. J. (2012). Post-Keynesian Institutionalism after the Great Recession. Working Paper No 724, Levy Economics Institute of Bard College. http://www.leveyinstitute.org

Chapter 8
Financial Layering

Introduction

As we have seen, the endogenous school had focused upon financial systems, not only as processes but also as institutions. In 2012, Charles J. Whalen saw these two foci about financial systems as converging: "In the mid-1970s, Wallace C. Peterson... argued that institutionalism and the economics of John Maynard Keynes can be viewed as 'two trains on parallel tracks toward a common destination'. Today, in the wake of the Great Recession (2007) —the worst global economic downturn since the 1930s—those trains have finally reached the station. Their arrival is none too soon for economics and the world economy. The common destination of institutionalism and the economics of Keynes, the latter of which is currently called Post-Keynesian economics, is Post-Keynesian Institutionalism (PKI)." (Whalen 2012)

Although credit–debt is the essential process of a Keynes–Minsky financial system, both Keynes and Minsky also emphasized a financial institutionalism. Minsky wrote: "...the dynamics of contemporary capitalism...characterizes all economic units by their financial portfolios. In all sectors, people and organizations constantly face the need to decide what assets to acquire and how to finance them. The result is a dynamic, paper world of financial liabilities, cash-flow commitments, and interrelated balance sheets—all dependent on expectations made against the backdrop of an uncertain future and an irreversible past" (Minsky 1969). Minsky was asserting that the economic rationality of financial agents depends upon their institutional context.

The emphasis on the actual behavior of financial agents had long been a tradition in economics called "institutional economics." In addition to Keynes and Minsky, it had many seminal writers, such as Thorstein Veblen, Walton Hale Hamilton, and Adolf A. Berle. They all challenged a traditional economic "idea" that all economic agents behave purely "rationally," where the rationality is independent of place and time and institution, purely logical without context. Instead institutional economists thought that institutional structures influence what agents, within the institutions, conceive of as "rational" behavior—how they should reason.

F. Betz, *Why Bank Panics Matter: Cross-Disciplinary Economic Theory*, SpringerBriefs in Economics, DOI 10.1007/978-3-319-01757-0_8,

For example, Charles J. Whalen wrote: "Conventional economics is constructed around the notion of a barter economy. The starting point is that of a village fair: Money, finance, capital assets, and production can all be added, but… (neoclassical synthesis) assumes that the central features of capitalism can be grasped without them. (However, neo-Keynesian Institutionalism insists that)…institutions, not impersonal forces or universal laws of nature,…balance (the) wheel of the economy… (For example) the Schumpeter-Minsky theory of capitalist development is institutionally grounded and finance driven. It holds that capitalist development is shaped by the institutional structure, and that this structure is always evolving in response to profit-seeking activity." (Whalen 2012)

Thus, next we need to construct an institutional model of finance, to complement the process model of finance. The model should include financial agents and financial markets, showing their interconnections. The conceptual basis for doing this was provided by Hyman Minsky in his idea of a "financial layering" of financial institutions (Minsky 1982). In a modern financial system, banks are only one part of a structure. Banks and shadow banks, together, form a kind of "layered" structure. Layered financial structures make "leverage" possible in financial processes. And as we have seen, it is an excess of leveraging which creates financial bubbles.

History: 1907 Bank Panic

We will next model a "layered financial structure"; and for this (also to historically ground Minsky's concept), we go back into the US financial history to the bank panic of 1907. In this case, the institutional relations in a layered structure are particularly clear. Also the legislation for a US central bank was later enacted based upon this experience. Ellis W. Tallman and Jon R. Moen wrote: "…the Bank Panic of 1907 disrupted financial markets to such an extent that it became an important catalyst for creating the Federal Reserve and the U.S. banking system…" (Tallman and Moen 1990)

In 1907, the structure of the US financial market consisted of several types of financial agents—New York banks and western banks, a New York bank clearing house, a New York stock exchange, New York stock brokerages, investment trust companies, and the US Federal Treasury. The New York bank clearing house was an organization established by private banks in New York to clear drafts and checks written by one bank and cashed in another—facilitating financial transfers between banks. It also could provide loans to banks, if the clearing house established a member bank needed a loan and was financially sound. By 1907, New York City had become the financial center of the nation. Banks in states corresponded with New York banking, for loans to finance agriculture, trade, and international financial transactions.

New York banks experienced annual fluctuations in the demand for money and credit. Tallman and Moen wrote: "…(the) New York money market faced seasonal variations in interest rates and liquidity resulting from the transportation of crops from the interior of the USA to New York and then to Europe." (Tallman and Moen 1990). In agriculture, crops were planted in the spring in the Midwest, and farmers needed loans from midwestern regional banks to purchase seed and gain support until harvest time (repaying the local banks at harvest). In the fall, buyers of crops then had to borrow money from Midwestern banks to purchase the crop and ship it east: "The outflow of capital (from New York) necessary to finance crop shipments from the Midwest to the East Coast in September or October usually left New York City money markets squeezed for cash." (Tallman and Moen 1990)

The 1907 bank panic happened in the autumn, when the New York banks needed cash for the seasonal crop shipment. Also at that time, the bank notes (money) in the USA and England were backed by stocks of gold, and so the flow of gold could affect the supply of money available in the USA or in the British Empire. Tallman and Moen wrote: " The U.S. base money stock (gold, greenbacks, national bank notes, and gold and silver certificates) was also affected by unusual variations in gold flows through foreign exchange markets." (Tallman and Moen 1990). These were conditions in place for the 1907 panic in the fall, as seasonal demand for credit for farm exports and the supply of money made the New York banks low in cash.

Also institutional arrangements would facilitate the panic. New York banks were connected together through interlocking boards of directors. Banks and stock brokerages were also interconnected by interlocking control (ownership or relationship). For example, F. Augustus Heinze (who, as we soon shall see, was key to triggering the bank panic) was the founder and major shareholder in the company of United Copper, while also on the board of directors of eight banks and two trust companies. His personal connections included being a brother to Otto Heinze of a stock brokerage house and also financial partners with Charles T. Barney (president of the Knickerbocker Trust Company) and Charles W. Morse (who controlled three banks). Together, Heinze and his brother and Barney and Morse used their control of banks to finance Heinze's attempt to corner the stock of United Copper. It was this "institutional interlocking" (of Heinze's eight banks, Barney's trust company, and Morse's three banks) which provided the banking "chain effect" to begin the 1907 panic: "Heinze's attempt to corner the stock of United Copper, a company of which he was president, eventually triggered the Panic of 1907." (Tallman and Moen 1990)

With these factors about money liquidity (process) and institutional bank interlocking (structure), there occurred the crisis event of "stock cornering." Abigail Tucker wrote: "The Panic of 1907...was a financial crisis that occurred in the USA when the New York Stock Exchange fell almost 50 % from its peak the previous year...The 1907 panic eventually spread throughout the nation when many state and local banks and businesses entered bankruptcy. Primary causes of the run include a retraction of market liquidity by a number of New York City banks and a loss of confidence among depositors, exacerbated by unregulated side bets at bucket shops (stock brokerages). The panic was triggered by the failed attempt in October 1907 to corner the market on stock of the United Copper Company. When this bid failed, banks that had lent money to the cornering scheme suffered runs that later spread to affiliated banks and trusts, leading a week later to the downfall of the Knickerbocker

Trust Company—New York City's third-largest trust. The collapse of the Knickerbocker spread fear throughout the city's trusts as regional banks withdrew reserves from New York City banks. Panic extended across the nation as vast numbers of people withdrew deposits from their regional banks." (Tucker 2008)

We review Heinze's attempt to manipulate (corner) United Copper shares. In 1869, Fritz Augustus Heinze had been born to immigrant parents, a German father and an Irish mother. At the age of nine, his father sent him to Germany to study. At the age of 16, he returned to the USA and studied at the Brooklyn Polytechnic Institute and then at Columbia University's School of Mines. In 1889 in Montana, he began working as a mining engineer for the Boston and Montana Company. In 1894, after inheriting $50,000 from his father, he opened his own company, Montana Ore Purchasing Company, to provide smelting for small mining companies. In 1895, he purchased a mine, the Raus Mine, which proved to be valuable in copper ore.

Fourteen years earlier in 1881, the largest copper company in the USA, Amalgamated Copper, had been formed. Marcus Daly had purchased a small silver mine (called Anaconda) near Butte, Montana. But a very large deposit of copper was found at the mine; and Daly was then able to buy up neighboring mines to form the Amalgamated Copper Mining Company.

In 1895, Heinze started a legal war with the powerful Amalgamated Copper. Tallman and Moen wrote: "Heinze, who owned a copper mine near the Amalgamated Mines, claimed that veins of copper from his mine extended under land owned by Amalgamated and that according to the 'apex law' he had a right to mine it… The matter was pursued in an extensive legal confrontation that was eventually settled out of court in February 1906, when Heinze sold his copper interest to Amalgamated for a reported $25 million… Heinze took his gains to New York City where he became involved in banking." (Tallman and Moen 1990)

The "apex law" was part of the earlier law of "The General Mining Act of 1872." This authorized and governed the "prospecting and mining" for minerals on federal public lands. It gave US citizens the right to locate a lode of hard rock or a placer of gravel for a mining claim on federal lands. The "apex" part of the law provided claim owners with the right to follow and mine a vein laterally, even if it went over into other owners' areas. Heinze won a settlement from Amalgamated, but he had also made an enemy who would not forget him.

In New York City, Heinze became a banker. Tallman and Moen wrote: "Elected president of Mercantile National Bank in February 1907, he immediately replaced the directorship with his associates. The Heinze group gained control of several other banks quite quickly through 'chain banking'… The group would buy stock in a bank and use it as collateral to borrow money, which was then used to buy stock in another bank or trust." (Tallman and Moen 1990)

But then Heinze leveraged too much: "Heinze's attempt to corner the stock of United Copper, a company of which he was president,…triggered the Panic of 1907… On Monday (October, 14, 1907) its stock had risen from $39 to $60… Heinze had purchased a large quantity of shares…through the brokerage house of his bother, Otto Heinze… He (also) ordered Gross and Kleeberg, a brokerage house started in 1904, to purchase 6,000 shares of stock at ascending prices…To punish the exchange houses that had gone short in United Copper stock, Heinze put out an order calling in all his United Copper shares." (Tallman and Moen 1990)

Heinze was buying large amounts of shares in his company, United Copper. As the stock price soared, he expected other brokers to bet against him by "shorting" the stock. Shorting a stock requires a broker to "borrow" stock from some owner in order to sell the stock at a given price (since a shorter does not own the stock, he/she is selling). By buying up most of the existing shares of United Copper in October, Heinze expected the short sellers on the stock to have to buy his shares to settle their accounts (if the price of the stock rose and did not fall). Heinze expected to make a profit by selling to short sellers his newly acquired shares at a higher price than Heinze paid for them. Tallman and Moen wrote: "Heinze hoped…(to) force short sellers to a settlement in a technique known as a 'bear squeeze'… By demanding delivery of his shares Heinze intended to force short sellers to come up with shares that they did not possess—and could not possess, unless they bought them from Heinze. Thus the settlement between Heinze and the short seller could be at almost any price and would clearly provide Heinze with a profit as long as there was no other source of United Copper shares." (Tallman and Moen 1990)

But unfortunately for Heinze, there was another source of United Copper shares. Tallman and Moen wrote: "On Wednesday (October 16, 1907), Heinze's corner attempt suffered the final blow. Gross and Kleeberg were forced to sell United Copper stock to pay for the shares purchased earlier (by Heinze) on margin. United Copper fell…to $10 a share…" (Tallman and Moen 1990). The short sellers bought shares to replace those they had shorted at a much lower price, making a large profit. Heinze lost a lot of money: "One commentator suggested that Amalgamated Copper interests, namely H. H. Rogers, Stillman, and other powerful financiers, were 'waiting in the wings' to deny Heinze an opportunity to corner the market in his stock…" (Tallman and Moen 1990). The financiers of Amalgamated Copper had not forgotten about Heinze, nor forgiven.

The collapse of the Copper shares also bought down the rest of the stock market. All in that market who had bought stock on margin were caught in a financial squeeze. Stock brokerages which had purchased the stocks on margin for customers were squeezed. Banks which had made the margin loans to brokerages had to call them from the stockbrokers. But as the stock prices fell, the collateral for the loans declined, and banks were squeezed. In addition, the trust companies which had pyramided the acquisitions of businesses through loans (collateralized) by their acquired business stocks were also squeezed. When stock prices dropped, all levered loans were called and their stock-collateral value (to the banks) dropped. A single effort to corner a particular stock in the market triggered a major drop in a highly levered stock market—jeopardizing the finances of brokerages, banks, and trust companies.

We recall this is the common pattern which Irving Fisher had called "debt deflation." Within a financial system, leverage of financial speculation connects from speculators to banks—through collateral of the loans—to the financial health of banks. Financial contagion can spread from a stock market event throughout a banking system. When stock is used as collateral for loans that provide the finance to purchase leveraged assets, the collapse of the stock market can then connect back to banks, through the leverage loans. We have seen before that this is how stock market collapses trigger bank panics, through leverage loans.

So it happened in 1907. At the time, O. M. W. Sprague wrote: "(Mr. Heinze)... at the beginning of the year had become president of the Mercantile National Bank... The resources of the bank seem to have been used to an increasing extent in the furtherance of (Heinze's)...speculation, and the failure of the copper corner brought matters to a head. The bank was unable to meet an unfavorable balance at the clearing house which assumed large proportions because alarmed depositors were shifting their accounts to other banks. The request (by the bank) for assistance from the clearing house was granted after examination to determine solvency of the bank, and upon condition that the president (Augustus Heinze) and entire board of directors should resign." (Sprague 1908)

The dates of the panic were:

Monday, October 14, 1907. Heinze has his brokerage, Gross and Kleeberg, buy large quantities of United Copper shares on margin. To finance the margin purchases, Gross and Kleeberg borrow money from two banks which Heinze controls, State Savings Bank of Butte, Montana, and Mercantile Bank in New York.

Wednesday, October 16. Heinze fails to acquire all the United Copper shares available to the New York Stock Market, and short sellers of United Copper buy stock from other sources, which collapses the price of United Copper to $10 a share. When the share price collapses, Gross and Kleeberg, which purchased stock on margin for Heinze, cannot pay back its margin loans and fails. Runs begin on banks controlled by Heinze and his associates, which loaned monies for the margin purchases of United Copper.

Thursday, October 17. The exchange suspends United Copper from trading. Heinze's bank in Butte announces it is insolvent. A run occurs at the Mercantile National bank, of which Heinze is president. Runs also begin at all the banks controlled by Heinze and by his associates, Charles Barney and Charles Morse.

Sunday, October 20. The New York Clearing House (which facilitates the transactions between banks in New York City) forces Heinze and Morse to resign from their directorate positions at their banks.

Monday, October 21. Charles Barney is forced to resign from the Knickerbocker Trust Company.

Tuesday, October 22. A bank run at Knickerbocker Trust forces it to close.

Wednesday, October 23. The banker J. P. Morgan provides a loan to another trust, Trust Company of America, to prevent its collapse.

Thursday, October 24. George Cortelyou, the US Treasury Secretary, deposits large amounts of Federal money in New York banks to help their liquidity. J.P. Morgan persuades bank presidents to loan $23 million to the New York Stock Exchange to keep it open.

Sunday, October 27. George Perkins, of the Morgan Bank, is told by New York City that the city will be insolvent by November 1, if they cannot raise new loans of $20 to $30 million.

Tuesday, October 29. J.P. Morgan purchases $30 million of New York City bonds, to prevent the city's bankruptcy.

Saturday, November 2. A major brokerage, Moore and Stanley, nearly collapses because its loans are called—loans backed as collateral by their stock in Tennessee Coal, Iron and Railroad (whose price has collapsed with the general decline of the New York Stock Market).

Monday, November 4. Morgan arranges the acquisition of Tennessee Coal, Iron and Railroad by US Steel. This creates a monopoly, but Morgan persuades the US President Theodore Roosevelt to approve of the acquisition, in order to shore up the stock market (despite Roosevelt's previous anti-monopoly policy).

Perceptual Space Analysis of the 1907 Bank Panic

We analyze the historical event in the observational framework of the cross-disciplinary societal dynamics perceptual space, Fig. 8.1.

> **Action**—Augustus Heinze failed in October to corner stock in United Copper. Triggered by Heinze's cornering failure, the New York Stock Market falls. Runs occur on the banks controlled by Heinze and his associates. Runs begin also on trust companies, funded by loans from these banks. Knickerbocker Trust fails. J.P. Morgan rescues Trust Company of America. Morgan and other bankers rescue other trusts. Morgan arranges the sale of Tennessee Coal, Iron and Railroad to US Steel. US Treasury Secretary, Cortelyou, deposits Federal funds in New York banks to increase their monetary reserves.

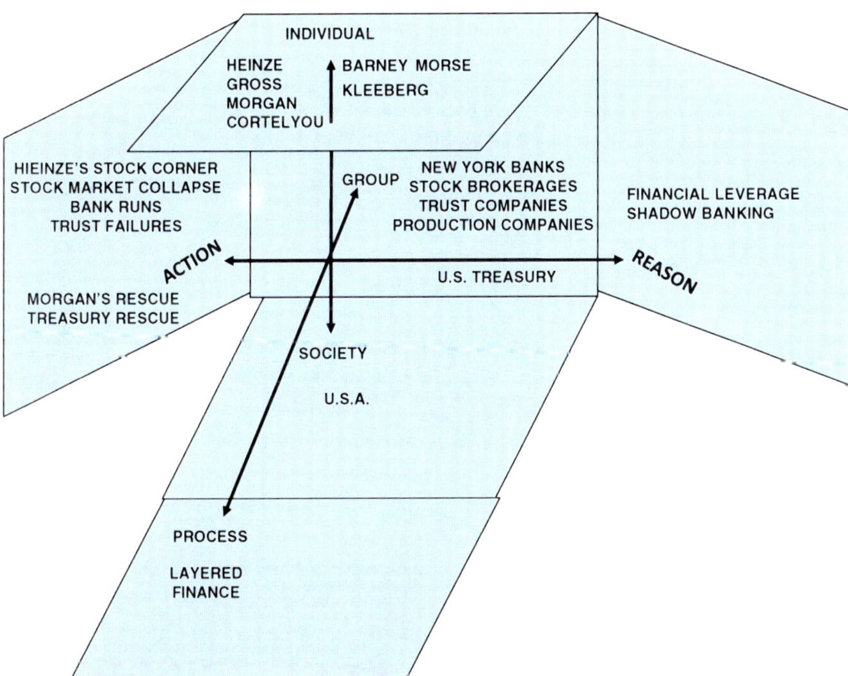

Fig. 8.1 1907 Bank panic

Group—The groups involved in the action included New York banks, New York Clearing House, stock brokerages, trust companies, copper companies, and the US Treasury.

Individual—Individuals involved in the action were as follows: Augustus Heinze, who was president of a bank and of a copper company, attempted to buy most of the stock (corner) of the US Copper Company. But in failing, this triggered a stock market collapse. The stock brokerage firms of Heinze's brother and of Gross and Kleeberg fail. Bank runs begin on banks controlled by Heinze and his associates Charles Barney and Charles Morse. J.P. Morgan, head of the Morgan bank, rescues the Trust Company of America, and Cortelyou deposits Federal money in New York banks.

Society—The society involved in the event is the US society and its financial system. Attempts to profit from the control of a company within the production system triggered a sharp stock market decline, which was followed by bank runs and trust company bankruptcy, which imperiled the New York financial system.

Process—The process involved in the action was one of financial layering in which intermediate financial institutions operated between the banks (key financial institution, such as the Morgan bank) and the production corporations (such as United Copper). The intermediate financial institutions included a stock market, stock brokerage firms, trust corporations, and a bank clearing house. These intermediate financial firms formed a "financial layer" between the financial banks and production firms. This has been called a "financially layered" system, with intermediate financial institutions between banks and production companies, processing levered loans for speculative trading by intermediate financial agents.

Reason—The reasoning (thinking) included two important concepts: "financial leverage" and "shadow banking." Financial leveraging is the way profits can be made on changes of the prices of "capital assets." The capital assets were the stocks (equity shares) in production firms (such as United Copper Company). The changes in prices of the stocks occur (1) through increased production and (2) through corporate control. Intermediate financial institutions can make money by manipulating corporate control. Heinze attempted to make a large profit through corporate control by "cornering" its shares. The cornering forced its price up in the stock market, without impacting its level of production.

Financial Layering

This manipulation of capital asset pricing (through financial leveraging by intermediate financial institutions) is now called "shadow banking." As a process, "financial leverage" creates the fragility of the financial system. As a structure, the leverage loans are supplied by banks—but used by financial institutions other than banks—structurally, a financial layer above and dependent upon the banks.

As earlier we noted, excessive financial leverage is always a reasoning (reflexivity) underlying a financial bubble (as was emphasized respectively by Fisher, Keynes, Minsky, and Soros). But financial leverage is only possible through layered institutional connections in a financial system—between banks at the bottom of the financial system and financial units above them—the financial layering.

Hyman Minsky described how financial firms which borrow money from banks create a "layering" of institutional finance (Minsky 1975). The bottom institutional layer of any financial system consists of commercial banks which derive their capital from depositors and make loans to borrowers. Borrowers can be consumers, productive businesses, or financial businesses. Above this bank layer is a higher layering of financial institutions, all of which depend upon the banks for financing. For example, in the 1907 panic, stock brokerage firms (Gross and Kleeberg) borrowed money (margin loans) from banks (e.g., Mercantile Bank) to finance the margin purchases of stock (United Copper stock). Also trust companies (e.g., Knickerbocker Trust) borrowed money from banks to purchase companies. Brokerages and trust companies formed a layer of finance above banks but dependent upon banks.

The principal financial process of this middle layer is "leveraging." Minsky wrote: "In a layered financial structure, the (financial) unit acquiring a liability (making an investment) may have liabilities of its own (borrowing money for the investment), and its ability to fulfill its obligations depends upon the cash flow it receives from its assets (investment)… (But) a financial unit may have the principle amount of some debt outstanding falling due and not have the cash or liquid assets on hand to meet the payment ('leverage'). In these circumstances, the firm may pay its amount due by issuing new debt, rolling over, or refunding, its debt." (Minsky 1975)

Speculative leverage is when the investment income from a debt cannot fully service the loan; and the loan must be refinanced.

Minsky wrote: "…our complex financial structure consists of a variety of institutions that lever on owners' equity and normally make on the 'carry', that is borrowing at a lower rate than their assets can earn" (Minsky 1975). The financial term "carry" means the "difference" in interest rate (that a financial firm can make from an investment) above the interest rate (the financial firm must pay to a bank to finance its investment). It is this "carry" which enables higher-level financial institutions to make money from leverage, during the time of a financing loan.

For example in 1907, the trust companies were financially layered above the banks (depending upon bank loans to finance their acquisitions of companies). The brokerage firms were financially layered above the banks (depending upon margin loans from the banks to finance their margin purchase of stocks for clients). It was their excess of leverage which created liquidity problems when the 1907 stock market fell, reducing the value of stocks held as collateral for the leverage loans.

Shadow Banking

Using Minsky's concept of financial layering, Paul McCulley in 2007 used the term of "shadow banking" to indicate the intermediate layer. McCulley wrote: "Unlike regulated real banks, who fund themselves with insured deposits, backstopped by access to the Fed's discount window, unregulated shadow banks fund themselves with un-insured commercial paper, which may or may not be backstopped by liquidity lines from real banks. Thus, the shadow banking system is particularly vulnerable to runs—commercial paper investors refusing to re-up when their paper matures, leaving the shadow banks with a liquidity crisis—a need to tap their back-up lines of credit with real banks and/or to liquidate assets at fire sale prices…" (McCulley 2007a)

Back in 1907, trust companies and not hedge funds (which were not invented until much later) principally constituted "shadow banking." Ellis Tallman and Jon Moen wrote: "The runs on deposits that sparked the Bank Panic of 1907 were at two of the largest New York City trust companies: Knickerbocker Trust and Trust Company of America… The main mechanism for the transmission of financial distress throughout the financial system was the contraction of loans, primarily collateralized loans, held by trusts." (Moen and Tallman 1992)

Then the trust companies were large. Ellis Tallman and Jon Moen wrote: "Trust companies rapidly emerged as important intermediaries in the New York financial market in the late nineteenth century. In the 10 years ending in 1907, trust company assets in New York State had grown 244 % (from \$396.7 million to \$1,364 billion) in comparison to 97 % (from \$615.2 million to \$1.8 billion) for those of national banks, and 82 % (from \$297 million to \$541 million) for state banks in New York. The disposition of trust assets was therefore significant in the New York money market… In panics before 1907—for example in 1873, 1884, and 1893—trusts had not yet become important intermediaries in New York City, so most of the financial distress was centered at banks. The Panic of 1907 was different in that it was concentrated in another large intermediary apart from banks." (Moen and Tallman 1992)

Tallman and Moen described: "Trust companies were state-chartered institutions. In New York, they were regulated less than national or state banks and had fewer restrictions on their choice of assets. For example, in contrast to national banks, trusts could own stock equity directly. They could also own real estate, although no more than 15 % of their total assets could be in this form. Trust companies could also make commercial loans like national banks. In short, while trust companies could compete with national banks in most banking activities, they also had investment opportunities that were prohibited to national banks… The contraction in financial intermediation that spread to the rest of the nation started in a specific intermediary that was less regulated than others operating in the same financial markets." (Moen and Tallman 1992)

Modern Shadow Banking

Here is an institutional pattern. In the Panic of 1907, the trust companies were a kind of an unregulated shadow-banking sector and spread the financial collapse. Later in 2007 in the global panic, they had been replaced by "hedge funds," another kind of shadow bank (also unregulated and highly leveraged). Trust companies triggered the bank panic in 1907. In 2007, hedge funds triggered the global panic. (We recall the panic began in the spring of 2007 with the failure of Bear Stearns hedge funds, which had marketed fraudulently rated, mortgage-based derivatives.)

Thus, shadow banking has continued, from 1907 through 2007 and on. Back in 2007 McCulley had written: "Shadow Banks are levered-up intermediaries without access to either FDIC deposit insurance or the Fed's discount window to protect against runs or stop runs. But since they don't have access to those governmental safety nets, Shadow Banks do not have to operate under meaningful regulatory constraints... The bottom line is that the Shadow Banking System (has) created explosive growth in leverage and liquidity risk outside the purview of the Fed." (McCulley 2007b)

Earlier we noted a convergence in theory between the "institutional economics" tradition with the "neo-Keynesian tradition." Here is the connection:

> *It is the institutional "financial layering" (institutional structure) in a financial system which enables and facilitates the "leveraging" of financial speculation (process). Lower-layer banks fund the speculative leveraging of intermediate-layer financial units, the shadow banks. When speculative excess occurs in shadow banking, a financial bubble happens.*
>
> *This connection—between financial layering (structure) and leveraging (process)—is the reason that both a monetarist and an institutional approach are needed for regulation theory (monetarist school and Keynesian school).*
>
> *The financial factor in economic theory concerns "process," money, and credit, and this is the "how" of banking—monetarists. The institutional factor in economic theory concerns "structure," governance of banks, and shadow bank, and this is the "who" of banking—institutionalists.*

Now we construct a topological model of a layered financial structure, Fig. 8.2. Graphically, we use a topological boxlike frame, for which the bottom layer indicates banks and the top layer indicates production companies and government treasury. The connecting middle panel indicates financial markets. On the sides and between the top level and bottom level is a middle level of the shadow system—financial traders and financial funds. These provide "shadow banking" as they operate upon financial leverage (based on loans provided by the bank lower layer). In the shadow left panel are hedge funds, money-market funds, and trust funds. (Trust companies existed for the 1907 panic, but they no longer existed by the 2007 panic, replaced by hedge funds.) In the shadow right panel are brokerage houses, trading desks, and mutual funds.

Base Bank Layer

At the base layer of the financial system, banks receive their funds from savings and deposits by customers (individuals and businesses); and they loan these funds to companies and to shadow-bank institutions in the financial trader sector and in the financial funds sector. The bank loans to the shadow-bank institutions create the "leverage" in the layered financial structure. *Bank loans to financial units in the shadow-banking panels provide the leverage to enable speculation by shadow banking, and excessive speculation creates financial bubbles.*

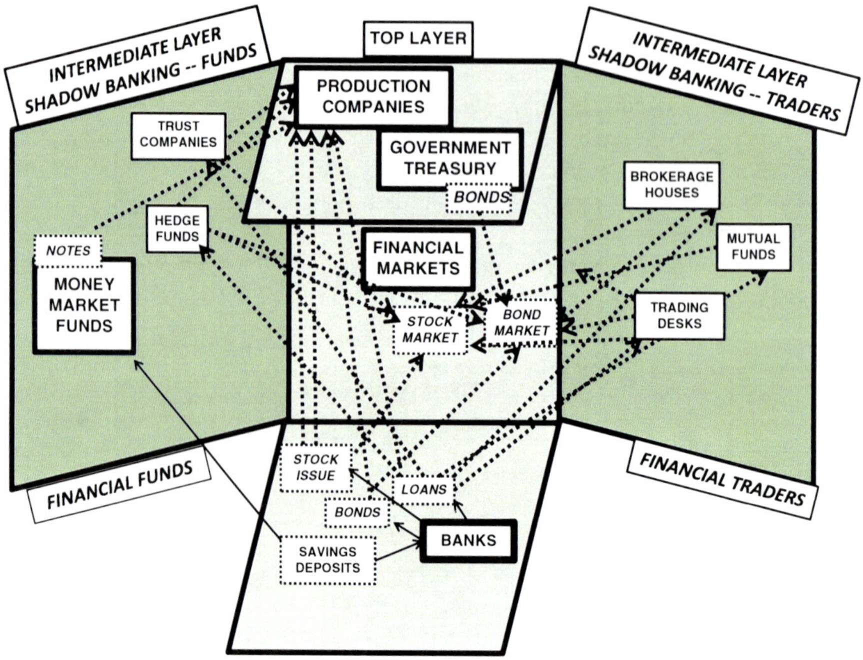

Fig. 8.2 Financial institutional model: layered financial structure

Shadow-Bank Intermediate Layer

In the shadow right panel are brokerage houses, trading desks, and mutual funds. Stock brokerage houses buy and sell stock for customers; they can borrow money from banks as loans to fund the buying of stock on margin for customers. (It was this use of bank loans by Heinze which brought down the bank of which he was president, the Mercantile National bank.) Brokerages may also provide stock offerings, providing money to a company for an offering and then selling that stock to the public; and to finance an offering, a brokerage will borrow money from a bank. Trading desks exist in brokerages to trade on the account of the brokerage itself; and brokerages also borrow money from banks to fund margin buying of stock for the brokerage. Mutual funds buy stock for customers, grouped into a fund. *Brokerages, trading desks, and mutual funds provide financial services for the public and act as a shadow-banking function, levered by bank loans.*

In the shadow left panel are money-market funds, trust funds, and hedge funds. Money-market funds are funds which accept savings deposits (like banks) from individuals and invest these in short-term loans to corporations. The funds pay a fixed interest to the individuals and gain a higher interest from the loans to corporations. These funds act like banks but are not regulated by Federal banking and therefore act as shadow banking. In 2007–2008, the Federal Reserve gave credit lines to the money-market funds to prevent their collapse.

Modern Shadow Banking: Hedge Funds

Trust companies existed for the 1907 panic, but they no longer existed for the 2007 panic, replaced by hedge funds. Hedge funds are partnerships of money managers and investors to make levered investments in trading and in buying companies. Hedge funds borrow money from banks to make larger profits in their trading and business acquisition transactions.

In buying a company, a hedge fund takes a public company private, borrowing most of the purchase price. This debt is then transferred from the hedge fund to the books of the acquired company. The company must then pay down the debt of its acquisition (by the hedge fund). Control by a hedge funds of a company aims to reduce costs to improve the appearance of the company and then to take the company public again, flipping the company. Hedge funds profit hugely in the "flip," the new public stock offering. Meanwhile, at each "flipping," a company is burdened with ever-increasing debt—not from "investments" in productivity but from "changes" in ownership.

In the USA, hedge funds became large in financial services during the 1980s. For example, from 1981 to 1985, approximately 25 % of US large corporations were acquired by hedge fund partnerships and loaded with debt. It was in this decade, when US manufacturing firms began outsourcing production to Asia, as they could not afford to take on debt for investments in manufacturing.

A famous example of a hedge fund acquisition of a large corporation occurred in 1988 when Ross Johnson, the President and CEO of RJR Nabisco, planned to take the company private at a share price of $65 (above the then share price of $49). This was to be financed with a gigantic loan, which then would be paid off by RJR Nabisco under the private ownership of Ross Johnson. Henry Kravis of the fund Kohlberg Kravis Roberts & Co. countered to the board of directors, with an offer of $80 a share (also financed with a gigantic loan). Finally, the hedge fund won the bidding, acquiring the company at $112 a share. This acquisition debt was then transferred to RJR Nabisco, which had to pay off the massive new debt loaded onto it by the Kohlberg Kravis Roberts fund. Later in March 1999, the fund made its profit by again offering stock to the public (taking the company public again). (Burrough and Helyar 1990)

In order to protect themselves from such corporate takeovers, CEOs of major US corporations in the 1990s turned to taking large stock bonuses as the principle form of their compensation. Stock bonuses provided the incentive to executives to increase share price in the short term, in order to benefit from such compensation. This short-term focus discouraged investment by corporations in manufacturing capacity. At the same time, many corporations outsourced their manufacturing from the USA to Asia, to avoid investments in manufacturing—thereby increasing profits and share prices. Yet by 1990 due to continuing advances in the technology of automation, labor costs in manufacturing had been less than 10 % of direct costs on average (or less than 5 % of overall costs). Thus in the USA then, outsourcing of manufacturing to Asia was probably not so much about labor costs but more about capital costs of investing in manufacturing.

The shadow-banking practice of hedge funds in the 1980s and 1990s (1) altered the form of executive compensation in the USA toward large annual bonuses and (2) increased management focus upon the short term and not long term of corporate life and (3) facilitated outsourcing of US manufacturing in the 1990s and 2000s.

Layered Financial Subsystem

Now we can replace the financial institutional model in the previous chapter with a layered-structure financial institutional model (Fig. 8.3). In this framework, all the partial models can be connected together to complete a whole model of an economic system. These connected partial models then fit into the larger societal framework as the economic system within a societal system model.

In this cross-disciplinary model of an economic system, one can see that the concepts of layered finance and of shadow banking are the keys to understanding how modern financial structures impact financial processes: (1) how leverage is supplied in a financial system, (2) how leverage can occur as unregulated and outside the control of bank regulation, (3) how excessive leverage can create financial bubbles, and (4) how the collapse of a financial bubble can create an economic recession.

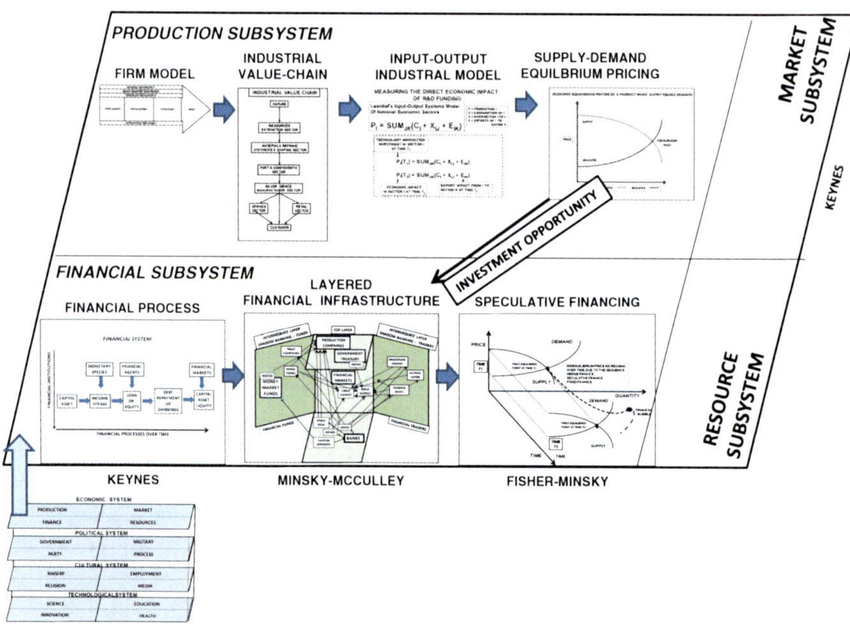

Fig. 8.3 Economic system plane of a societal model

Discussion

In a modern financial system, understanding the institutional structure is the key to understanding how leverage in finance operates. It is the leveraged finance which makes capital very profitable (provides an incentive to invest). A layered financial system is essential for the finances of a modern economy, and a layered financial system has institutions both of banks and of shadow banks.

> *The financial factor in economic theory concerns "process," money, and credit; and this is the "how" of banking—monetarism.*
>
> *The institutional factor in economic theory concerns "structure," governance of banks, and shadow banks; and this is the "who" of banking—institutionalism.*
>
> *Regulation/deregulation of both process (money/credit) and structure (governance) provides the "what" of banking—stability/instability.*

It is financial stability which stimulates economic growth and financial instability which creates bank panics. In 1999, instability in the US financial structure was reintroduced into US banking as "deregulation," when the previous Glass–Steagall separation of investment and commercial banking was repealed and permitted integrated banking. This deregulation allowed shadow banking to go down into the base layer of US banking, the banks too big to fail. Next by 2007, their shadow-banking activities of "securitization" brought down the world's financial system.

References

Burrough, B., & Helyar, J. (1990). *Barbarians at the gate: The fall of RJR Nabisco*. New York: Harper Collins.

McCulley, P. (2007a). Comments before the Money Marketeers Club. PIMCO. http://web.archive.org/web/20100206185224/http://www.pimco.com/LeftNav/Featured+Market+Commentary/FF/2009/Global+Central+Bank+Focus+April+2009+Money+Marketeers+Solitaire+McCulley.htm

McCulley, P. (2007b). Teton remarks. http://web.archive.org/web/20091124124300/http://www.pimco.com/LeftNav/Featured+Market+Commentary/FF/2007/GCBF+August-+September+2007.htm

Minsky, H. P. (1969). Private sector asset management and the effectiveness of monetary policy: theory and practice. *The Journal of Finance, 24*(2), 23–38.

Minsky, H. (1975). *John Maynard Keynes*. New York: Columbia University Press (reprinted in 2008 by Mc Graw Hill).

Minsky, H. P. (1982). *Can 'it' happen again? Essays on instability and finance*. Armonk, NY: M.E. Sharpe Inc.

Moen, J., & Tallman, E. W. (1992, September). The bank panic of 1907: The role of trust companies. *The Journal of Economic History, 52*(3).

Sprague, O. M. W. (1908, September). The American crisis of 1907. *The Economic Journal, 18*(71). http://www.jsotr.org/stable/2221551

Tallman, E. W., & Moen, J. R. (1990, May/June). Lessons from the panic of 1907. *Economic Review*.

Tucker, A. (2008, October 10). The financial panic of 1907: Running from history. *Smithsonian Magazine*. http://www.smithsonianmag.com/history-archaeology/1907_Panic.html.

Whalen, C. J. (2012). Post-Keynesian Institutionalism after the Great Recession. Working Paper No 724, Levy Economics Institute of Bard College. http://www.leveyinstitute.org

Chapter 9
Public Good and Private Good

Introduction

Regulation is a topic which has been studied in several social science disciplines. It has long been a topic in economic theory, addressed under economic concept as "public good." Regulation has also been studied as a subfield of sociology as the sociology of law. Regulation has also been studied in the interdisciplinary social science area of "political economy." In all views, there is agreement that formally "regulation" is enacted legislation which is administered to constrain rights and allocate responsibilities by participants in a societal order which is being regulated. In the topic of "administrative law," the term "rule-making" is used to characterize the process in which legislative and executive bodies create and implement rules of the game. Legislature sets broad policy mandates by passing laws, and then executive agencies create and implement detailed regulations. (See, e.g., Hall 2009.) In the USA, enacted on June 11, 1946, the Administrative Procedure Act (Public Law 79-404, 60 Statute 237) established how administrative agencies of the federal government may propose and establish regulations and how federal courts may review agency regulatory decisions (Administrative Procedure Act 1946).

It is this view on "financial regulation", which we here adopt and defines the "rules of the game" for the economic activity. Proper rules allow economic activity to be beneficial to the public good rather than harmful. A properly regulated financial system controls the supply and price of money and credit to facilitate economic production, trade, and consumption. An improperly regulated financial system allows economic cheating, fraud, theft, inflation of monetary value, and financial instability.

F. Betz, *Why Bank Panics Matter: Cross-Disciplinary Economic Theory*, SpringerBriefs in Economics, DOI 10.1007/978-3-319-01757-0_9,

Public Good

Economists use the phrase "public good" to indicate a product/service produced in a society which is shared by all members of society. This is in contrast to the term "private good" in which the product/service is consumed only by a particular member of society. A private good is an easier term to understand within the economics discipline, since private goods are produced and sold by businesses. Public goods are the domain of government; and government is studied outside of economics in political science.

Yet some economists do emphasize the importance of the concept, as Martin Wolf wrote: "Public goods are the building blocks of civilization. Economic stability is itself a public good. So are security, science, a clean environment, trust, honest administration, and free speech. The list could be far longer. This matters, because it is hard to secure adequate supply. The more global the public goods, the more difficult it is. Ironically, the better we have become at supplying private goods and so the richer we are, the more complex the public goods we need. Humanity's efforts to meet that challenge could prove to be the defining story of the century… (now) a central element of debate is how to avoid extreme financial instability. Such instability is a public bad. Avoiding it is a public good." (Wolf 2012)

Wolf defined the term: "What, for those unfamiliar with this terminology, is a public good? In the (economics) jargon, a public good is 'non-excludable' and 'non-rivalrous'. Non-excludable means that one cannot prevent non-payers from enjoying benefits. Non-rivalrous means that one person's enjoyment is not at another person's expense. National defense is a classic public good. If a country is made safe from attack everybody benefits, including residents who make no contribution. Again, enjoyment of the benefits does not reduce that of others. Similarly, if an economy is stable, everybody has the benefit and nobody can be deprived of it." (Wolf 2012)

This is a positive view of a public good, but not all economists have regarded the term as positive. Wolf wrote: "Public goods are an example of what economists call 'market failure'. The point is generalized in the language of 'externalities'—consequences, either good or bad, not taken into account by decision-makers. In such cases, Adam Smith's invisible hand does not work as one might like. Some way needs to be found to shift behavior. Public goods usually involve some state provision. Externalities usually involve a tax, a subsidy or some change in property rights. Free-market economists, such as Tyler Cowen of George Mason University, prefer the latter. But even that requires effective public action, if only via the apparatus of the law." (Wolf 2012)

In financial regulation, one public good is to prevent collapses. Wolf concluded: "Economists have tended to assume that the market economy is inherently stable. If so, stability is supplied automatically. Unfortunately, this is not so. A free-market economy can expand credit without limit, at zero cost. Since money supply is simply the liability counterpart of private credit decisions, instability is baked in the economic cake. For this reason, economic stability is a public good we find quite hard to supply. The consequences of the repeated failure to do so can also be dire. Even the late Milton Friedman believed that government intervention, via the central bank, was needed to prevent long chains of banking collapses." (Wolf 2012)

History: US Regulatory Reforms in 1913, 1933, 1999, and 2009

With this view of regulatory theory as a public good (and not as a market failure), we review the history of regulatory reform in the USA in the twentieth century. This occurred successively in the two stages of regulation (1913 and 1933), a later stage of deregulation (1995), and a fourth stage of partial reregulation (2009). Regulatory reforms were attempts to strengthen the public good of finance by defining better rules of the game for financial stability.

1913 Reform: US Federal Reserve System

In 1913, the US government established the Federal Reserve System as a central bank to be the national "lender of last resort." G. Gorton and L. Huang summarized the idea: "The most important function of a central bank is to provide liquidity to the banking system in times of crisis. The classic work on central banking, Lombard Street, by Walter Bagehot, published in 1877, offered the advice that in times of panic the central bank (Bank of England) should lend freely and continue to pay out currency." (Gorton and Huang 2006)

The reason it took until 1913 for the US government to establish a central bank was that the idea had been politically controversial, from the beginning. In 1782, Robert Morris was the superintendent of finance and in favor of a central bank. He helped to open the Bank of North America. In 1791, Alexander Hamilton, secretary of treasury, enabled the continuation of Morris's project as the First Bank of the United States, chartered by Congress and approved by George Washington. But in 1811, its 20-year charter was allowed to lapse by President Jefferson. In 1816, James Madison established the Second Bank of the United States. This bank ended in 1836, under President Jackson's executive order requiring all federal land payments to be paid in gold or silver (triggering a depression in 1837 which lasted 4 years). From 1837 to 1862, all banks were only state chartered and could issue bank notes against their own holding of gold and silver. In 1863, a National Banking Act was passed, intended to facilitate loans in the Civil War; and it created a system of nationally chartered banks.

Thus, it was only after the bank Panic of 1907 that a need for a national central bank was finally accepted. Nelson Aldrich was a senator from Rhode Island and republican leader in the Senate. He established a Commission, which visited the central banks in Britain and Germany. Aldrich proposed legislation to establish a central bank in the USA. His bill did not pass. But after Woodrow Wilson was elected in 1913, a new bill from the House and Senate Banking and Currency Committees, under Representative Carter Glass of Virginia and Senator Robert L. Owen of Oklahoma, passed Congress and established the Federal Reserve System.

As a central bank after 1913, the new Federal Reserve System was (1) to act as a lender of last resort to stop bank panics and (2) to control inflation by reducing or boosting the provision of bank credit (through lowering or raising the rate (discount) at which Federal Reserve banks loaned money to federally chartered private banks). Its structure consisted of a board of governors and 12 regional Federal Reserve banks. The public component of the System was the presidentially appointed board of governors; and the private component was the 12 Federal Reserve banks as private corporations (with boards partly presidentially appointed and partly privately appointed by private banks as owners of the 12 Federal Reserve banks). The objective of the Federal Reserve System was to prevent bank panics. As we earlier noted, later in 1930, leadership in the Federal Reserve had not acted to stop the bank panic (because they thought that "speculation" should be punished). Later in 2008, both the Federal Reserve and the US Treasury decided to try to stop the bank panic in the USA and avert another depression. They pumped 700 billion dollars into the banks too big to fail, with government as lender of last resort in the USA.

1933 Glass–Steagall Act

In March 1933, bank runs were everywhere in the USA, and the new President Franklin Delano Roosevelt ordered a "bank holiday," temporarily halting the panics. Following this, Congress enacted the Glass–Steagall Act. This Act (sponsored by legislators Senator Carter Glass and Henry B. Steagall) established the Federal Deposit Insurance Corporation (FDIC), which guaranteed the value of depositors funds deposited in US commercial bank accounts. It also separated commercial banking from investment banking. Commercial banks accept savings deposits from customers and make mortgage investment and provide business loans. Investment banks assist corporations in raising capital and issuing stocks and trade in various financial markets.

About federal deposit insurance, Charles W. Calomiris and Eugene N. White wrote: "The insurance of bank deposits has become a common feature of banking regulation in many countries, but until recently it was strictly an American phenomenon. Many countries adopted deposit insurance in imitation of the USA, where (with the exception of many economists) it is regarded as an institution necessary for the stability of the banking system and the protection of depositors… The widespread support for deposit insurance in the United States represented a remarkable change of public opinion. Until the early 1930s, there was no general interest in deposit insurance… In 1933, the USA had just suffered the worst economic contraction in its history, and proponents of deposit insurance offered it as a prophylactic against a repetition of the disruption and depositor loss that plagued America in the early 1930s. Had there been no Great Depression, it seems unlikely that the USA would have adopted deposit insurance." (Calomiris and White 1994)

1999 Gramm–Leach–Bliley Act

On January 4, 1995, as we earlier indicated, Representative James A. Leach introduced a bill to repeal the earlier Glass–Steagall separation of commercial and investment banking. On February 18, 1995, Robert Rubin, treasury secretary under President Bill Clinton, argued for passage of the bill. Former Federal Reserve Board Chairman Paul Volcker also favored repealing the Glass–Steagall banking separation. On November 12, 1999, Congress passed the Gramm–Leach–Bliley Act, allowing commercial and investment banks to merge, along with brokerages and insurance companies. President Clinton signed it into law.

And we recall that a year before the bill passed (and while still under Glass–Steagall law), there had been a merger of a commercial bank with an insurance company, Citicorp Bank with Travelers Group. By law, this should have been illegal, except the Treasury Secretary Rubin gave the merger a temporary waiver from the law (anticipating that it would be soon be repealed). The leader of this merger was Stanford Weill, chief executive of Travelers Group and CEO of the new Citibank. Weill had been lobbying for this change to the Glass–Steagall Act since 1995. About Weill's lobbying role, Gretchen Morgenson and Joshua Rosner wrote: "Happily for Weill, he had friends in positions of power to help him overcome these legal obstacles. Robert Rubin (was) the Secretary of Treasury, and former head of Goldman Sachs… Rubin left Treasury to return to corporate America. He landed a cushy job as vice chairman of Citigroup… Over the following decade Rubin pocketed more than one hundred million dollars as the bank sank deeper and deeper into a risky morass of its own design… Glass-Steagall's demise…opened the door to greater risk taking among banks." (Morgenson and Rosner 2011, p. 108)

2009: Dodd–Frank Wall Street Reform and Consumer Protection Act

After the financial crisis of 2007–2008, the US government in 2009 passed new financial reform legislation called the Dodd–Frank Regulatory Reform Act. It did not reinstate the separation of investment from commercial banking. But it had a provision, called the Volcker Rule, to forbid integrated banks to trade on their own account.

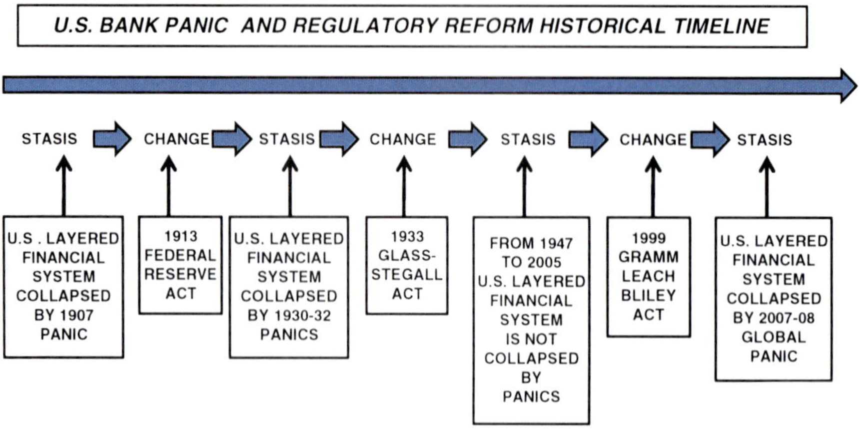

Fig. 9.1 US regulatory reform laws in the twentieth century

The Volcker Rule was a political compromise and a complicated attempt to go back a little toward the public good in the Glass–Steagall Act which had imposed banking separation. If the Glass–Steagall Act had been reinstated by law, then all the big US banks, like JPMorgan–Chase, would have had to break up.

Regulation and Financial Events

We can graphically summarize the history of US banking reform (in the twentieth century) within the framework of a societal dynamics historical timeline chart, Fig. 9.1.

Note that we have not placed another bank panic which occurred in 1985. This had been in the Savings and Loan (S&L) banking community and contagion was therein contained. It was another example where imprudent deregulation allowed bad practices, all of which led up to a banking collapse. See, for example, Emmons and Pennington–Cross (2006).

Public and Private Good and Ethics and Power

We next turn to political science as a cross-disciplinary way to enrich the economic idea of "public good." What can be meant by the metaphor about "public good" as a kind of "rules of the game"? Economic activity is not as innocent as a game. It is a serious business about livelihood in a modern economy, about wealth or poverty, and about survival or famine. Still this metaphor does point toward some kind of ethical aspect about regulation. We can pursue this by next turning to the discipline of political science, wherein the idea of "ethics" is explicit. In the economists' definition of public good, the idea of ethics is only implicit; but in political science, the idea of ethics is explicit—in the concept of a "civil society."

In the twentieth century, political theory turned upon two different ideas about the nature of society. Was society basically divisive and not civil? Or was society basically cooperative and civil? Was society empirically and normatively divisive (implacably divided)? Or was society empirically divided but integrative? The "divisive view" on society was held by communists; and the "civil view" on society was held by those advocating democracy.

Those who viewed society as basically cooperative and not one of internal war advocated democracy, a society governed in a representative form with elected officials from contending parties. Democratic ideology viewed all society as an integrative society, a civil society. For example, the political scientist, Bent Flyvbjerg, wrote: "...a strong civil society is a crucial condition of strong democracy. Empowering civil society is a central concern for the project of democracy... But what is 'civil society'?... Most writers on civil society agree...that civil society has an institutional core constituted by voluntary associations outside the sphere of the state and the economy. The fundamental act of citizenship in a pluralist democracy is in forming (voluntary) associations... The task of maintaining and redefining the boundaries between civil society and state are the two interdependent and simultaneous processes: the expansion of social equality and liberty, and the restructuring and democratizing of state institutions." (Flyvbjerg 1988)

The idea of a civil society allows the voluntary association of citizens in a state to act freely and independently of state institutions. Freedom of the citizen to voluntarily associate enables the democratic goals in the pursuit of social equality and liberty and limitation to the arbitrary exercise of state power. In an authoritarian government, all voluntary associations are controlled by the state, as well as controlling state institutions. There is no freedom for citizens in an authoritarian (e.g., communist) state, only the obedience to dictates of the state.

But the idea of a "civil society" introduces methodological complications in political science research. This idea of a "civil compromise" (civil cooperation) raises the problem about (1) the existence of power and (2) the distribution of power within society. *The idea of a "civil compromise" can have a normative implication: what ought to be a "civil compromise"?* This is the methodological problem of normative judgments versus empirical judgments—idealism or realism. Within contemporary political science in the last half of the twentieth century, this problem between the ideal and the real (normative or empirical) was the central methodological issue. And this was so, not only in political science but in all social sciences. What is real about the nature of society, and what is ideal? *The distinction between a societal reality and a societal ideal is the methodological fulcrum of societal theory.*

To illustrate this, Bent Flyvbjerg focused upon the writings of two influential political scientists of the late twentieth century: Jürgen Habermas and Michel Foucault. Flyvbjerg saw their differences as that of methodology: (1) Habermas approached research in political systems as a study of *idealism* in political theory—*normative theory*; (2) Foucault approached research in political systems as a study of *realism* in political theory—*empirical theory*.

Jürgen Habermas described political activities by focusing upon and identifying the political *ideals* around which people gather, associate, and identify. Habermas called this "discourse ethics" of the politics. By the term "discourse," Habermas indicated that social ideals are discussed openly in the politics as a justification of political action. By the term "ethics," Habermas was indicating that the ideal of the discourse provided an ethical agreement around which a group associates.

But also there is a reality about power in all political situations—the reality of how power is actually used, as opposed to how the power is justified. This is what Michel Foucault emphasized as an essential feature of social science methodology. Foucault argued that in any political situation (even focused around a *"discourse ethics"*), there was also another view about power—which is a "realism" about politics, an analysis of power, the *"power analytics"* of a situation.

For example, one of the ideals of American democracy is for equal opportunity and equal treatment under law—*Habermas's discourse ethics*. But in reality not every American has the same access to legal systems, education, safety, health, etc. People of means have better opportunities in life, and wealthy folk can hire more expert lawyers than can poor folk—*Foucault's power analytics*.

Flyvbjerg argued that these two approaches capture the modern political science methodological duality of idealism or realism: "The works of Habermas and Foucault highlight an essential tension in modernity. This is the tension between consensus and conflict… Habermas is the philosopher of Moralitat (morality) based on consensus. Foucault…is the philosopher of wirkliche Historie (real history) told in terms of conflict and power." (Flyvbjerg 1988)

A "consensus about power" in a group is constructed around an ideal expressed in the discourse ethics of the group (idealism). The "reality of how power is really exercised" in a group is expressed in the power analytics of the group (realism). *Public good is a discourse ethics theory of an economy (idealism). Private good is a power analytics theory of an economy (realism).*

One can place this cross-disciplinary view of ethics and regulatory theory within the societal perceptual space, as in Fig. 9.2.

This indicates that the view by an individual of an economic event is as a private good, the power capability of the individual (power analytics). Conversely, the view by society of the same economic event is as a public good, the discursive consensus on a society's ethics (discourse ethics).

> *A regulatory rule is a normative ethical statement—about what should be the benefit of an economic activity to society. The benefit of the economic activity to the individuals involved is a private good—a power analytics, an empirical statement about power of an individual.*
>
> *The challenge for regulatory theory is to match or balance the realism of an economic system (power analytics, private good) to the idealism of the economic system (discourse ethics, public good).*

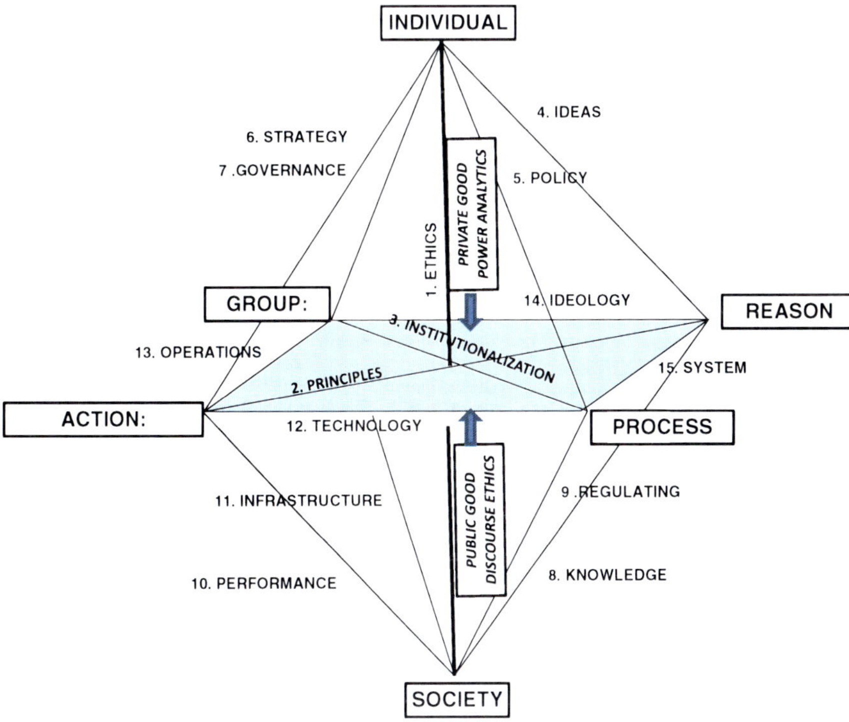

Fig. 9.2 Ethics in a cross-disciplinary societal perceptual space

History: 1997—The Reform That Never Was

An example of power analytics in the 1990s was the failure of the US government to regulate securitization of financial derivatives. In 1997, there had been an opportunity to regulate derivative transactions in the shadow-banking sector, but it was not taken on the advice by key regulatory officials of the US Federal Government. The Commodity Futures Trading Commission is a US Federal agency which regulates options and futures trading. The head of the Commission was Brooksley E. Born. Paul Goodman wrote: "Ms. Born was concerned that unfettered, opaque trading could 'threaten our regulated markets or, indeed, our economy without any federal agency knowing about it,' she said in Congressional testimony. She called for greater disclosure of trades and reserves to cushion against losses." (Goodman 2008)

But other Federal regulators, notably Allan Greenspan, chair of the Federal Reserve System, and Robert Rubin, Secretary of Treasury, did not wish to regulate derivatives. Goodman wrote: "Ms. Born's views incited fierce opposition from Mr. Greenspan and Robert E. Rubin… Treasury lawyers concluded that merely discussing new rules threatened the derivatives market. Mr. Greenspan warned that too many rules would damage Wall Street, prompting traders to take their business overseas." (Goodman 2008)

Later another member of the Commission, Michael Greenberger, commented how Greenspan viewed Brooksley: "Greenspan told Brooksley that she essentially didn't know what she was doing and she'd cause a financial crisis. Brooksley was this woman who was not playing tennis with these guys and not having lunch with these guys. There was a little bit of the feeling that this woman was not of Wall Street." (Goodman 2008)

The Secretary of Treasury, Robert Rubin, was strongly opposed to regulating derivatives. Goodman wrote: "In early 1998, Mr. Rubin's deputy, Lawrence H. Summers, called Ms. Born and chastised her for taking steps he said would lead to a financial crisis, according to Mr. Greenberger. Mr. Summers said he could not recall the conversation but agreed with Mr. Greenspan and Mr. Rubin that Ms. Born's proposal was 'highly problematic.' On April 21, 1998, senior federal financial regulators convened in a wood-paneled conference room at the Treasury to discuss Ms. Born's proposal. Mr. Rubin and Mr. Greenspan implored her to reconsider, according to both Mr. Greenberger and Mr. Levitt." (Goodman 2008)

Still Ms. Born believed derivatives needed to be regulated and decided to act. Other regulators appealed to Congress to prevent this. Goodman wrote: "Ms. Born pushed ahead. On June 5, 1998, Mr. Greenspan, Mr. Rubin and Mr. Levitt called on Congress to prevent Ms. Born from acting until more senior regulators developed their own recommendations. Mr. Levitt says he now regrets that decision. Mr. Greenspan and Mr. Rubin were 'joined at the hip on this', he said. 'They were certainly very fiercely opposed to this and persuaded me that this would cause chaos'." (Goodman 2008)

Then a trading disaster occurred in a hedge fund called long-term capital went bankrupt, due to leveraging a bad bet on Russian debt. This major loss on derivatives demonstrated to Ms. Born that regulation was indeed necessary. The secretary of treasury called together many large US banks to bail out the fund.

But such empirical historical events had no impact upon the ideological use of economic theory (perfect markets) then advocated by Greenspan and Rubin. They influenced Congress to block any regulatory action on derivatives by the Commodity Futures Trading Commission. Goodman wrote: "Despite that event, Congress froze the Commodity Futures Trading Commission's regulatory authority for six months. The following year, Ms. Born departed." (Goodman 2008)

Alan Greenspan, chair of the Federal Reserve, and Robert Rubin, Secretary of Treasury, continued to urge Congress to ban any regulatory action on derivatives. Goodman wrote: "In November 1999, senior regulators recommended that Congress permanently strip the C.F.T.C. of regulatory authority over derivatives. Mr. Greenspan, according to lawmakers, then used his prestige to make sure Congress followed through. 'Alan was held in very high regard,' said Jim Leach, an Iowa Republican who led the House Banking and Financial Services Committee at the time. 'You've got an area of judgment in which members of Congress have nonexistent expertise.'" (Goodman 2008)

Still some members of Congress had questions. In a hearing in 2000, Mr. Harkin asked about who would act if something went wrong in the derivatives market.

Goodman quoted: "'If you have this exclusion (of derivatives) and something unforeseen happens, who does something about it?' he asked Mr. Greenspan in a hearing." (Goodman 2008)

Greenspan was confident about the economic theory of markets being perfect, including Wall Street's financial markets. Goodman wrote: "Mr. Greenspan said that Wall Street could be trusted. He said, 'There is a very fundamental trade-off of what type of economy you wish to have. You can have huge amounts of regulation, and I will guarantee nothing will go wrong, but nothing will go right either.'" (Goodman 2008)

In all his testimonies to Congress, the chair of the Federal Reserve System continued to express his confidence in the "invisible hand of the market." Goodman wrote: "Later that year, at a Congressional hearing on the merger boom, Greenspan argued that Wall Street had tamed risk. Representative Bernard Sanders, an independent from Vermont, asked him: 'Aren't you concerned with such a growing concentration of wealth that if one of these huge institutions fails that it will have a horrendous impact on the national and global economy?' Mr. Greenspan replied, 'No, I'm not. I believe that the general growth in large institutions have occurred in the context of an underlying structure of markets in which many of the larger risks are dramatically, I should say, fully hedged.'" (Goodman 2008).

Congress passed and the President signed a bill which took derivatives regulation out of the purview of C.F.T.C. oversight. Derivatives went unregulated. But in 2007, the unregulated derivatives market in securitized mortgages crashed; and, with it, the global financial system collapsed. Paul Goodman pointed out: "The Wall Street debacle that swallowed firms like Bear Stearns and Lehman Brothers and imperiled the insurance giant American International Group has been driven by the fact that they and their customers were linked to one another by derivatives" (Goodman 2008).

Power Analytics and Discourse Ethics in Regulation

In regulatory actions, one can clarify the complexities of ethics and power by using a taxonomy of the two dichotomies (public good and private good and discourse ethics and power analytics), Fig. 9.3.

Financial regulation in economic systems is complicated by the two kinds of goods, public and private, and by the two aspects of ethics and power. Regulatory law is the expression of the discourse ethics in the public good of a financial

	PUBLIC GOOD	*PRIVATE GOOD*
DISCOURSE ETHICS	REGULATORY LAW	REGULATORY INFLUENCE
POWER ANALYTICS	REGULATORY PRACTICE	REGULATORY COMPLIANCE

Fig. 9.3 Ethics and power in regulation

institution. Regulatory practice is how law is actually administered within the context of political power. To optimize the private good in the exercise of regulatory practice, private financial institutions attempt to influence the political process for legislating and implementing regulation. Private firms can also exert their own private good to the extent they comply with the spirit of regulatory law (discourse ethics) in addition to the practice of regulatory law (power analytics). *Regulation exists in a context of both discourse ethics (public good) and power analytics (private good). Regulation should balance public and private good—in the idealism of ethics and in the realism of politics.*

Hyman Minsky emphasized that regulation, in the form of bank examination, had increased in importance as banks became larger: "With the attenuation of customer and collegiate surveillance as a result of the risk absorption by broadly defined central banking, bank examination becomes increasingly important as an instrument for constraining the exposure to risk of banks. Bank examination is largely perfunctory—the domain of accountants who look for proper procedures, documentation, and obvious fraud—rather than an inquiry into the economic viability and the exposures to risk of banking organizations." (Minsky 2008)

Regulation of the banking industry should attend to the "economic viability and risk taking" of the financial structure. Economic theory which is intended to underpin regulatory principles for financial systems should provide an empirical and normative grounding for financial regulation—both the "power analytics" and "discourse ethics" of economic systems. Issues which should be addressed include:

- The appropriateness of a *financial transaction* and the conditions under which it creates both private and public good (e.g., trading or gambling)
- The appropriateness of a *financial institution* and the conditions under which it creates both private and public good (e.g., bank or shadow bank)
- The appropriateness of *relationships between financial institutions* and the conditions under which they create both private and public good (e.g., internal shadow banking in integrated banks)
- The appropriateness of *financial market operations* and the conditions under which they facilitate both private and public good (e.g., unregulated derivatives markets)
- The appropriateness of the *relationships between the financial institutions and a central bank* and the conditions under which both private and public financial good are protected (e.g., financial institution access to Federal central bank "discount window" loans)

Historically (in 2013), it remained to be seen—would the US integrated banks perform for the public good, in the absence of the Glass–Steagall Act and only under the Volcker Rule of the Dodd–Frank Act? (Figs. 9.4 and 9.5). We recall that the systematic failure of the 2007–08 Global Financial Crisis was due to "unregulated derivative markets" and to "bad banking practices". We also recall that it was the "power analytics" (exercised by government officials) to repeal the prior separation of investment and commercial banking (of the Glass-Steagle Act) was argued under the economic ideology of "deregulation" —and this created the permission for the banks-too-large-to-fail, which brought down the world's financial sociotechnical system, seven years later.

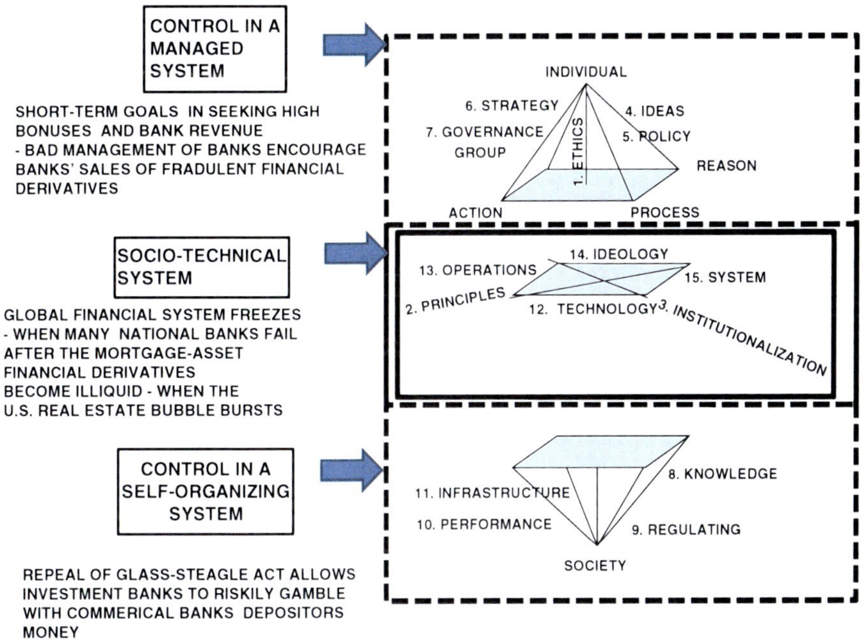

Fig. 9.4 Systems failures in 2007 global financial crisis

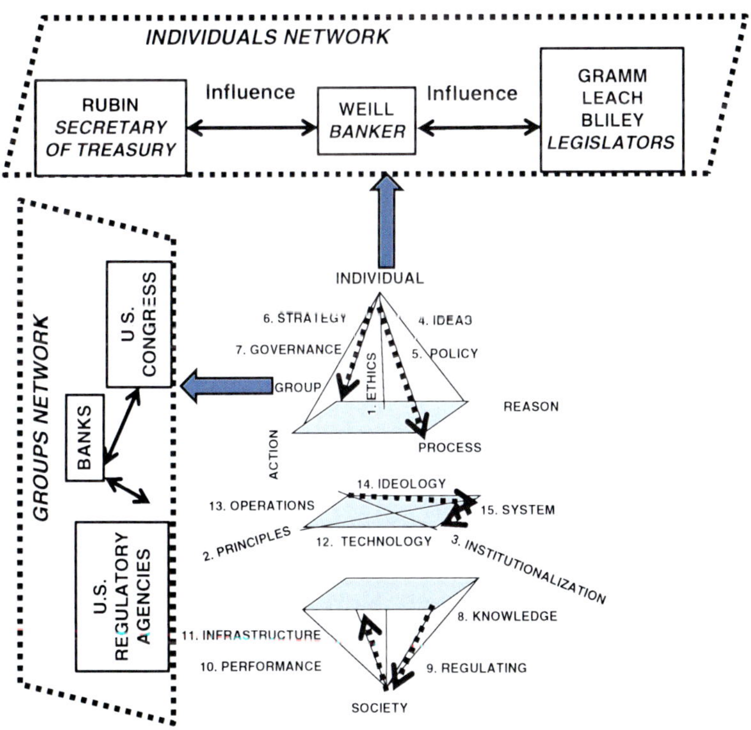

Fig. 9.5 Influence and societal impact

Discourse ethics in economic and regulatory theory is about 'idealism', what ought to be. Power analytics in economic and regulatory theory is about 'realism', what actually happened. The contexts of economic systems influence the realism of economic/regulatory theory. This has long been known in the economics literatures, but has been a item of contention in the schools of economics. For example, Peter Boettke focused on the role of context' in economic theory when he reviewed F. A. Hayek's contributions.

Peter Boettke wrote: " F. A. Hayek's realistic economic theory has been replaced by the formalistic use of equilibrium models that bear little resemblance to reality. . . . The first casualty of the formalist revolution (in economics) was the historically and institutionally rich tradition of economics still evident in the 1930s. Case studies of particular industries, for example, had been common. After the development of econometrics, however, the case-study approach was discarded in favor of large-sample data analysis. The second casualty of the formalist revolution was what might be called "the economist's way of thinking," the defining characteristic of the discipline in both its classical and early neoclassical renditions. The best of the earlier economics combined an appreciation for the particularities of institutional context, with theory grounded in the generalities of choice under conditions of scarcity." (Boettke 1997)

The cross-disciplinary formalism of societal dynamics facilitates economic modeling both of economic idealism and realism – theory and practice.

References

Associated Press. (1946). Report of the House Judiciary Committee, No. 1989, 79th Congress. BRUSSELS Administrative Procedure Act.

Boettke, P. J. (1997). What went wrong with economics? *Critical Review, 11*(1), 35–58. http://www.the-dissident.com/Boettke_CR.pdf.

Calomiris, C. W., & White, E. N. (1994). The origins of federal deposit insurance. In C. Glodin & G. D. Libecap (Eds.), *The regulated economy: A historical approach to political economy*. Chicago, IL: University of Chicago Press. http://www.nber.org/chapters/c6575.

Emmons, W. R., & Pennington-Cross, A. N. M. (2006, July/August). Lessons for federal pension insurance from the savings and loan crisis. *Federal Reserve Bank of St. Louis Review*. http://research.stlouisfed.org/publications/review/.

Flyvbjerg, B. (1988, June). Habermas and Foucault: Thinkers for civil society? *British Journal of Sociology, 49*(2), 210–233.

Goodman, P. S. (2008, October 8). Taking hard new look at a Greenspan legacy. *New York Times*.

Gorton, G., & Huang, L. (2006). Bank panics and the endogeneity of central banking. *Journal of Monetary Economics, 53*(7), 1613–1629. doi:10.1016/j.jmoneco.2005.05.015.

Hall, D. (2009). *Administrative law bureaucracy in a democracy* (4th ed.). Upper Saddle River, NJ: Pearson.

Minsky, H. (2008). *Stabilizing an unstable economy*. New York: McGraw Hill.

Morgenson, G., & Rosner, J. (2011). *Reckless endangerment: How outsized ambition, greed, and corruption led to economic Armageddon*. New York: Henry Holt and Company.

Wolf, M. (2012, January 24). The world's hunger for public goods. *Financial Times*.

Chapter 10
Casino Banking

Introduction

After the year of 2008 and its frightening global experience of inappropriate financial use of "technology" and bad "banking practice" and foolish "deregulation," then the world's banking system straightened up, didn't it? There were no more occurrences of bank "fragility" in the world. And this would be the happy ending to the world's banking problem. Right?

Wrong, as in 2012, Peter Eavis and Susanne Craig reported: "When will Wall Street stop springing these types of nasty surprises? Every big bank has risk controls. Teams of executives are assigned to manage and review trades to ensure the bank's safety and health. Yet trading debacles happen with surprising regularity. Last year, losses at two big institutions rocked the financial world. MF Global went out of business after making an ill-timed bet on European debt. Before that, a UBS trader in London lost the firm $2.3 billion. The 2008 financial crisis was the result of major risk miscalculations that brought down several big financial institutions, including Bear Stearns, Lehman Brothers, and the American International Group. Now, JPMorgan Chase faces its own mess. While JPMorgan has long been regarded as one of the nation's strongest banks, the circumstances surrounding its $2 billion trading loss (later raised to $6 billion) look depressingly familiar. Once again, a bank with large trading operations allowed a mixture of incompetence, risk-taking, hubris and complexity lead to an embarrassing and costly blowup." (Eavis and Craig 2012)

In the integrated US banks, trading had become a major source of revenue. Peter Eavis wrote: "Traders at the top Wall Street firms racked up nearly $80 billion of revenue last year (2012)... At large banks, sales and trading is a major source of revenue, often dwarfing the fees that they earn from arranging deals or managing other people's money. For instance, Goldman Sachs had sales and trading revenue of $18 billion last year, compared with $5 billion from activities like advising on mergers and handling initial public offerings." (Eavis 2013)

Casino banking is the name which has been given to the trading activities of integrated banks. Casino banking is a phenomenon of financial layering in an

F. Betz, *Why Bank Panics Matter: Cross-Disciplinary Economic Theory*, SpringerBriefs in Economics, DOI 10.1007/978-3-319-01757-0_10,

integrated bank. How did financial layering work in an integrated bank? That new era of "casino banking" continued in the world, after being introduced into the USA by the Gramm–Leach–Bliley Act of 1999.

Thus despite some of the banking reforms in the world after 2009, instability in US and European banks continued. Why did bank "trading" losses continue to occur, even after the rescue of the many collapsed banks in 2008? Would the Dodd–Frank reform act of 2009 be adequate to protect the public good in the US in its new era of "casino banking"?

History: JPMorgan Chase 2012 Trading Loss

As an example of casino banking, we examine JPMorgan Chase's large trading loss in 2012. JPMorgan Chase constituted within itself the whole of a layered financial system. Chase was a commercial bank taking in deposits from savers, while JPMorgan was an investment bank, providing corporate loans and including a big trading division.

We look at the technical aspect of their "trading" activity in that integrated bank. Details can be tiresome and difficult to understand but important in gaining accurate insight. In the case of "trading" by integrated banks, the "details" can be opaque and sometimes deliberately clouded with misinformation. The first detail we will understand is that "trading" in the integrated banks in 2012 did not constitute "trades" in any traditional economic sense—but was just "gambling." The Wall Street bankers called them trades because they didn't want depositors to know that they were gambling with their savings; instead they said they were "hedging" by "trades."

Karl Russell and Sergio Pecanha identified the 2012 JPMorgan "trade" as a bet on an index: "JPMorgan Chase is invested in various corporate debt. JPMorgan hedges its investment in that debt by buying insurance against losses on it. A major way it does that is by making bets with other investors on a basket of credit-default swaps, specifically an index of derivatives of about 120 companies' debt called CDX.NA.IG.9… This…grew so large that it became obvious to other investors who then saw an opportunity to bet against JPMorgan, which they viewed as cornered." (Russell and Pecanha 2012)

Daniel Wilchins and Carrick Mollenkamp further explained: "The source of JPMorgan's problems is an obscure group of indexes that track the performance of corporate bonds. One of the indexes, the Markit CDX NA IG Series 9 maturing in 2017, is essentially a portfolio of credit default swaps—contracts that protect against default by a borrower. This particular index is tied to the credit quality of 121 North American investment-grade bond issuers (including such names as Kraft Foods and Wal-Mart Stores). JPMorgan used that index…to bet that credit markets would strengthen. Because that position was widely known on Wall Street, many traders are betting the opposite way in the hope of profiting as the bank's losses increase. The index has been moving against JPMorgan in recent days." (Wilchins and Mollenkamp 2012)

The "move" against JPMorgan was made by other traders. This so-called "trade" was not a buying or selling of anything (as one normally calls a trade). Instead it was just a bet, a gamble on the direction an index was heading, up or down. Yet the investment bankers called it a trade, "index trading." They justified "gambling" by calling it a "hedge." This is a confusion of terms. Gambling is not trading. To make a "gamble" is still not a trade, but only a bet. One bet was that the cost of corporate bonds would go up, and the other bet was that it would go down. There was no "public good" in this bet, because it did not facilitate the issuing or assuring of corporate bonds. It merely moved money around from one gambler to another.

Also a "hedge" is an investment counter to one's other major investments, which pays off if the other investments lose money. Or conversely if the other investments make money, the hedge loses money. But was that Morgan "trade–gamble" even a hedge? Francine McKenna thought not: "When is a hedge not a hedge? Most of the talk about the losing JPMorgan derivatives trade has been nothing but trader chatter—long on speculation and short on facts. CEO Jamie Dimon may be spinning the trades as a 'hedge' but there's no hedge here for financial reporting purposes. JPMorgan's credit derivative positions did not qualify for hedge accounting and are, therefore, reported at fair value. Since the bank's credit derivatives didn't take advantage of hedge accounting treatment under U.S. generally accepted accounting principles, they're nothing, in my book, but a bet." (Mc Kenna 2012)

It was not a hedge and not even a trade. It was just a bet. Peter Eavis and Susanne Craig reported how one Wall Street executive called it: "'There is no safe way to getting risk management right because by its very nature risk is risk,' said one senior Wall Street executive who spoke on the condition of anonymity because he was prohibited from speaking publicly about the matter. 'The issue is how you manage it, and you need a strong aversion to directional bets and big bets.'" (Eavis and Craig 2012)

Was it just "trader chatter"? Did the Wall Street jargon fool its own people with its terminology? But whatever called, "casino banking" was seen as a quick way to make big profits. Such bets were leveraged by the deposited capital in integrated banks. Peter Eavis and Susanne Craig wrote: "Large banks continue to make trades with their own money, saying they are part of broader hedging strategy. The activities, the firms argue, are meant to offset various risks across the bank and to protect their profits. But at JPMorgan, the group responsible for its hedging activities, the so-called chief investment office, had gained a reputation in recent years for its trading prowess. In some ways, it became a profit center for the bank at a time when the industry earnings were under pressure. In the 3 years through the end of 2011, the unit racked up $5.4 billion of gains on its securities. Now, the group's fortunes have reversed, and the firm is paying the price. On Thursday, Mr. Dimon conceded that the trades were 'flawed' and 'poorly monitored.'" (Eavis and Craig 2012). In the year of 2012, the trading unit lost more money than it had made over the previous 5 years. But the Chase side of JPMorgan Chase provided a comfortable asset base, due to the huge amount of savings deposited, in the commercial side of the integrated bank.

Gambling (trading) upon small changes in an index with large amounts of money (leverage) can create large profits, or dangerously large losses

From 2011 to 2012, the direction of the Markit CDX NA IG Series 9 index went down and then up and then again down: "…in January 2011, investors began to have a more optimistic view of the global economy, thanks in part to the European Central Bank's decision in December (2010) to give European banks cheap access to 489 billion euros ($623 billion) of financing. The ECB followed in February (2012) with another 529 billion euros of funding. For a time that flood of money eased investor concern about the European debt crisis—and bolstered the view that corporations would be able to pay off their debt. Signs of strength in the US economy and job market helped, too. (That fall of 2011) the corporate credit index began falling, a sign of credit fears abating. In October, 2011 the index hit 182, meaning it cost $182,000 to insure against $10 million of default… By January 2012, the index had fallen to as low as 121. In late March 2012, the index hit 106. Those declines likely translated to healthy gains in the first quarter (for JP Morgan). But in April and May of 2012, the indexes began rising, as investors grew concerned about the durability of a recovery. The weakening credit market likely resulted in increasing losses for JPMorgan (which had bet upon the credit index falling). Matters worsened for the bank as hedge funds began betting against JPMorgan. That pushed up the index, giving the (JP Morgan) bank more losses. In the first 9 days of May 2012, the index climbed. On the 10th day of May, the (JP Morgan) bank stunned markets by announcing it had racked up more than $2 billion in losses." (Wilchins and Mollenkamp 2012)

Effectively, the JPMorgan trader was "betting" on good economic conditions for corporate credit. The bets were between "traders." It was like a poker game, with traders in the shadow-banking brokerages of Wall Street betting against one another. This was economically not a "perfect market" but a kind of "crap game" (like a game of dice).

Moreover, managing risk in trading is very different from managing risk in betting. In a trade, one can estimate from the conditions of the trade the likely profit from the trade from a knowledge of markets. However in gambling, one can only estimate from the history of the events the probability of a future event when the events are repetitive. The risk in betting on an index's direction depends upon an extrapolation from the index's past. And extrapolations can change. Betting on an "index" cannot be calculated as a probability, as it is a time-dependent extrapolation of a unique event. Probabilities can only technically be calculated for repetitive events. Thus gambling by traders cannot be risk managed, but only intuitively betted. Some gamblers are better than others. They have better gambling instincts. For example, an effective gambler knows when "to walk away"; but JPMorgan's trader did not know when to walk away. The trader might have lost only a billion dollars if he had walked and perhaps not the whole six billion (which he lost by staying).

In 2012 what did an integrated bank executive think about "gambling"? Andrew Rosenthal reported: "Jamie Dimon, the head of JPMorgan Chase, testified before the House Committee on Financial Services today: Rep. Gary Ackerman: "What is the difference between gambling and investing?" Dimon: "I think when you gamble you usually lose to the house." Ackerman: "That's been my general experience with investing." Dimon: I'd be happy to get you a better financial advisor." (Rosenthal 2012)

By Dimon's definition, when one gambles, one loses to the "house," the casino gambling house. But this is the problem about "casino banking." When a bank gambles on trading, it is not the casino house. It is only another gambler in a kind of "floating crap game" with other traders. In the casino gambling on indexes, J.P. Morgan was not the "house" and had not the advantage of casino house rules (ensuring that the house will always eventually win). This is why in "casino banking," losses frequently occurred (and large losses).

Financial jargon can be used to label a "private good" but also can be used to obscure a lack of "public good." It is important for proper regulation that language be used to clarify and make more transparent things—and not to hide the real economic nature of a financial transaction with terminology that obscures.

It took several months to determine the eventual size of the trading loss: "Jamie Dimon, chief executive of JPMorgan Chase, discussed the deal last week (June 28, 2012) before the House Financial Services Committee. Losses on JPMorgan Chase's bungled trade could total as much as $6 billion, far exceeding earlier public estimates..., the red ink has been mounting in recent weeks, as the bank has been unwinding its positions..." (Silver-Greenberg and Craig 2012)

Perceptual Space of the Morgan 2012 Trading Loss

We analyze this case in the observational format of societal dynamics theory, Fig. 10.1.

Action—The action was betting upon the direction of a financial index by some trading divisions and incurring large losses in failed financial bets.

Reason—The reason that index betting was occurring with large bets was the large profits, possibly by financial leverage. Sometimes placing a huge bet could make large profits, even if the index changed marginally—as long as the bet had been in the right direction of the index change.

Group—The groups involved were US integrated banks, such as the JPMorgan Chase, and other trading firms, such as hedge funds.

Process—A trading division of an integrated bank has traders who are permitted to trade bets with other financial traders on any financial index.

Individual—The principal individuals in the action were as follows: Jamie Dimon, the CEO of JPMorgan, authorized trade-betting activities of the bank and appointed a manager–supervisor for the activity. The Morgan trader who made the large index bet was nicknamed the "whale" because of his history of making large bets for banks which employed him.

Society—The US society's financial system was affected by the trading activities of large banks, even after the global financial collapse of 2007–2008.

Bank gambling can be a private good but seldom a public good as it does not facilitate productive bank investments. Casino banking certainly cannot be a public good, when the banks are backed with government deposit insurance.

In 2013, the New York Times reported: "A detailed report put out by JPMorgan Chase last week on how it lost $6 billion from ill-fated trading in 2012 should be required reading for policy makers and financial executives. The 129-page document serves as a case study of how excessive complexity and poor oversight still threaten many parts of the financial system more than 4 years after the failure of

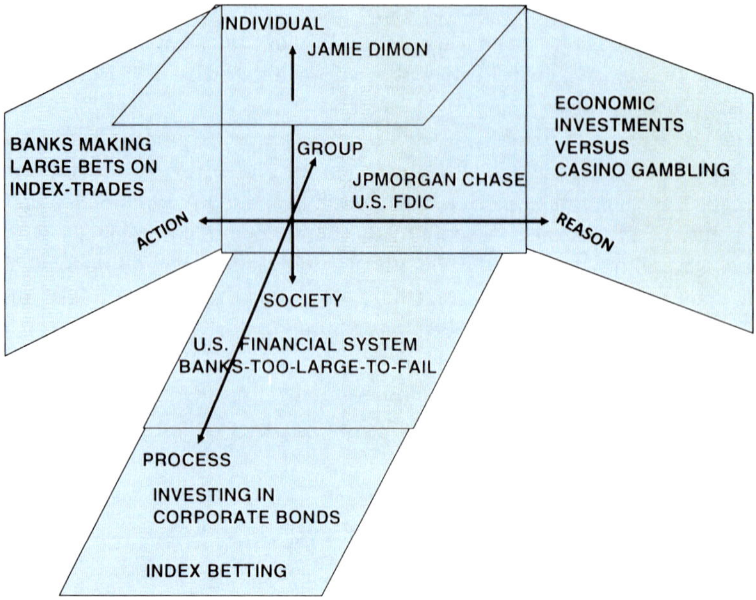

Fig. 10.1 JPMorgan chase index trade 2012

Lehman Brothers. The subject of the report is the bank's trading of complex derivatives known as credit default swaps that are similar to the instruments that forced the government to bail out the American International Group in 2008. At JPMorgan, the nation's largest bank and one of many that received government aid during the crisis, these investments did not threaten the institution's survival as they did with A.I.G. But they caused losses large enough to dent the bank's reputation for managing risk well…" (New York Times Editorial 2013)

The New York Times continued: "The report…provides important insights into why the losses took the bank and regulators by surprise. The main reason is that they were not paying attention to a small group of traders working for the bank's chief investment unit, which was supposed to be hedging, or protecting against future losses. In fact, far from mitigating the bank's risk, the London-based traders amassed a large, complex financial portfolio in the misguided hope that doing so would help the bank avoid a relatively modest loss of about $100 million, according to the report. As they dug themselves into a deeper and deeper hole, the risks they were taking were either kept from or ignored by senior managers and bank supervisors. But not everybody was oblivious. Investors at other banks and hedge funds, who were trading with JPMorgan, noticed and took advantage of the situation. They even dubbed the group's principal trader the "London Whale" because he took a very large position in the market. The report's findings suggest that some of the riskiest trading would have been either prohibited or at least better monitored had regulators finished drafting regulations about derivatives and short-term trading by banks that are required under the Dodd-Frank financial reform law." (New York Times Editorial 2013)

This example indicates the internal shadow-banking activities of J.P. Morgan's trading:

(1) "...a small group of traders working for the bank's chief investment unit, which was supposed to be hedging, or protecting against future losses." *This was a shadow-banking trading desk—a shadow-banking activity internal to the integrated bank of JPMorgan Chase.*
(2) "Investors at other banks and hedge funds who were trading with JPMorgan noticed and took advantage of the situation." *This was a shadow-banking market between trading desks external to JPMorgan—a floating crap game* (this term is one from the gambling community, and it describes a gambling game of dice which moves from location to location).
(3) "The report's findings suggest that some of the riskiest trading would have been either prohibited or at least better monitored had regulators finished drafting regulations about derivatives and short-term trading by banks that are required under the Dodd-Frank financial reform law." *This was a lack of regulation of integrated banks shadow activities, expected to be addressed in the implementation of the Dodd–Frank financial reform law (passed in 2009 but not yet implemented by 2013).*

Bank Integration and Casino Banking

Effectively, the 1999 Gramm–Leach–Bliley Act had permitted banks to bring shadow banking inside themselves—down into the base bank layer. It allowed casino banking (trading–gambling) in the integrated banks "too big to fail." The Act allowed the banking system to leverage itself as a shadow system—creating speculation-hedge financing internally into a base-layer bank. We can graphically describe the shadow-banking activities in an integrated bank in Fig. 10.2. Therein, we indicate that "shadow banking" was incorporated within the base layer of integrated banks as divisions of the bank—internal hedge funds and internal trading desks. Within this graph, one can see how an integrated bank added into its base layer some shadow-banking layer activities with internal "trading desks" and "hedge funds." Integrated investment and commercial banks were permitted by the Gramm–Leach–Bliley Act; and the "shadow world" of banking came within the banks themselves, down into the basic bank level.

We recall that when the 2007–2008 bank panic occurred, it began in the shadow banks (Bear Sterns, Lehman Brothers). But it was enlarged by shadow-banking activities in the basic bank layer (Citibank, Bank of America, Washington Mutual, Wachovia, JPMorgan Chase). And about that 2007–2008 financial crisis, we recall that in that December of 2007, Gillian Tett and Paul J. Davies had written: "A plethora of opaque institutions and vehicles have sprung up in American and European markets this decade (2000s). ...Until the summer, structured investment vehicles (SIVs) and collateralized debt obligations (CDOs) attracted little attention outside specialist financial circles. Through often affiliated to major banks, they were not always fully recognized on (the banks') balance sheets... By any standards, the activities of this shadow realm have become startling... The involvement of hedge funds, themselves highly geared (leveraged)...illustrates why shadow banking can have such an outsized impact on the supply of credit...(for example)

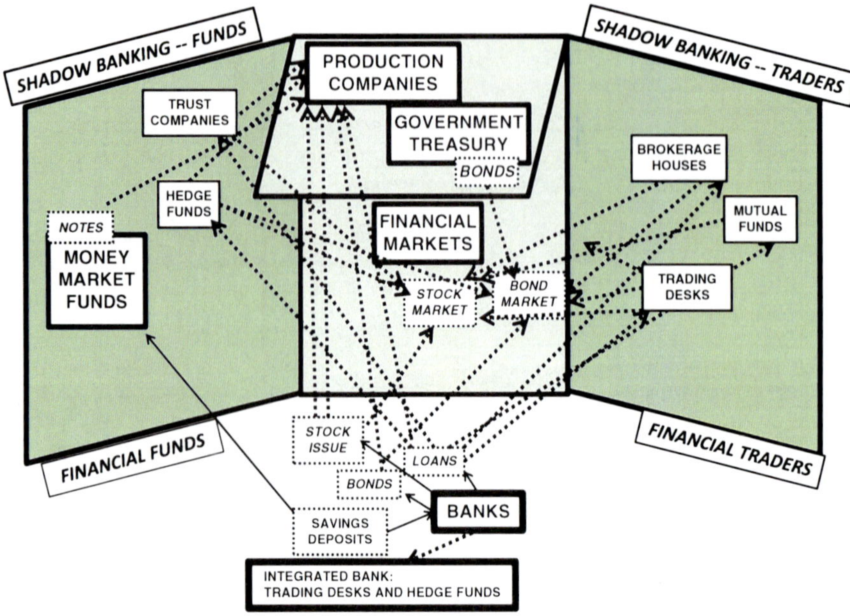

Fig. 10.2 Financial institutional model: layered financial structure and integrated banks

just $10 million of a real, unlevered hedge fund money supported a $850 million mortgage-backed deal. This means $1 dollar of real money is being used to create $85 of mortgage lending… Most of these vehicles, and the shadow banking sector as a whole, is supported by back-up liquidity lines with 'real banks'—(as) promises to lend money that bankers never imagined they would have to deliver on." (Tett and Davies 2007). And as the world learned, the integrated banks had to "deliver in 2008". The global banking system collapsed.

Even after 2008, trading continued in integrated banks—casino banking. The JPMorgan Chase integrated bank had been gambling on its index betting—making bets on financial indices composed of credit default swap contracts. Gambling on financial indexes is an example of casino banking. In JPMorgan Chase's trading, an integrated bank performed banking functions not only at the base layer of banking but also at the intermediate layer of shadowing banking, through its trading division. An advantage to an integrated bank in doing casino banking is that a large betting loss can be absorbed. An integrated bank can do casino banking with relative private safety, due to its large capital base in its commercial side.

Executive Bonuses in Integrated Banks

Thus even after the 2007–2008 bank panic, the too-big-to-fail integrated banks continued to emphasize their shadow-banking activities, particularly "trading." They made large bets, in order to maximize short-term bank profits. It was the trading desks within integrated banks which made "betting" a preoccupation for executives—as a source of profits for bonuses.

For example on April 4, 2012, Jamie Dimon received his pay for 2011: "JPMorgan Chase disclosed…that it paid its CEO $23 million in 2011. That was the same as last year, but it handily made Dimon, for the second year in a row, the best paid CEO in banking in 2011… Goldman Sachs CEO Lloyd Blankfein…pay dropped to $6 million for 2011, down nearly $4 million from the year before. The only CEO who was even close to Dimon was Wells Fargo's John Stumpf, who got a total pay package of just under $20 million… Dimon received $6 million of his $23 million in salary or cash bonus. The rest was paid in restricted stock and options, the first portion of which will start to vest in early 2014. And while Dimon was also the only JPMorgan executive who managed to avoid a pay cut in 2011, the pay of the other executives make it clear that big paydays are far from over on Wall Street. JPMorgan's investment banking chief James Staley, for instance, got paid $16 million for last year, including a $5.3 million cash bonus. JPMorgan's CFO Douglas Braunstein saw the biggest drop in pay to $6.5 million for 2011, down $3 million from the year before." (Gandel 2012)

Due to the trading loss of $6 billion in 2012, Jamie Dimon did receive less pay for that year, down to only about $12.5 million: "…the bank's trading of complex derivatives known as credit default swaps…did not threaten the institution's survival… But they caused losses large enough to dent the bank's reputation for managing risk well, and cost its top executive, Jamie Dimon, a 50 percent reduction in his 2012 pay." (New York Times Editorial 2013)

The behavior of particular individuals in positions of authority is an essential factor in explaining how managed systems (organizations) really perform—the power analytics of organizational performance. A part of the economics literature, called behavioral economics, has focused upon this. For example, Werner Erhard and Michael C. Jensen wrote: "There is a continuous and seemingly endless stream of reports of value-destroying behavior of individuals and organizations, often termed 'scandals', in the financial world… The progress in economics and finance over the last two decades—founded on the paradigm-altering insights from psychology…has allowed the profession to focus on the existence and significant impact of counter-to-interest behavior, often characterized unproductively as 'irrational behavior." (Erhard and Jensen 2012)

How executives are rewarded influences their behavior. Most bonus plans assume that the bonus will motivate the executives to behave for the good of the organization (discourse ethics of bonus plans). But reality can be determined by the structure of the bonus (power analytics of bonus plans). Kevin Murphy and Michael C. Jensen wrote: "Our research and consulting experience leads us to conclude that almost all CEO and executive bonus plans are deeply flawed. These flaws lead to highly counterproductive incentives and actions that seriously harm most firms." (Murphy and Jensen 2011)

The idea of a bonus plan is to align the private good of the executive (rewards) with the private good of the organization (performance). But the intention of the organization's private good may be distorted by how the plan calculates the bonus. Some flaws in bonus plans have been to focus the executives to short-term performance at the cost of long-term performance. For example, Murphy and Jensen described how "…bonus plans…(can) motivate executives to shift earnings from period to period …(Also) these plans teach CEOs and their subordinates to lie in annual budget negotiations… More generally, all 'non-linearity's' in the pay-performance relation affect incentives to take risks." (Murphy and Jensen 2011)

It is an important regulatory principle to understand how bank executives are rewarded for matching private to public good. When the twenty-first century began, the bonus plans of integrated banks created major incentives for short-term profits, even at ignoring long-term bank profits and survival. (We recall that this happened in Bear Sterns and Fanny Mae, leading up to the 2007–2008 collapse of both institutions.) Huge annual bonuses only incentivize short-term executive focus on the short-term, next year's annual bonus. Then the long-term profitability and survival of any institution becomes less important to such an executive who has already become, in the short term, a multimillionaire.

Traditional bank loans make profits over the term of the loan; but trading bets (gambling) can make profits immediately on the bet. Highly leveraged bets can immediately make large profits upon small immediate changes in the index upon which the bet is made. Thus the integration of banks (institutions) shifted US bank executives' incentives away from the process of long-term investments in economic production and more toward short-term trading, with highly leveraged bets.

Large annual bonuses for bank executives had encouraged their "irrational behavior" toward the long-term good of their banks. For example, Patrick Jenkins of the Financial Times wrote: "Bank regulation was a running theme of 2012, as it has been every year since the 2008 crisis… There was a little progress towards finalizing the Basel III global rule book on capital and liquidity. In Europe, the Liikanen committee published an EU-commissioned report on ring-fencing banks' trading operations. France announced a plan to ban speculative trading. US lawmakers inched forward with their implementation of Dodd-Frank reforms… But regulators spent far more of their time looking in the rear-view mirror. If 2008 was a year of bank failures, 2012 was a year of bank scandals. The Libor affair dominated with… twenty institutions coming under investigation (with the first two banks fined $1.95 billion)… The settlement documents exposed a culture of dishonesty and backslapping. In the most infamous Barclays' email exchange, one banker thanked another for manipulating Libor submissions: 'Dude. I owe you big time! Come over one day after work and I'm opening a bottle of Bollinger.'…Bob Diamond was forced out as Barclays' chief executive… HSBC paid US regulators $1.9 billion over its involvement in several illicit activities, facilitating the money laundering of Mexican drug runners. Standard Chartered paid a…$667 million fine over breaches of US sanctions on Iran. And In February, five banks agreed to a $25 billion settlement over the way they foreclosed on mortgage borrowers without following due legal requirements—Bank of America, JPMorgan Chase, Wells Fargo, Citigroup, and Ally Financial." (Jenkins 2012)

Erhard and Jensen emphasized that "integrity" in behavior (of both individuals and organizations) is needed for the long-run value of an organization. Without integrity, an individual (or organization) does not create value over time. Erhard and Jensen identified integrity with honor: "Integrity—Honoring One's Word.

Honoring-your-word means you are honest and straight forward… Without integrity nothing works." (Erhard and Jensen 2012)

Rational bank executive behavior is to manage with "integrity," to honor their word to serve both private and public good in finance.

Financial Integrity

The concept of "integrity for value over time" has long been a basic concept about finance. However in financial jargon, the term is "guaranteeing," which is based upon the idea of financial "integrity" in making a loan. For example, Hyman Minsky wrote: "Banking is not money lending… The fundamental banking activity is accepting, that is, guaranteeing that some party is credit worthy. A bank, by accepting a debt instrument, agrees to make specified payments if the debtor will not or cannot. Such an accepted or endorsed note can be then sold in the open market." (Minsky 2008)

Finance conducted in an honorable way in banking (financial integrity) is the guaranteeing of the credit integrity of a borrower—"accepting." This guarantee is based upon a banking procedure called "due diligence" in the processing of the loan. Due diligence creates the public good in banking as well as the private good of credit. The "public good" of banking lies in the bank's guaranteeing of the credit worthiness of the borrower.

"Accepting and guaranteeing" a debt is the fundamental act of banking integrity (honor). A financial debt without a bank guarantee (backed by the honor/reputation of the bank) is not acceptable to be sold in the financial market (lacks financial power). The banking system can break down on the behavior of banker acting without integrity in "due financial diligence," destroying the long-run value adding of the financial system.

Bank runs occur when public confidence is lost in the bank's integrity on their financial decisions.

Hyman Minsky also wrote: "Thus, the overall fragility-robustness of the financial structure, upon which the cyclic stability of the economy depends, emerges out of loans made by bankers. A cash-flow orientation by bankers is conducive to sustaining a robust financial structure. (In contrast) an emphasis by bankers on the collateral value and expected values of assets is conducive to the emergence of a fragile financial structure." (Minsky 2008)

The goals of financial regulation are the public goods of financial integrity and economic stability. It is financial integrity in banking (honor)—and not merely profitability (financial power)—which is the basis for stability of a financial system. Wealth is a form of power (power analytics). Wealth invested in economic productivity is a form of integrity and social honor (discourse ethics). Thus in economic thought, wealth has aspects of both power and honor—the power to organize production in business and the honor to provide employment in society. All this is indicated in Fig. 10.3. Financial integrity in banking requires leadership, with integrity (Ethics), by bank executives (Individuals). Responsible boards (Governance) should oversee that profits (Strategy) are generated with honesty (Ideas)—as the due diligence (Policy) of finance (Operations) with financial transparency (Institutionalization)—and using proper debt acceptance (Principles) in debt guaranteeing (Process). The banks (Group) should provide credit (Action) with financial stability (Reason). Information monitoring (Technology) is essential both to modern banking practices and to regulation of banking (System).

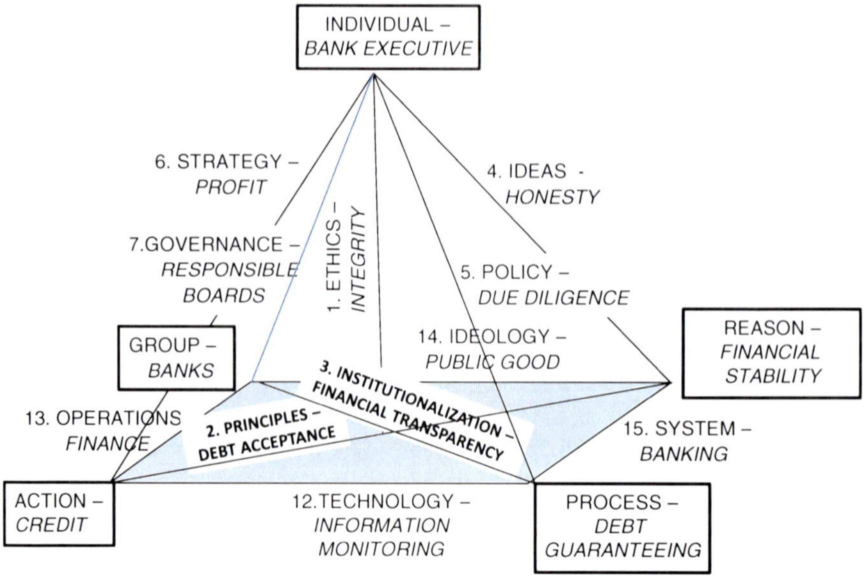

Fig. 10.3 Financial integrity in banking

References

Eavis, P. (2013, January 25). Making sense of Wall Street's trading revenue. *New York Times*.

Eavis, P., & Craig, S. (2012, May 11). The bet that blew up for JPMorgan chase. *New York Times*.

Erhard, W., & Jensen, M. C. (2012, September 18). Putting integrity into finance: A purely positive approach. Harvard Business School. http://ssrn.com/abstract=1985594.

Gandel, S. (2012, April). JPMorgan's Dimon gets $23 million for 2011 and bragging right. *Fortune*.

Jenkins, P. (2012, December 29–30). Scandals dominate bank sector. *Financial Times*.

Mc Kenna, F. (2012, May 17). The JPMorgan Whale's disastrous trades were no hedges. *American Banker*.

Minsky, H. (2008). *Stabilizing an unstable economy*. New York: McGraw Hill.

Murphy, K. J., & Jensen, M. C. (2011). CEO bonus plans: And how to fix them, chapter 8. In *CEO Pay and What to Do About It*, Harvard Business School Press. 2012 (http://ssrn.com/abstract=1935654)

New York Times Editorial. (2013, January 19). Lessons from the London Whale. *New York Times*.

Rosenthal, A. (2012). Jamie Dimon on gambling. *New York Times*.

Russell, K., & Pecanha, S. (2012, May 11). At JPMorgan chase, a complex strategy that backfired. *New York Times*.

Silver-Greenberg, J., & Craig, S. (2012, June 28). JMorgan trading loss may reach $9 billion. *New York Times*.

Tett, G., & Davies, P. J. (2007, December 16). Out of the shadows: How banking's secret system broke down. *Financial Times*.

Wilchins, D., & Mollenkamp, C. (2012, May 17). JPMorgan's future losses at the mercy of an obscure index. *Reuters*.

Chapter 11
Why Banks Panic

Introduction

As we have seen, there is no single cause of a bank panic; instead there are several factors which set the stage for bank depositors to panic about a bank and withdraw savings en masse, starting a bank panic. In general, what are the principal reasons for bank panics? We can now compare the set of historical cases, which we have been studying: US bank panics of 1857, 1907, 1930–1933, and 2007–2008 and Greek Cyprus bank panic of 2013. In this comparison we will see at least five main ways in which banks set themselves up for a potential panic: (1) funding excessive leverage in speculation, (2) lack of proper banking regulation, (3) bad banking practices, (4) lack of banking integrity, and (5) corrupt banking.

Review: 1857 US Bank Panic

We recall we analyzed the event of the 1857 bank panic in a cross-disciplinary perceptual space and identified the key factors, as shown in Fig. 11.1 (earlier Fig. 2.4).

> **Actions**—Actions included railroad construction, land speculation, immigration, and wheat market prices.
>
> Rail development in western USA generated stock offerings and bonds financed in New York banks, with connections to London banks. Western land speculation and immigration generated traffic for the railroads. Wheat grown in midwestern farms found markets in eastern USA and in Europe. Decline of demand for wheat in Europe lowered wheat prices, and competition among railroads lowered revenues. Immigration to Kansas slowed. The US Supreme Court's decision on the Dred Scott case opened Kansas to the possibility of becoming a slave state, and the land market declined. Railroads defaulted upon bonds and some went bankrupt. Some stockbrokers making markets in railroad stock collapsed, as banks called in loans and stopped withdrawal payment in species.
>
> **Reason**—Financial speculation expected price rises in land and railroads and also stimulated loans taken by securities brokers from banks for stock speculation.

F. Betz, *Why Bank Panics Matter: Cross-Disciplinary Economic Theory*,
SpringerBriefs in Economics, DOI 10.1007/978-3-319-01757-0_11,

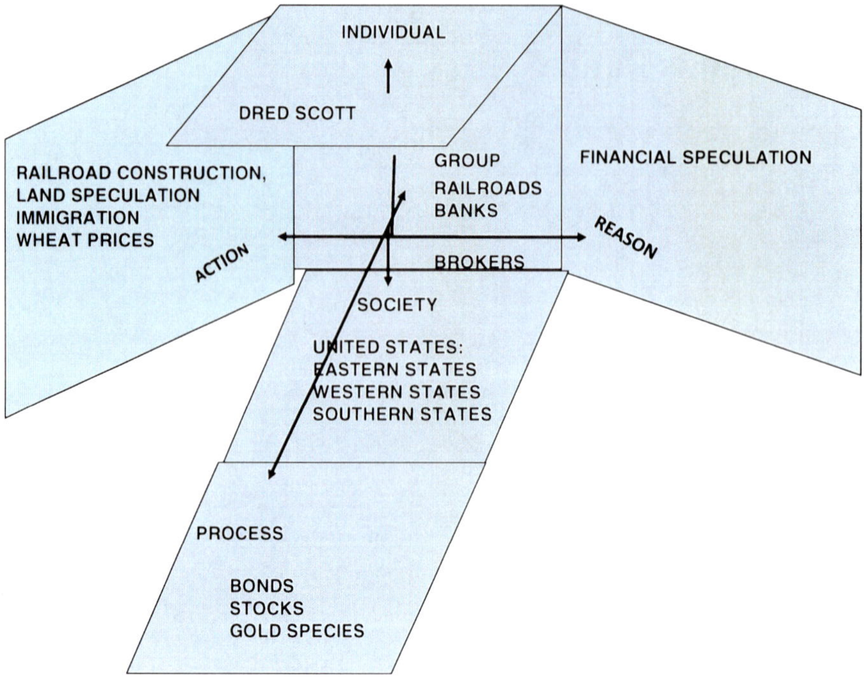

Fig. 11.1 Perceptual space of 1857 bank panic

Group—Railroads, banks, security brokers, immigrants, and London banks were some of the key groups involved in the event.

Process—Financial capital flows and firm bankruptcies were key processes in the event.

Individual—Dred Scott had filed a lawsuit for his freedom from slavery, but the Supreme Court denied it, making it a key legal decision to open up western territories as possible slave states.

Society—The society in the event was USA: with regional focus upon Eastern, Western, and Southern states.

In this event, we saw financial speculation in land and railroads financed by New York banks, which also financed stock speculation by securities brokers. We also saw financing by New York banks or agricultural trade; and monetary transactions about gold by New York banks for European banks.

Here we saw two of the reasons for the run on the New York banks (not causes, but reasons or explanations):

1. Excessive leverage of speculation funded by banks—*for funding speculation in railroad stocks and bonds*
2. Lack of proper bank regulation—*by having only a regional bank clearing house rather than a national central bank to deal with foreign monetary demands for gold*

Review: 1907 US Bank Panic

We analyzed the historical event of the 1907 bank in the observational framework of the cross-disciplinary societal dynamics perceptual space, Fig. 11.2 (earlier Fig. 8.1).

Action—Augustus Heinze attempts but fails to corner stock in United Copper in October. New York Stock Market falls, triggered by Heinze's cornering failure. Runs occur on the banks controlled by Heinze and his associates. Runs begin also on trust companies, funded by loans from these banks. Knickerbocker Trust fails. J.P. Morgan rescues Trust Company of America. Morgan and other bankers rescue other trusts. The US Treasury Secretary, Cortelyou, deposits Federal funds in New York banks to increase their monetary reserves. US Steel acquires Tennessee Coal, Iron, and Railroad.

Group—The groups involved in the action included New York banks, New York clearing house, stock brokerages, trust companies, copper companies, and the US Treasury.

Individual—Individuals involved in the action were as follows: Augustus Heinze, who was president of a bank and of a copper company, attempted to buy most of the stock (corner) of US Copper Company. But in failing, this triggered a stock market collapse. The stock brokerage firms of Heinze's brother and of Gross and Kleeberg fail. Bank runs begin on banks controlled by Heinze and his associates Charles Barney and Charles Morse. J.P. Morgan, head of the Morgan bank, rescues the Trust Company of America, and Cortelyou deposits Federal money in New York banks.

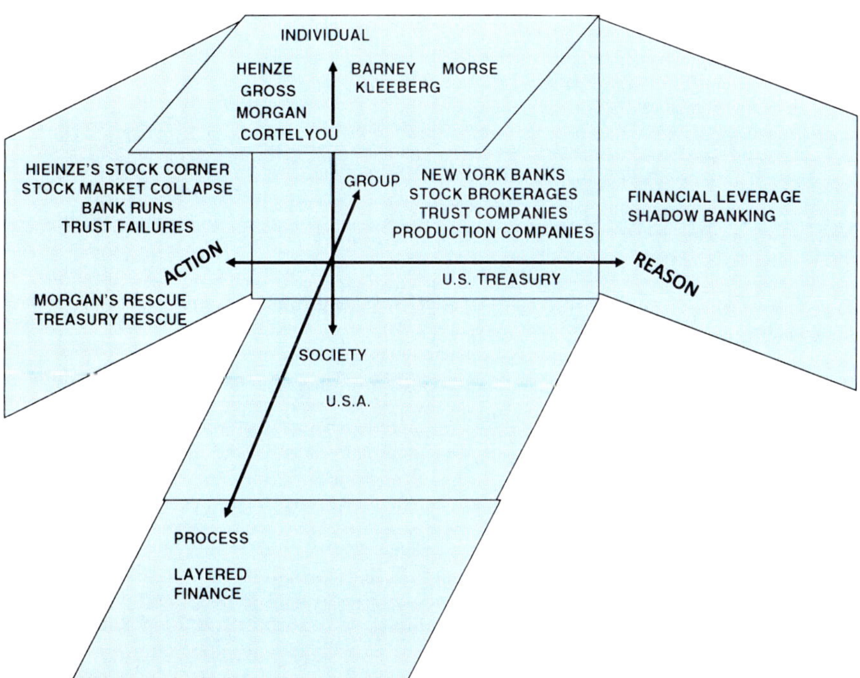

Fig. 11.2 1907 Bank panic

Society—The society involved in the event is the US society and its financial system. Attempts to profit from the control of a company within the production system triggered a sharp stock market decline, which was followed by bank runs and trust company bankruptcy, which imperiled the New York financial system.

Process—The process involved in the action was one of financial layering in which intermediate financial institutions operated between the banks (key financial institution, such as the Morgan bank) and the production corporations (such as United Copper). The intermediate financial institutions included a stock market, stock brokerage firms, trust corporations, and a bank clearing house. These intermediate financial firms formed a "financial layer" between the financial banks and production firms. This has been called a "financially layered" system, with intermediate financial institutions between banks and production companies, processing levered loans for speculative trading by intermediate financial agents.

Reason—The reasoning (thinking) included two important concepts: "financial leverage" and "shadow banking." Financial leveraging is the way profits can be made on changes of the prices of "capital assets." The capital assets were the stocks (equity shares) in production firms (such as United Copper Company). The changes in prices of the stocks occur (1) through increased production and (2) through corporate control. Intermediate financial institutions can make money by manipulating corporate control. Heinze attempted to make a large profit through corporate control by "cornering" its shares. The cornering forced its price up in the stock market, without impacting its level of production.

With the structural analysis of shadow banking, again we saw two of the reasons for the run on the New York banks (not causes, but reasons or explanations):

1. Excessive leverage of speculation funded by banks—*for funding speculation in stocks purchased on margin.*
2. Lack of proper bank regulation—*without a national central bank to deal bank runs, a private bank, J. P. Morgan played this role. And later in 1913, the US central bank was established as the Federal Reserve System.*

Review: 1930 Bank Panic

We recall that we analyzed the event of the 1930 bank panic in a societal perceptual space in Fig. 11.3 (earlier Fig. 6.2).

Individual—Prominent individuals in the USA expressed public concern about an overpriced stock market in the spring and summer of 1929.

Society—The society of the event was the nation of the USA.

Action—The action of the event was the steep decline of the New York Stock Exchange Market in October 1929, followed by additional declines and bank panics in 1930, 1931, 1932, and 1933.

Reason—Stock speculation was the reasoning which had driven the stock prices higher and higher.

Group—Groups involved in the event were banks, stock brokers, investment trusts, and utility holding companies. And also involved were the state public utility commissions, concerned about utility company profits.

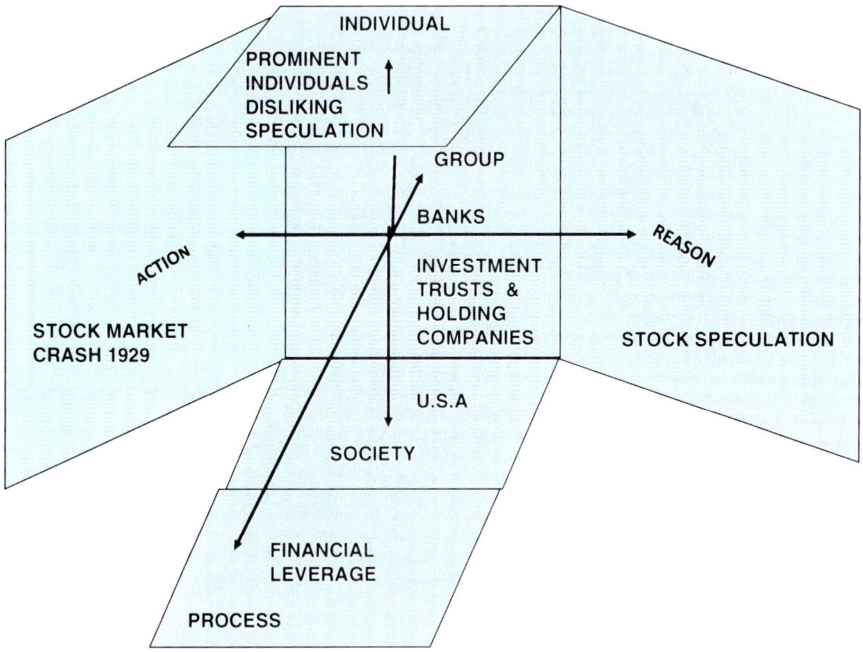

Fig. 11.3 Perceptual space of 1929 US stock market crash

Process—The financial process of "leverage" was important to the height of the price rise in the New York Stock Market. Stock purchases have been financed by the (1) banks which had provided stock issues and margin loans, (2) investment trusts which had purchased companies on leverage, and utility holding companies which acquired utility companies on leverage.

Again we saw two reasons for bank runs:

1. Excessive leverage of speculation funded by banks—*for funding speculation in stocks through purchase on margin.*
2. Lack of proper bank regulation—*the Federal Reserve System had not acted nationally to stop bank runs, with its leadership believing the speculation should be squeezed out of the system.*

Review: 2007–2008 Global Financial Crisis

We recall that then bank panics had grown from national events to global events because of the new information technologies applied to financial systems, computers, and the Internet. Yet despite the history and despite the new technology, major economists in the USA had thought the problem of bank panics was solved. Accordingly, in 1999, the US government deregulated some banking prohibitions in the Gramm–Leach–Bliley Act. This repealed the separation of commercial and investment banking. This allowed a merged commercial–investment bank to trade,

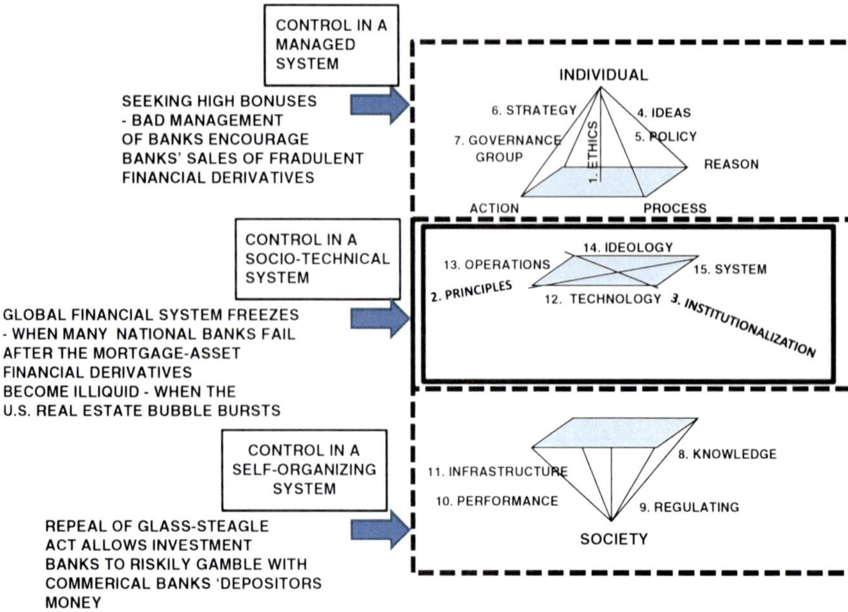

Fig. 11.4 Systems failures in 2007 global financial crisis

using depositors' funds. It created the "banks too big to fail." We had analyzed these systems failures in Fig. 11.4 (earlier Fig. 5.4).

Here we saw three reasons for the bank runs:

1. Excessive leverage of speculation funded by banks—*funding speculation by hedge funds in securitized derivatives from mortgage bonds*
2. Lack of proper bank regulation—*repealing the Glass–Steagall separation of investment and commercial banking and allowing the lowering of lending standards*
3. Bad banking practices—*banks lending "short term" to hedge funds to buy "long-term" mortgage bond, which also were fraudulently rated as to risk*

Review: 2013 Greek Cyprus Bank Panic

From the preface, we recall that global banking crises continued into the second decade of the twenty-first century, with the Euro-bank panics in Europe. Bank runs threatened in Greece, Italy, Portugal, Spain, France, and Greek Cyprus. Cypriot banks were serving as an "offshore" bank for tax evasion and money laundering. And exacerbating the harm was the leverage effect upon the Euro-bank system with the computerized Internet connection of Cypriot banks to Europe and Russia. We can analyze this action in a cross-disciplinary perceptual/observational space (Fig. 11.5).

Action—The collapse of Greek Cypriot banks required a European Union bailout to protect a euro–dollar member country.

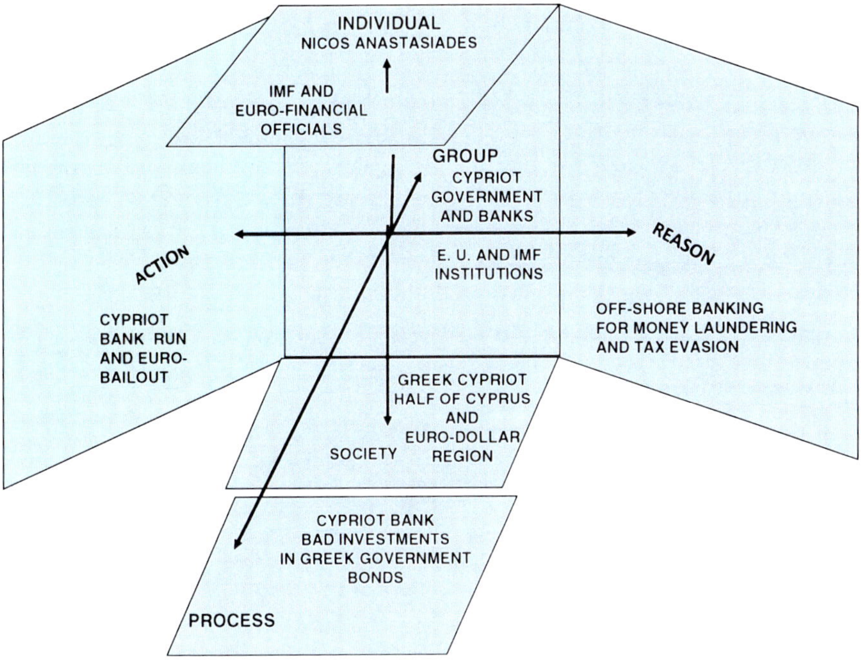

Fig. 11.5 Perceptual space of 2013 Cypriot bank bailout

Reason—The reason was bad investments in Greek government bonds by Cypriot banks using deposits from Russian oligarchs wishing to launder money and evade Russian taxes.

Group—The groups involved were the Cypriot government and Cypriot banks and the International Monetary Fund, the European Central Bank, and the European Commission.

Process—The process was a bank run on Cypriot banks after their purchases of Greek government bonds had been cut in value in the previous Greek bank panic.

Individual—The president of Greek Cyprus was involved with IMF and European Central Bank officials in negotiating terms of the bailout.

Society—Cypriot society was the Greek half of the island of Cypriots, divided earlier between Greek and Turkish citizens of the island.

Here we saw three reasons for bank panics:

2. Lack of proper bank regulation—*no Euro-wide bank regulation for countries banking in the EU system.*
3. Bad banking practices—*Cypriot banks buying too much Greek sovereign debt, so when the Greek government bonds declined, Cypriot banks collapsed.*
4. Corrupt banking—*The Cypriot financial system was set up to draw international deposits from questionable financial sources, such as tax evasion and money laundering.*

Review: 2012 Integrated Banks' Trading Losses

We recall that we analyzed casino banking in JPMorgan Chase, through the event of its large trading loss in 2012. We looked at the technical detail of their "trading" activity in that integrated bank. The "trading" in the integrated banks in 2012 did not constitute "trades" in any traditional economic sense but just "gambling." The Wall Street bankers called them trades because they didn't want depositors to know that they were gambling with their savings; instead they said they were "hedging" by "trades." This gambling event is analyzed in Fig. 11.6 (earlier Fig. 10.1).

Action—The action was betting upon the direction of a financial index by some trading divisions of large integrated investment–commercial banks and hedge funds and incurring large losses in failed financial bets.

Reason—The reason that index betting was occurring with large bets was the large profits, possibly by financial leverage. Sometimes placing a huge bet could make large profits, even if the index changed marginally—as long as the bet had been in the right direction of the index change.

Group—The groups involved were US integrated banks, such as the JPMorgan Chase, and other trading firms, such as hedge funds

Process—A trading division of an integrated bank has traders who are permitted to trade bets with other financial traders on any financial index.

Individual—The principal individuals in the action were as follows: Jamie Dimon, the CEO of JPMorgan, authorized trade-betting activities of the bank and appointed a

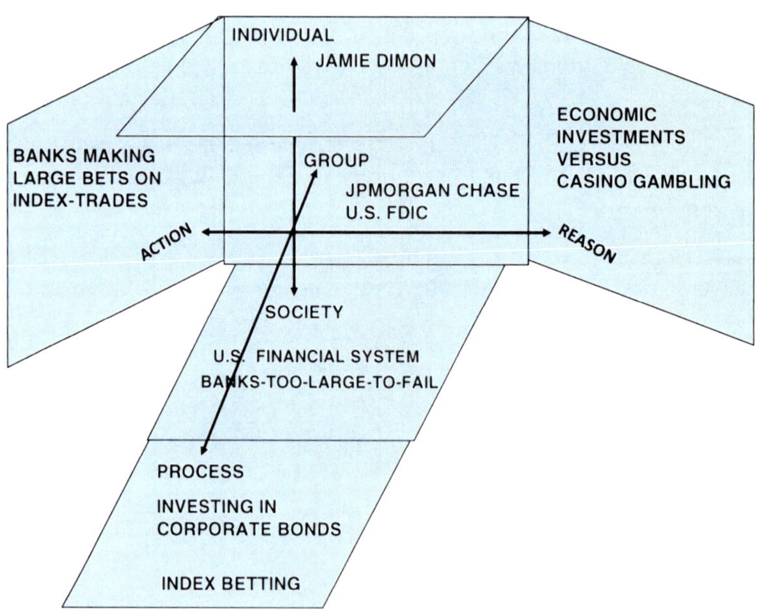

Fig. 11.6 JPMorgan chase index trade 2012

manager–supervisor for the activity. The Morgan trader who made the large index bet was nicknamed the "whale" because of his history of making large bets for banks which employed him.

Society—The US society's financial system was affected by the trading activities of large banks, even after the global financial collapse of 2007–2008.

Here we saw another reason which can trigger a bank run:

5. Lack of integrity of bank executives—*management focused on excessive bonuses, based upon short-term financial performance in casino trading (gambling).*

Discussion

From the review of the selection of bank run histories, we have identified five common reasons (explanations) for bank runs that have appeared in these events: *excessive leverage of speculation funded by banks, lack of proper bank regulation, bad banking practices, corrupt banking, and lack of integrity of bank executives.* We can indicate these as explanations in the cross-disciplinary perceptual space of societal dynamics (Fig. 11.7).

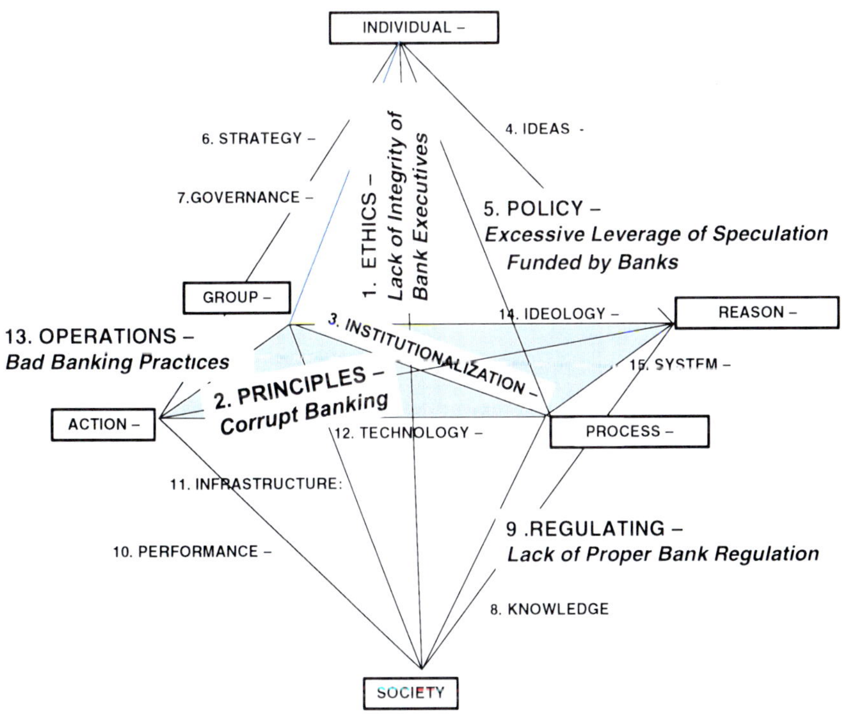

Fig. 11.7 Five common reasons/explanations for bank panic

In this scheme of societal explanation, we see the five common reasons for bank panic occur in the following explanations of a societal event:

5. Policy: excessive leverage of speculation funded by banks
9. Regulating: lack of proper bank regulation
13. Operations: bad banking practices
2. Principles: corrupt banking
1. Ethics: lack of integrity of bank executives

From this analysis, one can see that effective regulatory theory should be developed for controlling the banking system as a socio-technical financial system—*with special attention to banking policy, regulation, operations, principles, and ethics.*

Financial systems are complicated socio-technical systems led by executive banking management and regulated properly (or unregulated) by governmental central banking systems. Stability or instability in a financial system is influenced by the integrity of bank management and by the integrity of governmental regulation. Failures of integrity by one or both parties can jeopardize financial stability. So there are only five common ways of failing, and they are likely the most frequent reasons for bank runs. Of all the fifteen explanations in societal dynamics, empirically only five are the most important to attend to, in order to prevent bank runs.

This is not too complicated. Why hasn't the world devised a way to stop bank panics, instead of just trying to bail out banks after the runs? Better regulatory theory needs to be constructed and practiced, based upon a real (empirical) understanding of banking and a whole view on society. The reasons for bank panics has become clear, as we have been analyzing a sample of the histories of bank runs—all within the cross-disciplinary social science framework of societal dynamics. This has enabled us to view society as a whole, rather than seeing only a narrow slice through the glasses of one single social science discipline.

Economic theory cannot be about societal mechanisms (causes) but instead about societal functions (prescriptive).

In a cross-disciplinary framework, the whole of a society can be perceived and described as sets of interacting socio-technical systems, each with structure and function.

The challenge about control of a financial socio-technical system is to enable financial transactions with integrity, effectiveness, and stability—otherwise, bank runs occur.

Economic theory is a prescriptive rationality for the private good of individuals in the context of a free market.

Properly empirically grounded economic theory is important for sound economic policy.

Economic theory has consequences when regulators use them to justify policies.

Regulatory theory is a prescriptive rationality about a proper market structure, for market processes to provide the public good of a free market.

Commodity markets should be regulated for the public good of safety and environment.

Financial markets should be regulated for the public good of financial integrity and stability.

Bibliography

Alderman, L., & Jolly, D. (2013, March 26). Head of Cyprus's biggest bank resigns. *New York Times*.

Associated Press. (2013, April 17). EU approves bonus caps for bankers. *The Korea Herald*.

Bernanke, B. S. (1983). Nonmonetary effects of the financial crisis in the propagation of the Great Depression. *American Economic Review, 73*(3), 257–276.

Bernanke, B. S. (2004, March 2). *Money, gold, and the Great Depression*. Presented at the H. Parker Willis lecture in economic policy, Washington and Lee University, Lexington, VA. http://www.federalreserve.gov/boarddocs/speeches/2004/200403022/default.htm.

Betz, F. (2004). *Managing technological innovation* (2nd ed.). New York: Wiley.

Bierman, H., Jr. (1991). *The great myths of 1929 and the lessons to be learned*. Westport, CT: Greenwood Press.

Blinder, A. (2012). *After the music stopped: The financial crisis, the response, and the work ahead*. New York: Penguin Press.

Boettke, P. J. (1997). What went wrong with economics? *Critical Review, 11*(1), 35–58. http://www.the-dissident.com/Boettke_CR.pdf.

Calomiris, C. W., & Mason, J. R. (2003, December). Fundamentals, panics, and bank distress during the depression. *American Economic Review. 93*(5), 1615–1646.

Caporale, T., & McKiernan, B. (1998). Interest rate uncertainty and the founding of the Federal Reserve. *The Journal of Economic History, 58*(4), 1110–1117. doi:10.1017/S0022050700021756.

Carosso, V. P. (1987). *The Morgans: Private international bankers, 1854–1913*. Cambridge: Harvard University Press. ISBN 0-674-58729-4.

Dash, E. (2010, July 14). After crisis, show of power from JPMorgan *New York Times*.

De La Merced, M. J. (2012, July 25). Weill calls for splitting up big banks. *New York Times*.

Economist. (1929, November 2). 806.

England, R. S. (2011). Black Box Casino, ABC-CLIO, llC.

Erlanger, S., & Jolly, D. (2013, April 10). Hollande creates a prosecutor for fraud and vows to end tax havens. *New York Times*.

Flyvbjerg, B. (1998, June). Habermas and Foucault: Thinkers for civil society? *British Journal of Sociology, 49*(2), 210–233.

Forrester, J. (1971). *World dynamics*. Cambridge: Wright-Allen Press.

Friedman, M., & Friedman, R. (1980). *Free to choose: A personal statement*. Harcourt Brace Jovanovich.

Gamble, R. (1989). A history of the Federal Reserve Bank of Atlanta, 1914–1989. Federal Reserve Bank of Atlanta.

Gapper, J., & Kaminska, I. (2011, November 4). Downfall of MF Global. *Financial Times*.

Giles, C. (2012, May 5). The Court of King Mervyn. *Financial Times*.

F. Betz, *Why Bank Panics Matter: Cross-Disciplinary Economic Theory*, SpringerBriefs in Economics, DOI 10.1007/978-3-319-01757-0,

Gorton, G. (2009). Clearinghouses and the origin of central banking in the United States. *The Journal of Economic History, 45*(2), 277–283. doi:10.1017/S0022050700033957.

Gray, A., & Burgess, K. (2012, May 3). Investor fury at executive pay policies. *Financial Times.*

Gurusamy, S. (2009). *Financial services and system.* New Delhi: McGraw-Hill.

Hamilton, J. D. (1987). Monetary factors in the Great Depression. *Journal of Monetary Economics, 13*, 1–25.

Henry, D. (2012, May 14). JPMorgan execs set to leave, sources say. *Reuters.*

Herrick, M. T. (1908). The panic of 1907 and some of its lessons. *The Annals of the American Academy of Political and Social Science.*

Higgins, A. (2013, March 26). Europeans planted seeds of crisis in Cyprus. *New York Times.*

Huston, J. L. (1987). *The panic of 1857 and coming of the civil war.* Baton Rouge, LA: Louisiana State University Press.

International Monetary Fund. (2012). http://www.imf.org/external/pubs/ft/weo/2009/01/pdf/exesum.pdf

Jenkins, P. (2009, September 9). Goldman chief admits banks lost control. *Financial Times.* http://www.ft.com

Jones, S. (2012, April 14). Swiss clampdown on hedge fund industry unsettles money managers. *Financial Times*, 1.

Keynes, J. M. (1933, December 31). An open letter to President Roosevelt. *New York Times.* http://newdeal.feri.org/misc/keynes2.htm

Lee, C-S. (2011). *Park Chung-Hee: From poverty to power.* KHU Press.

Lowenstein, R. (2010, December 5). Jamie Dimon: America's least-hated banker. *New York Times.*

Lowrey, A. (2013, April 16). A study that set the tone for austerity is challenged. *New York Times.*

Lynch, J. (2011, February 17). JPMorgan gives Dimon a $17 million payday. *New York Times.*

Martin, W. (2008, April 8). Why Greenspan does not bear most of the blame. *Financial Times.*

Mercier, L. (2001). *Anaconda: labor, community, and culture in Montana's Smelter City.* Champaign, IL: University of Illinois Press.

Meyer, A. R., & Mackenzie, M. (2011, November 4). MF Global client funds turn up at JPMorgan. *New York Times.*

Minder, R. (2013, March 3). Swiss voters approve a plan to severely limit executive compensation. *New York Times.*

Mishkin, F. S. (1978). The household balance sheet and the Great Depression. *Journal of Economic History, 38*(4), 918–937.

Moggridge, D. (1981). *The collected writings of John Maynard Keynes* (Vol. 20). London: Macmillan.

Monaghan, A. (2012a, May 18). Northern Rock could cost taxpayers £2bn, National Audit Office warns. *The Telegraph.*

Monaghan, A. (2012b, May 21). Sir Mervyn King scrutinized as Bank of England orders review. *The Telegraph.*

Morgenson, G. (2012a, May 12). At JPMorgan, the ghost of dinner parties past. *New York Times.*

Morgenson, G. (2012b, October 1). JPMorgan unit is sued over mortgage pools'. *New York Times.*

National U.S. Commission. (2011). *The financial crisis inquiry report.* National Commission on the Causes of the Financial and Economic Crisis in the U.S. Government Printing Office.

Nocera, J. (2012, July 6). Libor's dirty laundry. *The New York Times.*

O'Grady, S. (2009, March 28). Mervyn King: At the top of his game. *The Independent (London).*

O'Neil, W. D. (2009). The Great Depression in facts and figures. http://www.analysis.williamdo-neil.com.

Parsons, T. (1937). The structure of social action. (1967 edition, Free Press).

Persons, C. E. (1930). Credit expansion, 1920 to 1929, and its lessons. *Quarterly Journal of Economics, 45*(1), 94–130.

Protess, B. (2012, May 21). Jamie Dimon shows some love for Volcker rule. *New York Times.*

Radzici, M. J., & Taylor, R. A. (2008). Origin of system dynamics: Jay W. Forrester and the history of system dynamics. U.S. Department of Energy's Introduction to System Dynamics. Retrieved October 23, 2008.

Richardson, G., & Troost, W. (2005). *Monetary intervention mitigated banking panics during the Great Depression*. Working Paper, Federal Deposit Insurance Corporation. http://www.fdic.gov/bank/analytical/cfr/2005/nov/CFRSS_2005_richardson.pdf

Schartz, N. D., & Silver-Greenberg, J. (2012, May 17). JPMorgan's trading loss is said to rise at least 50%. *New York Times*.

Sobel, R. (1968). *Panic on Wall Street*. New York: Macmillan.

Sorkin, Andres Ross, & De la Merced, M. J. (2013, February 4). U.S. and states prepare to sue S.&P. over mortgage ratings'. *New York Times*.

Soros, G. (2004, February 25). Interview with Buzzflash.com.http://www.buzzflash.com/interviews/04/02/int04012.html

Soros, G. (2012). *Financial turmoil in Europe and the United States: essays*. New York: PublicAffairs. ISBN 1-61039-161-0.

Soule, G. H. (1947). *Prosperity decade, from war to depression: 1917–1929*. New York: Rinehart.

Steindl, F. G. (2012, February 5). Economic recovery in the Great Depression. Economic History Association. http://eh.net/encyclopedia/article/Steindl.GD.Recovery

Stiglitz, J. (2010, April 22). The non-existent hand. *London Review of Books*, *32*(8).

Stone, A., & Brewster, M. (2002). *King of Capital: Sandy Weill and the Making of Citigroup*. New York: Wiley. ISBN 0-471-33015-9.

Treanor, J. (2011a, February 14). New outrage over billion-pound bonus plans at Barclays and RBS. *Guardian*.

Treanor, J. (2011b, February 24). RBS bankers get £950m in bonuses despite £1.1bn loss. *Guardian*.

Tully, S. (2009, February 27). Will the banks survive? *Fortune Magazine/CNN Money*.

Volcker, P. (2010, January 30). How to reform our financial system. *New York Times*.

Wicker, E. (1966). *Federal Reserve monetary policy: 1917–1933*. New York: Random House.

Wicker, E. (2001, September 4). Banking panics in the US: 1873–1933. EH.Net Encyclopedia (R. Whaples, Ed.). http://eh.net/encyclopedia/article/wicker.banking.panics.us

Index

F. Betz, *Why Bank Panics Matter: Cross-Disciplinary Economic Theory*, SpringerBriefs in Economics, DOI 10.1007/978-3-319-01757-0,

Printed by Publishers' Graphics LLC